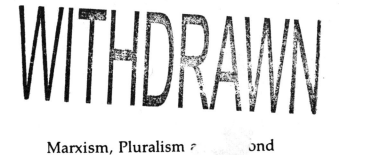

WITHDRAWN

Marxism, Pluralism and Beyond

For Mary and Gordon

Marxism, Pluralism and Beyond

Classic Debates and New Departures

GREGOR McLENNAN

Polity Press

First published 1989 by Polity Press
in association with Basil Blackwell.

Editorial Office:
Polity Press, Dales Brewery, Gwydir Street,
Cambridge CB1 2LJ, UK

Basil Blackwell Ltd
108 Cowley Road, Oxford OX4 1JF, UK

Basil Blackwell, Inc.
3 Cambridge Center, Cambridge, Massachusetts 02142, USA

ISBN 0–7456–0350–5
ISBN 0–7456–0351–3 (pbk)

British Library Cataloguing in Publication Data

A CIP catalogue record for this book is available from the
British Library.

Library of Congress Cataloging in Publication Data

A CIP catalogue record for this book is available from the
Library of Congress.

Typeset in 11 on 13pt Palatino
by Hope Services, Abingdon

Printed and bound in Great Britain by
Marston Lindsay Ross International Ltd,
Oxfordshire

CONTENTS

PREFACE

There has been a 'debate' between marxism and pluralism for about a century. Analytically speaking, it is one which forefronts the relationship between economic and political power. In its normative dimension, it is about the compatibility or otherwise of socialism and representative democracy. These topics are so immediately resonant with practical connotations, and have been so momentous in the history of the twentieth century, that to characterize the juxtaposition of such major political options as a case of 'debate' must initially strike us as altogether too academic, too anaemic. Yet on reflection, that way of seeing things is quite appropriate, partly because the discursive and rhetorical aspect of political activity and imagination is something which has been forcefully brought out in recent social theory. More specifically, though, part of the very substance of marxism-versus-pluralism concerns precisely the scope and role of theoretical concepts in the articulation of programmatic visions. The term 'debate' thus serves well to capture not only the element of active *engagement* between marxism and pluralism but also the necessarily intellectual fabric of that confrontation.

The objective of this book is to clarify and extend the contemporary dialogue between marxism and pluralism considered as bodies of social and political thought. Some work of clarification is essential, because the traditions we are dealing with are no longer (if they ever were) monolithic blocs. Rather, they are diverse and living formations of theory and practice, whose several doctrinal strands and analytical implications require careful delineation. In offering a reconstruction of the past and present of the debate, I try to highlight elements both of continuity and of change. However, this cannot be achieved by way of simple description or chronology, since the notion of development *within* each tradition, as well as the changing relationship *between* them, requires an interpretative baseline to work from. To that end, I set up a simplified model of sheer antagonism, using this as a vehicle for progressively complicating matters to the point of (uneasy) compromise at which I think things now stand.

In arriving at this characterization, I draw out the differences amongst important variants of each paradigm, and between the two traditions as a whole, in terms of three interconnected levels of abstraction. First, there is the dimension of the manifestly *political*, concerning the way in which marxism and pluralism respectively construe the nature of parties, campaigns and institutional forms. Secondly, the sociological context of political life is given a distinct grounding in each theory. Whether in terms of social classes or interest groups, marxism and pluralism share the project of a 'sociology of politics'. Thirdly, I draw attention (more than in most works on the subject) to the philosophical dimension of debate. Time and again we will see how substantive arguments about democratic organization or social forces spill over into 'meta-theoretical' reflection on the ontological and epistemological status of the primary entities or causal processes which are invoked.

In depicting the debate across these three domains, it is clear that the effort of clarification merges into critical assessment. Through Part I, I promote the idea that the 'outcome' of the debate between marxism and pluralism depends very much on *which* variants of each perspective we choose to focus on, and upon which level of abstraction we have in mind when any such comparison is undertaken. Overall, I argue that the generalized antagonism between marxism and pluralism has dramatically weakened of late. However, no scenario of straightforward 'convergence' is available, largely due to the intractability of the philosophical rather than empirical strand of theorizing. The portrayal of a series of 'essential tensions' is thus a feature of my presentation: tensions between the traditions themselves, between those variants of each perspective which produce markedly different 'resolutions' to the debate, and between the sometimes contrary impulses of substantive and epistemological commitments.

When these tensions are fully elaborated, it appears unlikely that the debate can ever be definitively resolved. Yet there are more and less productive ways of addressing the impasse or, better, the continuous *dialogue* which emerges. One unproductive type of resolution involves affirming the unqualified victory of one paradigm (conventionally understood) over the other. Apart from anything else, such views appear steadfastly to ignore empirical and theoretical shifts of the utmost importance in the late twentieth century. A second type of resolution is unsatisfactory for just the opposite reason. This is the view that marxism and pluralism, separately and jointly, have run their course. On this line the debate is not only very familiar, it is thoroughly outmoded. Whether at the substantive or meta-theoretical level, the new sparks of social thinking appear to be coming from somewhere else – somewhere *beyond* marxism-and-pluralism. Especially in the second part of the book, I argue that such views are premature and unconvincing. Some of the ostensibly novel and iconoclastic alternatives to the tired old paradigms in effect involve re-runs of very similar issues, only couched in more up-beat terminology. Other contributions towards a 'synthetic' programme for social theory are valuable and important, but they seldom register the wholesale advance that is sometimes claimed as their achievement.

If these points can be made to stick, then for all its familiarity and instability, the marxism-pluralism exchange can be defended as still ranking amongst the most urgent and consequential arenas of discussion and prognosis. Additionally, this continued relevance cautions us to note that the borderlines between 'merely eclectic', 'synthetic', and 'genuinely novel' developments in social theory are often far from distinct.

The development of a critical perspective on persistent issues of this kind is seldom conducted from a neutral standpoint. My own preferred perspective on, and within, the marxism-pluralism debate is one which conjoins historical materialism, taken as a broadly-interpreted substantive theory, to a 'scientific realist' methodological outlook. Such a combination seems to me well suited to understand the substantial place for causal and normative diversity within a wider integrative framework. However, it is worth saying at the outset that I do not see the book as *establishing* this theoretical position. One of my purposes is to provide a kind of epochal review, in which a series of issues are related together and dealt with head-on, but where the style of exegesis and evaluation remains as accessible as possible to non-specialists. The attraction to historical materialism and realism is therefore a matter of inclination rather than elaborate demonstration. Indeed, in the course of the argument of the text, it emerges that these vantage points are themselves ensnared in the general problems highlighted, and like other available options negotiate them imperfectly. In the state of stimulating uncertainty which marks social theory today it is desirable that all assumptions should be critically reviewed – even where provisional choices must be, and are, made. In that spirit, there are many firm evaluations in what follows, but no grand solutions.

GREGOR McLENNAN
EDINBURGH 1988

ACKNOWLEDGEMENTS

As all authors know, writing a book involves very peculiar pleasures and disciplines, the proper shaping of which requires the help and patience of other people. For their contributions to this book, I would like to express warm thanks to: Stuart Hall, Tony Giddens and Bob Jessop for their incisive opinions on various drafts or parts; to Desmond King, who was good enough to read two (rather different) versions and offered rigorous commentaries on both; to Margaret Liston, who expertly produced the manuscript and provided much general administrative back-up during the period of writing; and to David Held, who convinced me at the start that it was worth doing, and throughout the project gave supportive and judicious editorial advice. The book is dedicated, with love and gratitude, to my parents, who have practised an admirable blend of marxism and pluralism all their adult lives. Finally, my greatest personal debt is to Suzanne Battleday, whose love and commitment have sustained me through this work and helped keep it in perspective.

PART I

A Tale of Two Traditions

1

HISTORIC OPPOSITIONS, CONTEMPORARY QUESTIONS

1. Why 'marxism and pluralism' today?

There are several reasons for developing an account of, and an argument about, the 'marxism versus pluralism' debate. But it has to be conceded from the outset that these reasons are partly shaped by the shadowy presence of a question mark which hangs over the terms of reference of this 'debate'. For is it not the case, some will ask, that marxism and orthodox political theory are each in a state of crisis, and indeed in process of decomposition? And is it not equally the case that the comparison and critique of these two once-eminent 'paradigms' in social science have been thrashed out many times as a text-book subject?

The thinking behind such questions as these is seldom innocent. The first embodies accurately the dual sense of uncertainty and movement in current social theory. In many quarters, there is an itch to be 'moving on' from the various dogmas of the post-war period, and a frustration with approaches which try to 'rescue' those propositions and beliefs which are seemingly beyond recall. The second question is a related one, though it seems, culturally speaking, less urgent, and more pedagogic or academic. Here, the assertion is that as a debate within political and social theory, marxism versus pluralism is exhausted. Every student of politics is, or should be, by now aware of the key points of critique and counter-critique. In my view, both these suggestions are mistaken. The student primers, for one thing, tend to treat marxism and pluralism as rather static entities, generally fixed in a posture of antagonism towards each other. As we will see, there is a lot to be said for this picture. Nevertheless, there is a real problem of caricature in the approach in that it tends to eliminate the subtleties and ambiguities within the theoretical perspectives. It also tends to *freeze* the latter into 'essences', making it hard for us to think of them as developing and to an extent open-ended outlooks. I too think that there are 'central' propositions on each side, and that these are irreconcilable, if portrayed in a certain light. But today, unlike the favoured method of the 1970s, it is probably more fruitful to see theoretical perspectives as broad *traditions* rather than logically sealed paradigms or 'problematics'.

Conceived as such, there may well be important, and growing, areas of overlap and convergence between marxist and pluralist problems and concepts. Whilst this claim is perhaps rather obvious to observers of real-world events and processes, it should be pointed out that the most taxonomically exhaustive textbook of recent years allows no point of contact whatsoever between marxism and pluralism in its diagrammatic representation of political science issues (Dunleavy and O'Leary 1987: 322–3). The *fact* of overlap is not, then, obvious to all; and the nature and significance of any potential convergence is a difficult matter for anyone to assess.

It is an interesting paradox, for example, that 'pluralism' as a theoretical term and as a set of cultural movements now strikes some 'empirical democratic theorists' as considerably more *problematical* than before; whilst marxists and socialists appear to be rediscovering the virtues of pluralism. The multiplicity of demands placed on the democratic state by a range of social groups becomes a dangerous predicament of government *overload* for erstwhile pluralist theorists. For many marxists, on the other hand, the recognition that socialism without partici- pative *democracy* is not worth having has led to a more positive valuation of pluralist diversity, both in socio-cultural life and political organization.

This sense of political development gives rise to a second neglected aspect of the debate. The very *meaning* of pluralism is not something to be taken for granted, and is considerably more fluid than is often allowed. The *term* does not appear, for example, in Mikhail Gorbachev's 'new model' Soviet philosophy (Gorbachev 1987), but the issues behind the term constantly threaten to break the surface of the rationale for 'glastnost' and 'perestroika'. One of the reasons the term does not appear, I suspect, is that although its rhetorical potency is considerable, its exact scope is unclear, and the 'pluralization' of Soviet society is something which will cause theoretical and political controversy for some time to come. Pluralism can, for example, be designated as a question of official party political competition, or as social stratification, or as cultural diversity. There are important differences between these meanings. However it is in the end conceived, the traditional view that pluralism 'belongs' exclusively to the capitalist democracies or that it has been entirely replaced for the better by people's democracy in the socialist bloc can be sustained only by ideologues of each system.

A third dimension of the debate which is generally missing or underplayed in the literature of political science is the philosophical aspect of theoretical comparison. Often the marxism-pluralism contrast is couched in terms of how they each attempt to explain concrete phenomena such as elections, or interest groups, or the state. Of course, this is probably the major task in teaching political studies. Yet in my view, the crisis of the major analytic traditions is as much a philosophical and epistemological one as it is substantive and political. 'Marxism versus pluralism' is a live confrontation precisely because it poses fundamental problems about the nature of adequate social science explanations, and about the validity of our reconstructions of the political past and futures. Is the social world to be imagined as an integrated totality or as a series of diverse and discrete factors? Does a theory of politics require a theory of history? This kind of 'meta-empirical' issue, I would argue, is more closely interwoven with concrete thinking about politics and society than is often credited.

The last point is a useful pivot on which to turn back towards the first provocative suggestion as to why the marxism-pluralism debate is decrepit. For it seems to me the case that the recent dissatisfaction with familiar theoretical debates is as much of philosophical inspiration as it is of substantive discovery. That is to say, a fresh awareness of the limitations of particular *types* of explanation, and an awareness of the diverse *goals* of social thinking is a powerful trigger in giving a new lease of life to substantive political analysis. Thus, for example, the tendencies to *functionalism* or *reductionism* in orthodox political theory are frequently cited as problematic, and these are, interestingly, weaknesses that marxism and pluralism are held to *share*. This kind of suggestion, and the concomitant hope that a non-reductive social theory can be constructed, lies behind a number of challenging contributions to the debate and its (alleged) aftermath. In the course of the book I discuss some of these alternatives, for example, 'post-marxist' conceptions of radical democracy, the 'statist' perspective on social development, and the structurationist strand of sociological reasoning. Just to cite these instances of challenge reveals that they each operate upon a slightly different problem or domain. Yet I hope to persuade the reader that together they also draw upon or help make concrete the general philosophical bent which I term, for shorthand and as convention now dictates, *post-modernism*.

I make no apology, therefore, for moving between different 'levels' of social theory in analysing marxism and pluralism. The philosophical aspect of the traditional debate is, I maintain, central to it, and the contemporary crisis of the various political orthodoxies is also in part a somewhat inchoate climate of philosophical doubt. Infused by these concerns, the marxism-pluralism debate itself can be regenerated and moves on. Yet the challenges do require a response which goes beyond expositional reformulation. My first instinct is to join in the excitement and enthusiasm which the declamatory demolition of familiar set pieces inevitably kindles. But we need to be as suspicious of sheer novelty as we must be of leaden orthodoxy. A more considered response is therefore called for, and my strategy is threefold. I think we need (1) to re-emphasize the difficulty and dynamism of the conventional questions, questions which innumerable commentaries have not succeeded in making finally uninteresting; (2) to emphasize where appropriate the incompleteness of any novel alternative; and (3) to point out where necessary that many of the dilemmas and points of reference in the marxism-pluralism spectrum sometimes reappear in the fabric of the ascendant projects.

That, at least, is the tenor of my text, and I want to begin the process of analysis and assessment by outlining what is certainly the most common 'scenario' for the marxism-pluralism debate; a scenario of historic opposition or antagonism. This, I would argue, is more of an ideal type than an accurate intellectual history, but it remains a potent and indispensable baseline from which to develop some further reflections.

2. A historic opposition

The marxism-pluralism debate can conveniently be set out as one of mutual antagonism. This antagonism can be regarded either as basic logical incompatibility or more generally as a matter of some residual conceptual contrasts which sharpen and ease according to the historical climate. Whilst there are grounds for keeping these two understandings separate in any full assessment of the debate, the temptation to bring them together is a powerful one. Thus, moments of heightened tension between the key, historic 'representatives' of marxism and pluralism can be taken to *embody* the essential and ineradicable differences of priorities between two coherent political systems. Above all, this process occurs in the period of the 'Cold War' during the 1950s. By that time, the marxist tradition was overwhelmingly dominated by the official 'Marxism-Leninism' of the CPSU, whilst the pluralist thrust of liberal thought seemed geared to the defence of the post-war American way of life.

In this interpretation, each camp has a clear conception that social theory and political practice are intertwined. Indeed, the intrinsic rationality of the respective systems of ideas are seen as being concretely and progressively 'lived out'. The question of 'progress' is especially significant in pursuing this contrast, for both North American pluralism and 'orthodox' marxism tended to ground their beliefs about the nature of *democracy* (the crucial political concept) on an overall conception of the development of human civilization.

Marxists aspire to bring the theory of modern capitalist society, as outlined by Marx and Engels themselves, to bear on socialist political practice in the service of a communist future. The central theoretical and political tenet of marxism is that the political forms of a society are governed and constrained by the mode of economic production and the class structure which emerges from it. In the modern era, the growth of democracy has been intimately bound up with the fortunes and contradictions of capitalism as a social system, and the attendant class struggles between, first the aristocracy and bourgeoisie, then between bourgeoisie and proletariat. These struggles are held to be endemic, generated in the development of the capitalist forces and relations of production. For marxists, capitalism undoubtedly creates some important preconditions for a democratic society, such as universal suffrage and the socialization of productive resources and technology. Yet capitalism is in essence an exploitative system, producing systematic inequalities in wealth, power and status in society. These antagonisms, these divisions of effective resources and influence amongst the people, are therefore structural features of capitalist society, not merely contingent ones. They are ineradicable, in other words, short of a transformation of production relations themselves. Only when the people in general, and the working class in particular, are free *from* exploitation and free *to* pursue a creative and self-directed life can genuine democracy prevail. In the meantime, the very partial democracy of capitalist society can be seen as, at best, concessions to the historic emergence and struggle of the working class and other oppressed social groups; at worst, the ideology of democracy is just another way of pacifying or disarming the working class by offering it the shadow of political autonomy.

For marxists, then, democracy cannot be restricted to the formal equality of electoral competition – this being the most common association of the term in capitalist societies. Rather, it is about the substantive socio-economic *conditions* of effective and equal participation in democratic forums. For marxists, only a socialist society can secure those conditions. The practical commitment of marxists to socialist movements is thus central to understanding the historical antagonism between the marxist and pluralist traditions of democratic thinking. In the lives and works of the marxist founders an enthusiasm for democracy, including 'bourgeois' democracy, was tempered by a profound critique of the capitalist system which enveloped it. Early marxist theory and politics provides a rich seam of argument and action in which socialist attitudes to bourgeois-democratic forms (parliaments, parties, elections etc.) were formed. Whilst, in my view, no unanimous or decisive attitude towards socialist participation in these institutions can be discerned in the period before universal suffrage was established, marxists have usually argued that limited representative institutions are the vehicles of bourgeois class ascendancy.

The original marxist scepticism towards formal electoral systems in the 'advanced' countries was consolidated and extended with the domination of socialist politics in the twentieth century by the CPSU. The Bolshevik, and subsequently Stalinist, inflexion of the marxist engagement with democratic politics has been profound, for it forefronts the question of how far political centralization and the state can be taken as vehicles of *proletarian* class ascendancy. In particular, the development of a strong Soviet state was supported by the theory that socialism could be achieved only through a 'dictatorship of the proletariat'. Bourgeois democracy, in the Marxist-Leninist view, itself embodied a progressive contradiction. It was the means by which the capitalist class came to exercise political power; yet it was also the most 'advanced' type of political regime to date. Many early marxists, including Marx, were enthusiastic about the potential for full democracy which the progressive side of that contradiction contained. The hallmark of later marxist, and particularly Leninist, thought is to dwell on the fact that what is *apparently* democratic in liberal institutions is precisely a form of class rule: in effect a dictatorship. By openly revealing the class content of particular political institutions, Marxist–Leninists could at least be seen to be honest about the nature of the political contradiction involved. The 'dictatorship of the proletariat' was thus conceived as a form of *explicit* class rule. Democracy was still limited, but for the first time in history the institutions of political domination were to be those of the *majority* class, the working class. Marxist politics, in this understanding, is decisively different in its goals and concepts from liberal politics. The latter is thought to promote a harmonious, classless democratic idiom in order to conceal social conflict and inequality. A socialist extension of democracy, paradoxically, would have to involve a more openly class-based idiom of struggle, with the interests of the minority ruling class being rigorously identified and suppressed.

This Marxist-Leninist theory thus fundamentally rejects the liberal understanding of political democracy as unconstrained institutionalized choice between competing parties. Pluralism does accept this understanding. Pluralism, though, develops the further claim that the essential foundation for a successful democracy is the existence of a range of citizen groups within the wider society. For pluralists of the post-war US school, modern liberal societies generate a remarkable array of groups and associations, free to develop their own interests and organizations. On these grounds, by comparison with the 'totalitarian' states, the western liberal nations were thought to have come close to attaining an optimum level of social diversity and political freedom, given the constraints of a dynamic and complex industrial society.

The logic of the latter is that it generates a division of labour and division of social responsibilities which is at the same time increasingly specialized and yet interdependent. This leads to the formation of specific social groups, whose separate interests are distinct, yet whose functional roles are closely bound up with one another. When they take on a political expression, such group interests may be recognized as legitimate representations of hitherto unrepresented social constituencies (as with the historic emergence of the labour movement, for example). Or they may be considered as further claims on the part of already-represented interests. In either case, still more interest groups will tend to emerge or re-emerge with demands of their own, and a developing diversity of concerns and political expressions results. Pluralism conceives of this array of interests as relatively balanced within civil society itself. Correspondingly, at the level of the political system, the 'voice' of any one interest group is generally counterbalanced by that of other social groups, separately or in combination.

Equilibrium at the level of the state, therefore, is achievable because of the tendency to equilibrium within modern democratic society at large. Since the dynamism of democracy comes principally from the socio-economic sphere, the role of the democratic state is responsively to reflect the balance of interests. The ideological implications of this theoretical picture is that since pluralism – the voluntary formation and interaction of groups and their representation at the level of the state – was what the Communist bloc did not have, the latter could not be accepted as being democratic. The 'West' , by contrast, did have pluralism, and so was (at least relatively) democratic and free.

One important proposition behind this general deployment of pluralist theory in support of the US system is that serious social conflict in the west, and with it any need for class ideologies, has largely ceased to exist. The end-of-ideology theorists believed that in conditions of pluralist democracy, politics would become a classless and therefore rational exchange of considered moral views. Social theorists could therefore afford to be more than a little proud of the affluent society which is born of capitalism and conducive of democracy. The brashness of the American way of life was not something to shy away from:

> America has been and continues to be one of the world's most democratic nations. Here, far more than elsewhere, the public is allowed to participate widely in the making of social and political policy. The public is not unaware of its power and the ordinary American tends to be rather arrogant about his right and competence to participate . . . The people think they know what they want and are in no mood to be led to greener pastures. (Hacker 1967: 68)

In the works of 'official' Communist marxism, these claims of the pluralists amounted to capitalist ideology pure and simple. They function to bolster the individualist ideas which sustain capitalist enterprise. 'People's democracies', for their part, have no need of the veneer of bourgeois democracy. Competing parties are not at all, in this view, a sign of free pluralist association. Rather they are a sign of the continuing, wracking antagonisms between class forces (Kelle and Kovalson 1973: 175–6). If a socialist society is in the business of *abolishing* classes, it cannot accept an organizational arrangement (i.e. party competition) which by definition *presupposes* the legitimate persistence of class division. Socialism has to develop other means by which popular democracy can operate (Soviets, workers' committees, residents' groups etc.). Socialist democracy, then, in this Marxist–Leninist argument, is about finding the proper representative form for a classless people. A one-party state, contrary to bourgeois propaganda, is thought to be a serious attempt to create a forum wherein an active consensus for *all* the people can be forged.

At this point the 'debate' has so visibly sharpened that we must wonder whether any line of thought can break the apparently intractable deadlock of theory and politics between pluralism and marxism. Historically (at least until the 1970s) official Communism has regarded pluralism principally as capitalist ideology and as having little valid to say about the political forms of the socialist state. For pluralists, marxism involves a transcendental determinism in which economic conflict and class interests wholly govern the alleged political 'necessities' of historical epochs. This appears to do away with essential tenets of western thought and culture: historical contingency, freedom of political choice and an open-ended future. More specifically, the marxist suspicion of party competition confirms the pluralist impression that marxism is an inherently undemocratic philosophy from which the authoritarian characteristics of marxist regimes follow perfectly logically. As far as pluralists are concerned, this association continues to place a large question mark over the sincerity of those modern Communist parties in the western world that claim to accept, and indeed promote, a democratic and parliamentary road to socialism. Is it possible, pluralists will ask, for marxist parties voluntarily to accept the result of an election whereby a socialist government and system is rejected by popular vote? The pluralist suggestion is that the answer is no.

For marxists, the burden of proof is quite the reverse. The capitalist class is typically prepared to sponsor democracy and to give its blessing to official oppositions only just as long as the legitimacy of the capitalist system itself is not at issue. In that eventuality, the socialist argument runs, democracy becomes entirely expendable. Each argument along these lines has recourse to history as a way of showing the inevitability of the outcomes projected. Lenin, it will be recalled, disbanded the Constituent Assembly in 1918 following a popular election in which the Bolsheviks gained only one quarter of the votes cast. On the other hand, in 1973 in Chile, the democratically elected socialist (and marxist) president, Allende, was killed in a successful military coup which had the backing of the business cartels, together with the CIA. These two cases are amongst the best-known illustrations of the theoretical logics outlined, but the last 150 years is rich in similar events elsewhere.

This sketch of ideological contrasts can be capped by the fact that, philosophically speaking, marxism and pluralism aspire to different sorts of explanatory theory. Pluralism, at least in its post-war American version, is a species of 'empirical democratic theory'. Pluralists are accordingly interested in describing and accounting for the character of modern democracy. Their declared focus is more the operation of political systems than, as with marxism, the development of the entire modern social structure. The marxist attachment to holistic explanations and 'depth' models of 'surface' phenomena is as suspicious in pluralist eyes as any economic determinism they espouse. Indeed, there might be nothing intrinsically wrong with the latter, as long as it could be specified in systematic empirical terms.

The philosophical tempers of marxism and pluralism are thus quite different. The latter involves a commitment to particularistic, observable propositions about the workings of democracy today. Pluralists do not aspire to seek out the fundamental processes in the evolution of society. In that sense their social ontology is extremely thin. Marxists, to the contrary, are interested in the underlying structures and causal mechanisms in society which might reveal its overall rationale and possible directions. This involves a hankering after 'scientific' explanation rather than 'mere' description. Marxists are also, relatedly, concerned with ascertaining a determinate *hierarchy* of causal relationships whether in historical evolution, the social structure, or in immediate political events. They see life as a coherent totality, though undoubtedly a complex one. Pluralists, on the other hand, generally back off from big explanations, preferring piecemeal and multi-factorial empirical connections. Their universe is necessarily heterogeneous and diverse, though they might acknowledge having to regard it for some purposes as if it were a unity. With this contrast between the respective conceptions of the social scientific task the schematic opposition between pluraliŝm and marxism is about complete. It is, of course, a caricature to some extent, but the power of caricatures in social theory should not be underestimated; they can be discovered doing active conceptual work at all levels, from the undergraduate essay to the latest statement of a new brand of thinking. Accordingly, the marxism–pluralism contrast appears to go all the way down, from approaches to the philosophy of history to the analysis of the latest election. In the rest of the first part of this book, I will be trying to fill out the model of antagonism in order to see how far it works and the ways in which it might be subverted. For one thing, it may not be either valid or useful to take as the exemplars of the two traditions the Bolshevik variant of marxism and the 'empirical democratic' school of US social science. The traditions are richer and broader than either of these narrowings suggest. Secondly, we should note that the fixed lines and basic concepts of the debate as sketched contain little room for ambiguities and silences *within* each tradition. What if, as well as being more variegated than the model of antagonism suggests, marxism and pluralism are also more internally contradictory, and, moreover, *increasingly* so? Whilst the full exegetical basis for qualifications of this kind cannot be set out in a book of this type, I will be offering a series of interpretations which do severely qualify the schematic model of all-out opposition as an accurate rendering of the current theoretical climate.

A final point is worth making about the way in which a strong model in social theory is deconstructed or modified. The idea that theoretical traditions or paradigms *do* always reveal an internal logic in which concepts at different levels of abstraction mesh and mutually support one another is an attractive one, and the opposition I have set up involves a logic of this kind. Whether going by the name of 'paradigm', 'problematic' or 'conceptual framework', much of 1960s and 1970s social theory relied on fairly tight theoretical boxes of this sort to enable choices and arguments to be made. In the case of some traditions, especially holistically-inclined ones such as marxism, there is plain ground for making connections between, for example, its philosophical conception of history and its approach to immediate empirical phenomena. In the case of a more piecemeal approach to social science, such as pluralism, the procedure of constructing a whole package of reinforcing assumptions, concepts and ideological outcomes is less obviously valid, since it may be that no major pluralist writer overtly makes those kinds of linkages.

Other recent commentators have noted this problem, but have pressed ahead regardless in the construction of a typical pluralist world-view (Graham 1986: 132, Alford and Friedland 1985: 47). My own view is more compromised by impulses in 1980s social theory which imply that what is interesting or challenging in certain parts of 'global' theories can be held relatively separate from its status as part of any wider theoretical or political project. By the same token, writers who do *not* happen to subscribe to the idea of the all-pervasive theoretical totality (arguably, this is the case with the pluralists), have some right not to be unilaterally assigned to such a pre-set paradigm, thence to be held responsible for its sins, or lauded for its virtues.

My own inclination is thus to say that some notion of a plausible 'connection' between the various logical levels of a perspective is indeed important. I would not otherwise have sketched out the model of marxist–pluralist antagonism. I also think that parts or phases of the traditions we are concerned with *do* have a fairly clear conceptual logic, whether or not any particular writer is aware of it. Nevertheless, the cautionary note is necessary at this stage because part of the changing relationship between 'grand theories' such as marxism and pluralism is precisely a greater common attention to the *problem* of characterizing theories (and even individual authors) as coherent logical totalities. The latter understanding of a perspective works against the identification of hesitancies and discrepancies which may well be of as much interest as the consistency between concepts and levels of abstraction. For that reason, a more flexible term than paradigm, model or problematic seems advisable, such as 'tradition'. Part of the necessary interrogation of our model of antagonism between marxism and pluralism, therefore, is to note that it is a device which irons out difficult issues. A model of simple convergence between the two traditions, as we will see in due course, would be objectionable on the same grounds.

2

CONVENTIONAL TO CRITICAL PLURALISM

1. Introduction

According to the scenario of antagonism, marxism and pluralism sharply differ in their conception of social structure and agency, in their political analysis and prognosis, and in their philosophical conception of social explanation. In this chapter, I want to begin to ascertain just how intractable the implied deadlock is once closer attention is paid to the arguments and changes within each tradition.

In the case of pluralism, the exact nature and span of its dominance within western political theory is more problematical to assess than is often assumed. Moreover, while the main elements of the pluralist outlook as sketched so far can indeed be substantiated by reference to well-known texts and authors, there are other propositions in those same works which cut against any simple characterization of this main pluralist variant. Indeed, many of the cogent radical critiques of orthodox or conventional pluralism have since been accepted and extended by erstwhile pluralists themselves. Accordingly, we should regard pluralism today as an evolving and in many respects *critical* set of texts and reflections on contemporary democracy. Interestingly, conventional North American pluralism developed as an offshoot of a philosophically minded European current which was influential in the early twentieth century. When the history and conceptual breadth of pluralism are treated in this more varied context, the generalized opposition between pluralism and marxism is considerably mitigated.

2. Conventional pluralism: elements and criticisms

The main features of conventional pluralism can be summarized as:

- A sociology of competing interest groups.
- A conception of the state as a political mechanism responsive to the balance of societal demands.
- An account of the democratic civic culture which sets a realistic minimum measure for the values of political participation and trust.
- An empiricist and multi-factorial methodology of social science.

2.1. Interest groups and the political market

From the early work of A. F. Bentley through to the more sophisticated writings of Robert Dahl and Charles E. Lindblom, pluralists have forefronted the role of societally constituted interest groups. In his keynote text *The Governmental Process* (1951), for example, David Truman started from the proposition that the conflict and rivalry between social groups was not to be lamented as amounting simply to anti-social sectionalism. On the contrary, the formation of, and interaction between, groups expressed some of the deepest tendencies in human psychology and modern history. Truman believed that group life represented man's essentially social nature, involving inextricable elements of both domination and co-operation (Truman 1951: 505). In any society, for Truman, we should expect the pattern of group relations to be central and, to some extent, to be quite complex. Whilst every society is to be seen as a 'mosaic of overlapping groups' (1951: 43), it is in specifically industrial society that individual membership of a number of diverse groups and associations is most pronounced. Within the fabric of group life in modern society are elements which make for interest rivalry and conflict; but this is offset by the stabilizing influence of group *overlap* and inter-negotiation. It is the task of the modern polity actively to seek to harmonize the various interests (1951: 313) and to maximize the *number* of interest positions taken into account. The latter consideration is important for Truman because unorganized as well as organized interests have to be catered for. In his notion of 'potential groups', Truman develops an argument that governments and institutions are guided in their decision-making as much by the ever-present *potential* of group-formation as by actual group demands. Should serious evasions or distortion of public issues become obvious, or blatant miscarriages of even-handed democracy occur, a powerful interest group presence can be expected to emerge where there was none before. Truman argues that, like the phenomenon of overlapping membership, potential group formation places considerable and ever-rising pressure on government decisions.

Interestingly, this positive theoretical account of groups in Truman's theory does not find equivalent expression in his comments on the resolution of practical matters. In the latter context, what comes over is that social demands only have to be met *minimally* by the state and that groups themselves come to learn, through socialization, to accept the rules of political compromise (1951: 515, 524). Truman's account has been described as 'the first full articulation of the modern pluralist viewpoint' (de Bets 1983), but the characteristic social imagery can be found equally well expressed in a number of earlier and later texts. Truman's book, in fact, was a conscious revival of themes in Bentley's *The Process of Government* (1967, original 1908). Bentley developed the notion that political ideas can only be analysed in terms of the behaviour of interest groups, and that the state of society at any given time simply *is* the balance of group pressures and resistances, and of government adjustment to those pressures (Bentley 1967: 259, 264). Writing a year later than Truman, Earl Latham offered similar thoughts on groups, only this time in terms of evolutionary biology rather than in Bentley's physics of group forces. Latham thought a social mechanism akin to environmental selection would determine which groups would come through in a social world which appeared as 'an aggregation, a collection, an assemblage, a throng, a moving multitude of human clusters, a consociation of groups, a plurality of collectivities, an intersecting series of social organisms, adhering, interpenetrating, overlapping . . .' (Latham 1952: 49). A representative later text to draw from is Nelson Polsby's defence of pluralist methodology. Polsby rebuffed radical critics by restating the case for regarding American society as being 'fractured into a congeries of hundreds of small special interest groups with incompletely overlapping memberships, widely differing power bases, and a multitude of techniques for exercising influence on decisions salient to them' (Polsby 1963: 118).

Dahl and Lindblom seldom resorted to such unrestrained prose, but they too conceived the political effect of interest groups as central, in five ways (Dahl and Lindblom 1953: 304–5). In the first place, groups are more politically effective than individuals, and this encourages greater all-round participation in voluntary associations. Secondly, group organization facilitates healthy political competition, the condition of a democratic public sphere. Third, the group bargaining process creates a barrier to extremism and provides a springboard for responsive political negotiators to emerge, in a climate conducive to the formation of alliances. Fourth, overlapping membership of social groups discourages unilateral thought and action. Fifth, an extensive network of social groups helps to ensure the spread of information and communication channels. In Dahl and Lindblom's eyes, these postulates do not by themselves guarantee democracy, since there are procedural, cultural and technical prerequisites too (Dahl 1956: 71, Dahl and Lindblom 1953: 280). But the central sociological agency for pluralists is the interest group, and balanced interaction between these units of political motivation constitutes the foundation of advanced democracy.

In terms of the debate with marxism, US pluralists from the first tended to posit a multiplicity of groups rather than a concentration of society into *classes*. Truman urged us not to think of group claims as the product of crass self-interest. He also moved against seeing groups as organized along class, caste or occupational lines of cleavage. Indeed, were a sectional and selfish conception of interests to come to dominate political affairs, a 'pathogenic' or 'apoplectic' paralysis of the democratic norms might ensue (1951: 526). The antidote to sectional interests is therefore an agreed pattern of interest-bargaining, and the marginalization of disruptive group 'voices'. In this respect, Truman again followed Bentley, who regarded Marx's focus on class struggle as empirically mistaken, or, at best, as a crude approximation to pluralist group theory itself (Bentley 1967: 465). Dahl and Lindblom for their part were happy to accept social class as one basis of social differentiation, but only as one of many (1953: 329), while Dahl took a stronger line in the face of later criticism, strenuously rejecting the reductionism of class analysis (1971: 106).

Generally speaking, the conventional pluralist literature reveals a fear that society will simply be torn apart, and democracy rendered impossible, by the concentrated workings of a small number of social divisions. Part of the affirmative tone many writers adopt when describing the near infinitude of social diversity stems from their belief that multiple group membership provides the very glue which binds society together (Berelson 1954: 406), whereas class divisions constantly threaten to pull it apart again.

The aversion to taking class as a major basis of group differentiation is one possible source of pluralism's tendency to accept a capitalist economic framework as the natural setting for democratic advance. Another reason is the pervasive inclination to see group interaction as a process akin to the jostling and bargaining of customers in a political market place (Kelso 1978: 13). Many of the main pluralist texts adopt this kind of free market imagery. The train of thought appears to be that since interest groups are perceived as in a sense spontaneous growths in modern society, they will emerge and fade according to the natural ebb and flow of social demand. When they do emerge as political customers with unmet needs, groups engage in a process of 'bargaining' with each other, often striking a deal between competing consumer interests. This prospect of social agents behaving as equalizing forces, bargaining and exchanging preferences which are born of a primitive social utility curve reflects exactly the dominant motifs of the capitalist market and its reflection in orthodox economic theory since Adam Smith. Thus Dahl and Lindblom conceived the role of the politician in pluralist democracy as that of a 'broker' and a 'bargainer' who acts on behalf of the clients (Dahl and Lindblom 1953: 333). At one point, even the President of the United States is recruited to the political enterprise as a 'general manager' (1953: 351).

When the state is brought into this picture of competing, exchanging groups, the polity is represented as driven by a tendency to equilibrium (Easton 1953: 268f.), one in which the 'preferences' of interest groups can be expressed and to a large extent satisfied. A variety of such images have been cited as actively at work in the pluralist conception of responsive government. The state is regarded variously as the broker, the cipher, the switchboard, or the weathervane which acts in accordance with the balance of interest groups in society. There are undoubtedly many subtle differences between these metaphors with regard to how *active* the government's own role in this balancing operation actually is (Dunleavy and O'Leary 1987: 41f.), but the conception of the state as more or less disinterested, more or less responsive to the impact of multiple group demands is a prominent one. The vocabulary of 'equilibrium' imparts a further technical and systemic aura to the business of democratic decision-making. Much more than (for example) the ideas of social peace or latent conflict, equilibrium conveys the sense of an evolving system or mechanism with political balance as its prime quality and end point. Indeed, in conventional pluralism, the origins, goals and determinations of 'the state' as such are seldom considered, and its non-representative branches are of much less concern that the representative ones. Pluralists thus tend to speak of the political system or governmental process, terms which work to reinforce a neutral understanding of the state's role and of its identity as a factor in a self-maintaining system. This notion of a balanced evolving organism is one which pluralism in political theory shares with functionalist sociology.

The pluralist/functionalist account, it can be charged, lacks serious historical bearings or a feel for the tremendous human and environmental turmoil which accompanied (and still accompanies) the evolution of modern society. The latter from the first has been a society in which pervasive inequalities are generated, a society which has emerged in a very particular part of the globe, and one which advances neither relentlessly nor in equilibrium. Rather, development is essentially uneven, contradictory and halting. The functionalist assumptions of smooth upward evolution, of disembodied technological imperatives, of class harmonization and uniform benefits can each be firmly countered. Social scientists are under at least an equal obligation to show the conflicts, contradictions and human agencies at work within society. And there is a considerable historiography which shows that the development of modern society has been an altogether messier and interest-bound process than the functionalists make out.

This radical critique of the form and content of the functionalist model which pluralists sometimes appear to adhere to can be shared by marxists and non-marxists alike. But the marxist critique is more specific than the general radical one. 'Modern society' is really a synonym for *capitalist* society, in this view. It is the capitalist mode of production which ignites the potential of technology in the modern era; a capitalism which, according to Marx, shows an inherent tendency to replace living labour (people) by dead labour (machines) in its drive to maximize profits and secure the conditions of its own reproduction. The very impetus of technological growth, hence, is indissolubly part of capitalist production, not 'modern' society *per se* (Marx 1976, Hobsbawm 1969). In that context, democracy itself is an unevenly developing, historic form of political organization. It is much more intrinsically connected to the class aspirations and compromises between classes and class fractions than the pluralist literature allows (cf. Therborn 1977, Moore 1969). Some pluralists, it should be said, accepted that certain sorts of groups emerge in a stronger bargaining position than others. The idea that one set of interests generates *countervailing* powers might not be a naturally produced balancing act. On the contrary, the importance of the democratic polity is that discrepancies of power and resources at the societal level can be offset only by carefully-wrought political arrangements (Galbraith 1952, Key 1964: 102, Dahl and Lindblom 1953: 351).

The radical response to this turn in the logic of the argument is to say that if social inequalities are indeed serious, it is quite unrealistic for pluralists to think that the formal political process will by itself rectify them. In pluralism, that system is essentially responsive not proactive: it allows those groups to be heard who make themselves heard. And the ones who do make themselves heard are those already privileged by the socio-economic structure. Therefore the pluralist 'sensitivity' to underlying inequalities is without real impact in their theoretical system, because the conceptual separation of political system and social structure together with the neutrality of the former means that inequalities are not eradicated or balanced out; at best they are tempered and defused.

Turning to the very concept of social interest groups, a number of telling objections can be drawn up. For one thing, pluralists seldom make clear just what collectivities of agents comprise interest groups. Hesitations over the meaning of 'interest', how various types of group allegiance are achieved, and how the various categories of groupings relate to one another in a social ontology are apparent throughout the pluralist canon. Bentley, for example, was prepared to entertain that blondes and brunettes could be seen as forming a distinct interest antagonism, provided only that they acted as such (Bentley 1967: 212). Without further specification of the subjective and objective constitution of an interest, this flourish only begs the question. Bentley did gesture towards distinctions between parties and organizations, pressure groups and latent interests, voluntary associations and civic orders, and above all underlying and surface interests (1967: 444f.). However, these points are never systematically ordered and the overall rationale of group theory becomes less clear the more the insightful differentiations pile up.

Truman did not improve the clarity of group theory in this respect. Indeed, he seemed to hold to a second-hand psychology to the effect that group-life intimately and intensely expresses the form of our essential sociality, binding together inherent elements of domination and co-operation (Truman 1951: 505). Such an assertion of the social character of human dispositions could be seen as either virtually tautological or deeply mystical, depending on one's own anthropological inclinations. But either way, it does not appear to ground a specific substantive sociology of interests. When that issue looms, Truman tends to resort to generalities which convey the instability and proliferation of social phenomena. 'The total pattern of government over a period of time . . . presents a protean complex of criss-crossing relations that change in strength and direction with alterations in the power and standing of interests, organized and unorganized' (Truman 1951: 508). The kind of perspective outlined does tend to favour a 'socialization' approach to human interaction, and the family in particular is sometimes singled out as a crucial basis for participation in wider social relations. Latham was certainly drawn to this kind of line (1964: 40–3). Yet in the face of the almost infinite potential for specifying group types, a more structural and independent basis for identifying the relevant context in which groups and agents interact is necessary. This important insight was put forward early in the debate around pluralist categories by David Easton (1953: 189) and slightly later by Stanley Rothman (1960).

Another source of criticism of conventional pluralism is its implied equality between interest groups, and between the members of a single interest group. It is impossible to read the standard works without getting the sense that resources, information and the means of political communication are openly available to all citizens, that groups form an array of equivalent power centres in society, and that all legitimate voices can and will be heard (Dahl 1956: 145). This thesis has been criticized as overlooking the massive concentration of power in the hands of those with structural economic advantages (especially *business* groups), and professional staffs who make a living by developing lobbying techniques. *Within* groups too there tends to be an iron law of oligarchy, whereby individuals or factions with inbuilt advantages (wealth, office, or professional skills) effectively wield power over the rank and file. Instead of an array of balanced, open-access groups, we find a 'plurality of entrenched oligarchies' (Kariel 1961: 68).

Finally, in this context, pluralism's focus on interest groups in civil society at large ignores the role of interest groups within the state itself. One of the visible tendencies of modern history is that the nation state has developed a powerful semi-autonomous agency with interests of its own and there are key groups within the state, it might be suggested, which are not at all concerned to reflect societal interests. Rather, they have objectives and self-reproducing strategies which go precisely *against* those of the civil society.

2.2 Normative requirements and implications

Pluralism's sociological remit is not simply the theory of groups of societal interests. It is rather the influence of these on a democratic polity which is central to conventional pluralism as I have defined it. This is because, whilst some pluralist theorists seemed to hold that political equilibrium could be effected by the autonomous process of group emergence and inter-negotiation, it is clear that a Hobbesian vision of a destructive war of all against all is just as plausible an outcome of sectional interests. There arises within pluralism, therefore, the need to supplement group theory with, first, an account of the contribution of the political system, and secondly a specification of the normative requirements for a stable and harmonious expression of interest group exchange in a democracy. It is in this respect that another major contribution of 1950s US political sociology comes in, namely the analysis of the *civic culture* of modern democracy.

The analysis of the civic culture has not always been thought to be directly connected to pluralism. Pluralism is only one aspect of the investigation of normative agreement, whilst some interest group theories highlight rational self interest as the basis of political behaviour, not subjective identification with the general socio-political fabric. But the power of the concern with democracy in pluralist theory, and its obsession with an effective balance between groups, created a widespread concern to ascertain the level of commitment of agents and groups to the system which allows all legitimate voices to be heard (Moodie and Studdert-Kennedy 1970: 72, Almond and Verba 1980: 20). In that sense pluralism begins with an ethic of competition and steadily moves towards a concern with consensus (Lively 1978: 197, Key 1964: 12). One of the principal researchers into political participation summed up this logic when he asserted that for political democracy to survive

... intensity of conflict must be limited, the rate of change must be restrained, stability in the economic and social structure must be maintained, a pluralistic social organization must exist, and a basic consensus must bind together the contending parties. (Berelson, in Kariel 1970: 70)

The central text which reported on the extent of citizen participation and allegiance to the western democratic culture was Almond and Verba's *The Civic Culture*, a comparative survey of values across five nations. The authors saw in the very idea of an open polity backed by a civic culture of democratic participation, man's discovery of a humane and conservative way of handling social change (Almond and Verba 1965: 7). The conservative emphasis is vital here, as it was seen to be in Truman, since the mitigation of social strife requires a particular cultural construal of the value of participation, one in which democratic activity is tempered by its necessary limitation (1965: 240, 243). A high subjective perception of the citizen's influence has thus to be counterbalanced by a relatively low level of *actual* ground-level input (1965: 346). This wariness of activism is not necessarily an expression of contradiction or cynicism in the pluralist outlook, for inactivity can be further interpreted as the free choice of citizens *not* to participate. Indeed, in a satisfactory democratic system we might even *expect* group demands to exist merely 'potentially'. Were the system not to be working effectively, the argument implies, people would quickly cease to be apathetic, turning their potential influence into real group muscle. As· in Truman's scenario, then, a set of norms which serve to regulate expectations and actions – a civic culture – acts as a check upon any tendency for political elites to act without due reference to the interests, demands and opinions of the wider society.

Given this 'law of anticipated reactions' (Almond and Verba 1965: 353), the indices of popular participation and democratic competence in the citizenry – at least in the USA and UK – seemed promising. Almond and Verba linked this enhanced democratic activity with a strong pattern of overlapping interest group membership: 55 per cent of US respondents who belonged to civic organizations, for instance, belonged to more than one. Almond and Verba's criteria for estimating democratic allegiance specified that the latter should be of an 'affective' as well as cognitive nature. This enabled them to register indications of small-scale dissatisfaction with the functioning of democracy, whilst emphasizing that, in a deeper sense, the virtue of the system is the fact that it *allows* for a range of conflicting pressures to be both expressed and absorbed. On the whole, they felt able to assert that the contemporary western society had come close to achieving 'a pluralist culture built on communication and persuasion, consensus and diversity' (Almond and Verba 1965: 6).

Conventional pluralists were not mere apologists for western democracy. Indeed, they were primarily interested in charac-terizing the nature of the *imperfect* democracy which existed in the modern world. Dahl and Lindblom spoke of the terrifying drive almost everywhere in the twentieth century *away* from effective control of leaders (1953: 276). For all that, pluralists were hopeful that where pockets of democracy (or at least 'polyarchy') existed, their ingredients could be specified and fostered. All governmental systems are in reality, they concluded, combinations of hierarchy, polyarchy and anarchy. Yet the point on the scale between democracy and dictatorship reached by particular societies is felt to be immensely important, and can be measured by, for example, the fact that there were, according to some calculations in the 1950s, 10 million prisoners in the USSR, but only 162,000 in the USA (Dahl and Lindblom, 1953: 276). For Dahl, actual democracy may be seen as quite limited, as little more than the 'steady appeasement of relatively small groups' (1956: 143). But the theory of interest groups does specify necessary, if not sufficient, conditions for democracy, and a culture of democratic trust reinforces it. The dominant sentiment is that whilst democracy might be imperfect, it is still worth having. Dahl did hold that there was a strong element of voluntary and rational allegiance to the polyarchies amongst the people. He speculated:

> Probably this strange hybrid, the normal American political system, is not for export to others. But so long as the social prerequisites of democracy are substantially intact in this country, it appears to be a relatively efficient

system for reinforcing agreement, encouraging moderation, and maintaining social peace in a restless and immoderate people operating a gigantic, powerful, diversified and incredibly complex society. (1956: 151)

This note of optimism chimes in with the belief of other sociologists that gradually the irrational drives associated with the sway of class ideologies was giving way to rational adjustments of interests for the sake of the public good. Seymour Lipset concluded that democracy, so conceived, was the good society in action, and that it had been largely achieved in the USA (Lipset 1960: 403f.). For other pluralists, the danger of 'immoderation' could not be eradicated by merely anticipating the spontaneous emergence of an appropriate civic culture. Berelson for one was clear that the values of democratic stability had to be trained into the child 'before it is old enough to care about the matter' (Berelson 1970: 72). Dahl too endorsed the idea that 'total social training in all the norms' might be necessary (1956: 76). The overall impression is that the pluralist structure and civic culture of American democracy should be defended, but that it also requires to be strenuously reinforced.

There are several reasons for questioning the entire 'civic culture' enterprise. The extent of these writers' reliance on a speculative theory about the positive function of apathy is indicated by the fact that the empirical results of the surveys do *not*, in the event, provide much for pluralists to cheer about. For example, only 39 per cent of the survey's British respondents felt that individuals ought to play some kind of active role in the community (Almond and Verba 1965: 127). Only 21 per cent of American respondents reckoned it was part of a citizen's duty to try to understand things and keep informed (129). And we should note that the researchers took as their base-line of participation the remarkably low-level attitude that 'one ought at least to take an interest in what goes on in the community' (128). Whilst 72 per cent of Britons did endorse this requirement, one feels that more could be learned about democratic responsiveness from the 68 per cent of Italians who seemed unable even to go along with this bland formulation.

The figure of 55 per cent for 'overlapping group membership' in the US was cited earlier as something that impressed Almond and Verba. Yet in the UK, this figure slips to 34 per cent, and in any case only one quarter of the Americans interviewed did actually belong to *one* organization (1965: 264). Moreover, it is a speculative hypothesis that membership of any sort of voluntary or civic organization *does* enhance the political culture. The secretary of the local whist drive for example could well be seen as directing valuable participatory energies *away* from politics and into the private domain of personal gratification.

In general, then, the idea of a vibrant democratic culture comes from arguments which link low criteria of participation with the best available figures, and which posit a connection (largely hypothetical) between minimum activity in associations and political competence. At best, these pluralist arguments highlight the contribution of *deference* or non-hostile inactivity to the stability of the system (Pateman 1980: 65). But a series of sociological studies over the last twenty years or so shows how precarious it is to associate compliance with the norms of a political culture with its legitimation in the eyes of ordinary people (cf. Mann 1973, Abercrombie, Hill and Turner 1980, Held 1984). Indeed some pathbreaking voting studies within US political science (Berelson et al. 1954, Campbell et al. 1960) conducted during the ascendancy of pluralist thought themselves lead to conclusions which go well beyond the 'deference' thesis. Ordinary American voters come out of these surveys of political competence as ill-informed, inactive and basically uninterested. The pluralists have, in fact, two contrary and unconvincing responses to this state of affairs. On the one hand, the 'law of anticipated reactions' can be brought in to give a remedial account of the lack of overt participation. Yet this theory involves a serious mistake about motivation. It can plausibly be counter-asserted that people are apathetic not because elites in power are responsive, but because they are *not*. Moreover, uninterest in the political system as people know it does not necessarily entail uninterest in all forms of politics (Hart 1978, Graham 1986: 130). Rather, a 'positive' assessment of the political implications of apathy are more likely to lead to revolutionary conclusions.

But perhaps this is just the point: as long as apathy exists rather than a revolutionary counter-culture, then the liberal democratic regime is at least *stable*. One criticism of the bias of pluralism is that under the guise of seeking indications of democratic participation it settles for something considerably less than the classical ideal of direct rule for and by the people themselves. A related point is that, ultimately, for many pluralists, *stability* is more important than participation. Apathy, regarded thus, can be construed as a force for stability, whereas democratic participation and revolutionary rebellion alike threaten to upset the prized and carefully evolved equilibrium of western societies. Quentin Skinner has chided critics of pluralism for pulling out of pluralist texts those occasional political gestures which seem to condemn the authors for failing to adhere to 'genuine' democratic values. He suggests that since true democracy is something of a chimera, the pluralists' revised sense of democracy might be as defensible as any radical alternative (Skinner 1973: 298). But it is the pluralists themselves who wrestle with the concept and measure of participation as a central indication of democratic legitimacy. Their conclusions are not favourable on this score, and indeed their own order of political values – perhaps in view of the results – does not have democracy unambiguously at its head. 'There must be involvement in politics if there is to be the sort of participation necessary for democratic decision-making; yet the involvement must not be so intense as to endanger stability' (Almond and Verba 1965: 240). Latham (1964: 48), Berelson (1970: 71), Truman (1951: 524), and Dahl and Lindblom (1953: 287f.) all similarly promote the functional role played by consensus in a stable liberal social order – a consensus which might be freely formed, but which can if necessary be secured by way of 'indoctrination' (Dahl and Lindblom's term).

In summary, it could be said that alongside the weaknesses identified in the theory of group interests, pluralism passes off a stunted political culture as a major western achievement. Moreover, the implicit support given by pluralists to 'democracy American style' (Margolis 1983) is arguably a concern less for participative democratic values than for a stable liberal social system.

2.3. Pluralist methodology

The descriptive ambitions of conventional pluralism are rooted in a *behaviourist* tradition of positivist empirical analysis (Lukes 1974: ch. 2). Much of Bentley's major work for example was concerned to rid political theory of 'spooks' and even 'ideas' – unless they could be pinned down in behavioural terms (1967: 172). So the investigator takes for his or her object of study the manifest actions and conscious beliefs of a sample population, then takes note of their observed causes and outcomes. In the case of pluralism, the object of study is political in quite a narrow sense, being concerned with group influences on the official decision-making process.

This empiricism has the advantage of eliminating meta-physical speculation from political observation. On the other hand, to focus only upon observable events as the causes and data of political analysis is an impoverished conception of social explanation, since it appears to pass over such vital social forces as unspoken belief systems and structural social pressures in determining the character of a political regime. Empiricism also operates with a weak social ontology. Group interaction is conceived by pluralists as a protean morass of surface data covering a whole range of different sorts of intentional motives and social categories. There is little awareness that social theory can or ought to develop an account of *which* groups are fundamental over the long term, or just how the structure of society operates to foster particular types of interaction. The theory of 'modern society' which pluralists draw upon states little more than that technological growth creates a complex world of specialization and progress. It is a curiously *formal* and excessively general theory which, as such, has limited concrete explanatory value. The empiricist concern to observe and deduce rather than to *explain* social phenomena leaves the relation between pluralism's sociology and its political objects vague, the former standing as 'background' only. But with a widening of the kinds of political phenomena to be explained, and a greater sense of their contradictions, a richer and more causally specific social theory could be projected.

Pluralism also carries at the back of its sociology some

relatively undeveloped assumptions about human beings in general. For example, it tends to presuppose that 'man' is a social animal whose attachments take hold most naturally in the context of small groups, and whose needs and aspirations are likely to be diverse. Truman (1951: 505) and Latham (1952: 1) begin from the standpoint that small groups express man's deepest psychic needs, and constitute his home in the world. Civic culture analysis, for its part, highlights the importance of the 'affective' conditions of political identity. These apparently harmless and commonsensical notions of cultural identity and belonging can, without extensive supplement, be dangerously simplistic. Apart from the general, ongoing debate about whether we can even speak of a settled human nature, recent work in social psychology (Harre 1979) and discussions of human attributes in relation to conceptions of ideology (Hirst and Woolley 1985) suggest the need for a much richer sense of the contradictory, multi-levelled process by which the subjects of political action are formed. The whole relationship between subjects, individuals and their identity as members of certain social categories is one which has been dramatically unsettled in recent social theory. Clearly, conventional pluralists cannot be written off just for failing to anticipate what has since become a widespread awareness of the strengths and pitfalls of a developed social ontology. But the empiricist conception of science which pluralism reflects does tend to undermine the importance of structural and often unobservable powers, forces and tendencies. It is an enhanced appreciation of the various *layers* of social causality and personality structure that is missing from behaviourist political science and this absence counts heavily against it. Pluralists, in fact, share with other empiricists a resistance to the very idea that the philosophical basis of explanatory social science requires coherent theorization. Temperamentally, they might baulk at the suggestion that this is what they ought to be doing, for the (plausible) reason that a useful political theory does not *have* to be grounded in an elaborate philosophy. A theory of democracy can, according to this line, achieve many of its aims without incurring an obligation to provide meta-theoretical justification. All the same, the social forces, constraints and conditions which necessarily envelop ideas about democracy cannot stand as optional background data only. They require a more extensive treatment both conceptually and in terms of the empirical measures which could be thought to control them. If this is so, the rather general and ambiguous pluralist accounts of the nature of social groups, their patterns of interaction, and their embodiment in contemporary political life each stand in need of considerable clarification and revision. These tasks, it is now recognized by many social researchers, are hindered by the retention of an empiricist epistemology.

An important by-product of adopting an empiricist approach to social life is pluralism's tendency to multi-factorialism, that is, the working belief that there are normally a great many relevant causes of events and phenomena in a particular domain. Moreover, the objects and theories of one domain can be kept strictly separate from those in another. This partly accounts for the pluralist inclination to keep political analysis distinct from any conclusions about economic organization. The empiricist project is a piecemeal one, which strenuously avoids the temptation to see contingent connections as necessary ones, and which regards the construction of a totality of knowledge as inherently speculative. Rather, in the pluralist picture, we discover bits of knowledge, largely by way of observation. While these can be systematically brought together in a descriptive way, they cannot be regarded as mapping the essential structure of the real world. The latter remains an infinite source of data and suggestion, no one factor among which can be singled out as primary.

3. Varieties of pluralism

The foregoing elaboration of conventional pluralist tenets and the radical criticisms that can be made of them captures much of the spirit and content of the opposition between pluralism and marxism. On the other hand, at important points the discussion continued to veer towards caricature. In redressing this tendency by spotlighting some overlooked discrepancies and ambiguities, my purpose is not to rub out the strong lines of the debate. The amendment of a caricature does not suffice to call off the contest between pluralist and radical theorists of democracy by declaring 'a plague on both their houses' (Skinner 1973). Conventional pluralists do come out of the amended version looking less apologetic; but their discourses are by the same token rather more contradictory. So the discussion is not intended to 'rescue' or 'retrieve' conventional pluralism (cf. Hirst 1987). Rather, by adding the theoretical complications in conventional pluralism to further reflection on its past history and subsequent development, we get a broader and more interesting picture of pluralism as a modern political current.

3.1. The 'reign' of conventional pluralism

One difficulty we face in pigeon-holing pluralism is that it is hard to find a text of the conventional variant which explicitly articulates or defends something called pluralism. As noted, many of these writers' allegiance was to 'empirical democratic theory', and within this umbrella term were to be found a range of studies concerned to investigate, for instance, voting patterns, cultural norms, comparative indices of democratic stability, pressure group formations, local government decision-making, and so on. Two of the most illuminating writings of the 1950s, texts which are sometimes taken as typical of North American political science, can only be seen as representative if we strain our interpretative categories to the limit. Dahl's *A Preface to Democratic Theory*, for example, oft-cited as a classic of pluralism, says relatively little about the social basis of democracy. It is true that the two main planks of pluralism as I have defined it – that a range of interest groups make their mark on the political process, and that there is a consensus in democratic nations around the virtues of responsive government – are to be found in Dahl. But these propositions are not perceived as a logical pairing (Dahl 1956: 145, 76). Dahl's main objective is to assess realistically the minimum conditions for effective decision-making in modern democracies, and social pluralism appears as only one of several equally-weighted conditions. Indeed, perhaps surprisingly, no work of Dahl is cited in Stanley Rothman's extensive list of the 'more notable' recent interest group studies (1960).

David Easton's *The Political System* is another work sometimes taken to be typical of US political science during the rise of pluralism. In fact, this unusually rigorous book contains the germs of some of the main criticisms of pluralism already mentioned. It examines, for example, the bias of the equilibrium model (Easton 1953: 268f.) and the imperative to look at the structural context of group interaction – the latter being recommended in part through a sympathetic summary of Marx's significance (1953: 189). Furthermore, while certainly cast in an empiricist idiom, Easton's treatment of the issues of value-free social theory and the problem of relativism (1953: 96, 264–5) is not amenable to crass philosophical bracketing. In short, if Easton's work is typical of 1950s political science, then the latter is not typically pluralist in any narrow doctrinal sense.

It has even been argued along similar tracks that the writings of Truman and Latham cannot be taken to be specifically pluralist (Garson 1978: 71). I would not want to go that far, but we can say that pluralism does not receive a systematic definition and exposition in the period of its supposed dominance. It *is* explicitly defended or retrieved at a later stage (Polsby 1963, Dahl 1980, 1982), but always with hindsight and only in part. So there is a considerable question about just how dominant conventional pluralism ever was, and about how *long* it occupied centre-stage in US political theory. The schematic version of our debate places pluralism as very much a post-war phenomenon, partly in order to clinch its role in legitimating US leadership of the 'free world'. The related proposition that pluralism represents an important shift away from the study of politics conceived as the grand march of ideas and institutions is, to be sure, testified in some reviews of the discipline (e.g. Eckstein 1979). On the other hand, Easton, writing in 1953, notes the 'deluge of interest group studies in the last 25 years' (1953: 173) and he generalizes that for most political scientists since Bentley, 'political life is primarily to be viewed as group life' (1953: 175–6).

In a sense, the pluralism question begins with the founding of the USA itself. The core of James Madison's articles in *The Federalist* (Madison 1966, original 1788) was that the basis of political factions resided in self-interest, and that the latter in turn stemmed from different sorts of property ownership (and human nature). The political issue, for Madison, was to devise a constitutional form which could express yet contain the interests of the factions. Madison above all wanted the interests of the *majority* to be institutionally contained. In that sense, he was very much a reluctant democrat (Held 1986: 66), and the pluralists can be seen as having turned his emphasis around in the proposition that the political system can compensate for social disadvantage. All the same, the links between property, group interests, and political expression are sketched out and fiercely debated in that early American moment.

The focus on group formation and societal interests, then, suggests that pluralism even in its US incarnation is not a creature of the 1950s. However, pluralism's other constitutive element – the civic culture of a modern democratic nation – does place it squarely in that decade. At this point, pluralism's heyday can be made to seem surprisingly short. Regarded not as a social physics of group pressures, but as a concern with the political bargaining process at government level within a democratic consensus, the dominance of pluralism could be seen as spanning the years 1956–9 only (Garson 1978: 90f.). But if we take this line, we should concede that the focus on government and culture must have been introduced partly in order to remedy the *weaknesses* of the pure theory of groups.

Moreover, by the later 1950s, many of the most incisive rejections of pluralism had already been tabled. E. E. Schatt-schneider's (1935) radical demolition of pressure group theory's explanation of taxation policy can be seen as an important forerunner of things to come, and its impulses were picked up and developed in the work of Floyd Hunter (1953), C. Wright Mills (1956) and others during the early 1950s. By the early 1960s, to turn Easton's phrase around, a deluge of *critiques* of interest group studies had been unleashed and Henry Kariel was already announcing 'the decline of American pluralism' (Kariel 1961, 1970, Bluhm 1965, Munger and Price 1964). The force of the critical reaction is indicated by the fact that the special (1960) 'Bentley revisited' issue of the *American Political Science Review* was strongly anti-pluralist in content (Garson 1978: 107).

3.2. Original pluralism

The point of that brief exercise in revisionist intellectual history was not to expound a thesis about 'the pluralism myth'. It is, though, a necessary part of qualifying the understanding of pluralism as a precise and coherent theory, and as a comprehensively conservative tradition. That task is taken further by recalling the impact of an influential current of pluralism in early twentieth-century European dabate – a current I will dub 'original pluralism'.

The main thrust of original pluralism was to develop an account of the forms of political association which might challenge and possibly replace the sovereignty of the political state. The pluralists' project was politically and philosophically radical in several ways. It emerged principally as a critique of *monistic* state theory as developed from Hegel by British idealist philosophers such as T. H. Green and Bernard Bosanquet. These thinkers were in turn responding to the crisis in Victorian laissez-faire, seeking to lay the ethical basis for some degree of general state intervention in culture and society. A philosophical defence of political sovereignty as embodied in the unified state involved a resurrection of such notions as the general will and the common good, ideas which could help redefine the scope of legitimate state action. Though their work was unashamedly abstract, the idealist philosophers were undoubtedly part of the important movement towards a new collectivism in late nineteenth-century Britain, the most notable political expression of which was the New Liberals' realignment of the political terrain from the 1880s (cf. Hall and Schwartz 1986).

The political radicalism of the pluralist reaction to these developments lay in its simultaneous rejection of idealist state theory and the atomistic individualism which the latter superseded (Nichols 1975: 10, Hsiao 1927: 8f.). The presumptions that the state expressed a collective will and a legal personality were, it was argued, dangerous metaphysical fictions. There was no guarantee, whatever that these would result in an adequate representational form for modern social democracy (this was the period of the struggle for universal suffrage): the greater likelihood was a latter day secular absolutism. The main fault of idealism in this respect was to provide the theoretical basis for regarding the state as coextensive with, and the only formal expression of, the entire social fabric (Hobhouse 1918: 75). The implications of that identification were thought to be distinctly undemocratic, since the accountability of the state to the particular sets of people who make up society's real life is vague and indirect.

The most coherent aspect of British pluralism lay in a common opposition to this monistic theory of sovereignty. A series of works by, amongst others, G. D. H. Cole (1914–15), Harold Laski (1917, 1919), and Ernest Barker which sought to expose 'the discredited state' (Barker 1915) laid out the essence of pluralist objections. Cole's version of pluralism was more imbued with a vision of developed associational self-government than others, but this summary of his important paper captures much of the wider pluralist spirit:

> Its key features were an awareness of groups and associations as the depositories of loyalties and obligations; of the principle of function as the central differentiating criterion in society; of the state as one functional association amongst others; and of the need to create an organizational structure which recognized the rights of associations to substantial self-government whilst harmonizing the relation between the associations themselves to meet the requirements of the community as a whole. (Wright 1979: 39)

The elements of original pluralism were thus an account of group identity and political obligation, a functional concept of political representation, a critique of the monistic sovereign state, and, I would add, philosophical pragmatism. The argument against the monistic state and for the idea of associational organizations was simply that as concrete individuals, we live and work among similarly situated individuals, and our primary loyalties and duties are towards social *groups* of that kind. The state, pluralists urged us to remember, was a fictional collectivity: human groups, by contrast, were perfectly real. On the latter point, much was taken from the 'realist' legal theories of Otto von Gierke and F. W. Maitland (1900) who brilliantly developed a critique of the categories of Roman law as being profoundly out of keeping with the inexorable tendencies to cultural diversity in modern society. Pluralists insisted that the state had no corporate personality of its own, but social groups did. Political sovereignty, therefore, should be vested in the latter not the former.

Following the derivation of sovereignty from the reality of social groups, the original pluralists emphasized functional representation as the politically appropriate form of a democracy. A franchise based only on territorial residence, they argued, inadequately reflects our collective social existence, and sets up a structure whereby the all-powerful state retains control and sovereignty over a mass of isolated individuals. Functional representation, on the other hand, allots political rights, and devises voting structures for people, according to their membership of groups which perform social functions of one kind or another – notably groups of workers. This second arrangement allows for a genuinely dispersed power system, since functional associations would themselves be effective self-governing democracies. A pluralist system of this kind would also be in the nature of the case a more direct and participatory form of democracy than the parliamentary-territorial system.

The philosophical context of this political debate was extremely important, as of course it was for the 'statist' thinkers. A pluralist philosophy involves a generalized epistemic hostility to all forms of monistic explanation (Breitling 1980). Where monists emphasize singularity and one-factor modes of explanation and justification, pluralists insist on heterogeneity and multi-factorialism. At bottom, plural simply means more than one. In the perennial philosophical oscillation, going back to the Greeks, between the One and the Many, pluralism seems unambiguously on the side of the latter. Assertions of abstract unity and totality are thus to be questioned in all spheres of thought and life, and instead a preference for concrete diversity is established. This set of connections not only enabled a critique of *political* monism to be undertaken, but prompted important reflections on religious obligation and the relationships between church and state (Figgis 1914). In general, we might even want to posit a pluralist philosophical *temperament,* one which is attracted by modalities of 'flux, diversity and contest' (Solomon 1983: 6).

In none of these dimensions of original pluralism was there any eventual theoretical unity – perhaps in keeping with the temperamental traits just alluded to. Politically, the initial pluralist challenge to the sovereign collectivist state resulted in a number of currents which could not easily be reconciled: guild socialism, socialist collectivism, social democracy, and liberal anti-statism. Theoretically, the pluralists did not succeed in pursuing to the finish the critique of a totalistic conception of sovereignty. Cole moved away from the idea of the 'real personality of groups' (having once even flirted with the concept of the 'group soul' (Nichols 1975: 59)). Furthermore, his sense of the need for a distinctive socialist co-ordination of functional groups has led critical commentators to see his work from at least *Social Theory* (1920) onwards as reintroducing a form of the very general will which earlier was emphatically denounced. Laski's intellectual biography reveals a similar movement, giving rise to the general proposition – one we will have to return to – that ultimately socialism cannot easily be squared with the fragmentation that pluralism entails. This proposition, though, should not be confined to socialist· discourse, for after the initially positive impact of pluralism on mainstream political theory, a general concern can be witnessed to take what is valuable in original pluralism and rework it into some wider sense of an ethical totality. The state is not, after all, just one association amongst others but an indispensable vehicle for overall community cohesion (cf. MacIver 1926, Hsaio 1927, Barker 1928).

In terms of the argument about representation, there was an interesting degree of disagreement and confusion amongst pluralists. In spite of movements towards full liberal democracy at the time, the pluralists' important case was that territorial-individual representation was not adequate to the democratic ideal. Industrial democracy was one recommendation which many pluralists supported, but how exactly would it be organized? And what *other* democratic forms would have to be introduced? In one of the most interesting texts of that era, Mary Follett (1918: 10) argued that for proper pluralist diversity it was insufficient to base a franchise upon occupational functions only, for example, or upon some more general consumers' or producers' range of interests. Follett's commitment to the psychological and personal aspect of political identification led her to advocate a neighbourhood-based principle of association, giving priority to the needs and psychic potential of daily community life. This would entail a move away from both what she scornfully termed 'ballot-box democracy' and from the guild socialist emphasis on workplace organization. In some respects, this strategy prefigures the turn towards feminist and communitarian priorities in radical politics from the 1970s (cf. Held and Pollitt 1986). Her work certainly illustrates the difficulties of some of the questions the original pluralists were grappling with.

Philosophically, original pluralism also comprised interestingly varied impulses. While Hegelian idealism was their *bête noire*, what they stood for beyond the general temperament indicated a moment ago is hard to pinpoint. Certainly, the influence of group personality concepts led pluralists away from nominalism and methodological individualism. The search for some principles of coherence and order in social life, moreover, rather works against the celebration of infinite diversity and flux which a radically pluralist ontology invokes. Perhaps it is better to see the original pluralists as seeking a way *beyond* the conceptual oscillations between totality and infinity, unity and difference. Philosophically minded though they were, no systematic elaboration of these possibilities emerged from the European pluralists.

Some of them did, though, draw inspiration from the work of William James. Among his many other ideas, James attempted to invert the Hegelian principle of reading into the diverse empirical forms taken by a phenomenon its *essential* form as given by pure conceptual reflection. Instead, for any object of investigation, James sought to move analytically from the knowable part to the constructed whole, conscious that the latter is always to an extent a fictional aid to further applied thinking. This epistemological instrumentalism aided the pluralists in their demonstrations against legal and political applications of Hegel's philosophical procedures. Beyond this, it is hard to say how far the pluralists accepted James's pragmatism. Since it was not of the traditionally sceptical empiricist variety, and since James's prose had an attractive 'real life' feel to it, pluralists undoubtedly found it congenial.

But the question of whether pragmatism as such reinforces empiricism or entirely subverts the whole process of epistemological reasoning (whether rationalist *or* empiricist) continues to engage cultural theorists today. James's *œuvre* provides no easy answer to that question, so it is not surprising that few unambiguous philosophical lines are drawn from James by the pluralist political theorists.

The original pluralist connection with James, and his strenuous attempt to rid philosophy of unnecessary essences, does have another important aspect in our general interpretive narrative. This is the rationale for the shift from philosophically-minded pluralism to empirical democratic theory in US political science. The positivist reaction to idealism involved a hostility to extraneous metaphysical entities in positive science and a firm commitment to the descriptive study of what people actually do, rather than a speculative study of what ideas they might have, or what concepts their actions embody. American pragmatism, with James enlisted as one of its founders, was particularly concerned to eschew philosophical argument, regarding politics as a relatively self-defining area of human behaviour with few motivating ideals and many competing real-world interests. Accordingly, the elements of original pluralism which are transported to the US context are the analysis of social interest groups, anti-idealism, and some part of the concern about democratic participation. What gets lost in the transatlantic crossing are the critique of sovereignty in particular and of liberal democratic society in general; the interest in forms of functional representation; and a sense of the necessity of philosophical elaboration in substantive theory. Conventional pluralism replaces the theory of state legitimacy with the study of group pressures on the democratic political system.

3.3. Critical pluralism

When added to the criticisms of conventional pluralism outlined earlier, this picture of a stimulating and politically engaged current of original pluralism serves to make the former look very conservative indeed. However, there are indications in conventional pluralism that this impression is not wholly fair. Moreover, there has been an important 'critical turn' in recent pluralist work.

The force of at least two of the standard sets of criticisms of conventional pluralism need to be deflected to some extent. First, there was the issue of the different sorts of interest group brought under the same heading for analytic purposes. The problem with conventional pluralist analysis is *not* that the need for distinctions was ignored, nor that inequalities between groups were considered insignificant. Bentley finally plumped for a kind of materialism in arriving at a manageable categorization of the basis of group life. His 'underlying' groups were, in effect, principles of potential social stratification and included those based on differences of environmental conditions, race, wealth and trade (Bentley 1967: 462). Writers such as Pendleton Herring and Peter Odegard in the 1930s developed an approach to group analysis which deliberately undercut any all-purpose usage of the notion of interests. Under later pressure from critical voices such as those of Schattschneider and Easton, the pluralist persistence with the notion of interest groups was not so much a naive and uncritical levelling of differences as the retention of a convenient label within which more detailed distinctions and comparisons could be made. Dahl's argument against marxism, for example, was not that class was unimportant, but that when considered as somehow more 'real' than other bases of social differences, the importance of the latter (e.g. language, religion, race) was undermined (Dahl 1971: 106–7). His argument – at least as reviewed in retrospect – was that the undeniable persistence of class division in modern society did not entail that class was always and everywhere the major determinant of politics (Dahl 1982: 62). In this context, Dahl is probably right to dismiss as 'rather absurd' the charge that the conventional pluralists theorized groups as being equally open, equally well resourced, and equally heard at the political level (Dahl 1982: 208–9).

Some pluralists, certainly, were more aware of group inequalities than others. V. O. Key, for example was an influential 'empirical democratic theorist' whose wry tone and clear mind were not conducive to mystification. Key (1964, 1st edn. 1942) looked at a range of pressure groups with a view to their potential for coherence and internal division. He pointed out that while sectional interests cut across the business community, the latter was able to achieve solidarity on political questions due to their special powers of class unity in the face of challenges to their control of wealth (Key 1964: 73f.). Business, however, is a minority interest, so in a democracy the problem for businessmen (which they generally overcome) is to generate the kind of public opinion that acquiesces to their high status in the economic order (1964: 91). For Key, an element of 'economic determinism' here is quite palatable – provided it does not obliterate other, non-economic sources of interest-conflict (1964: 103).

A second objection to pluralism – that it ignores the organized power of the state – also stands in need of modification. It is true that group theory does play down 'the state' as a concept and focuses instead on the representative and responsive political system. But this is not merely a 'bias' of pluralism since the tradition in the US from the early part of this century has been unimpressed by idealist concepts of the general will and common good which the state was held to 'represent'. The turn to group interests was a more empiricist and behavioural approach, but it was also a substantive sociological impulse which can be defended as such. Additionally, it does not follow from pluralists' relative neglect of the state that they were wholly unaware of interest-group activity *within* the level of the political system. On the contrary, Latham for one pointed out the perpetual 'group struggle' within officialdom itself (1952: 35). And Dahl's whole concern was to establish the political as well as the social prerequisites for polyarchy, since societal pluralism could not of itself guarantee that a range of interests would be taken up by parties and leaders. The frequency in pluralist writings of terms such as 'leaders' as marking a contrast between the groups represented and the political representatives in a polyarchy indicates the pluralist awareness of self-interest on the parts of officials and politicians. Dahl's major empirical study of the interest group influence on local decision-making, *Who Governs?* (1961), comes out with quite 'anti-pluralist' conclusions, if pluralism is taken in any pure sense. The city government of New Haven is clearly perceived and portrayed by Dahl as an independent agent and the various interest groups identified do not appear to have great impact on the outcome of the political process (1961: 5–6).

The condensation of pluralist thinking on the state into a convenient metaphor suggesting responsive representation can therefore be misleading. Truman, for example, described the 'weathervane' picture, in which government as a single entity is moved this way and that by the balance of forces amongst social interests, as 'much too simple' (Truman 1951: 106). Latham not only saw officials as constituting interest groups, he accepted that in some sense the state had to act independently as the 'custodian of the consensus' (1952: 14). Clearly, this conception, like Dahl's continual assertion of the imperfections of modern democracy, entails a powerful semi-autonomous governmental interest. The bargaining amongst the various powers, interests and organizations in pluralist theory is not, after all, an even-handed process. Some groups in society are in a stronger position to bargain than others, and those in the political system itself are often in a position to brush off the pressures created by social constituencies.

The main critical charges against pluralism are therefore relative ones. It is true that in comparison with other types of political theory 'the state' is *relatively* neglected. It is true that in *some* expressions of pluralism, democratic consensus is assumed to operate and the impression is given that all serious interests can be both balanced out and partially satisfied. *Occasionally* pluralists tend to take suggestive images and parallels for real: the state as broker or umpire, for example, or the social system as tending to equilibrium. Overall, though, it is the contradictoriness of pluralist discourse which is striking, and this does involve a culpable theoretical forgetfulness. For example, in spite of his acute analysis of class interests amongst the most powerful group in society, Key is able to generalize – in a characteristic pluralist phrase – that power remains widely dispersed and that groups interact in a 'complex and kaleidoscopic manner' (1964: 8). In parallel, and in spite of the recognition of the autonomy of political elites, the pluralists do frequently return to the constraints on leadership imposed by a variety of social interests and indeed the norms of the democratic culture.

This lack of a stable set of conceptual hierarchies is one

reason why pluralism is seldom expounded as a specific theory. It also explains why attempts to definitively pin down conventional pluralism tend to run into trouble. For example, two recent commentators have argued that pluralism presents an 'image of society as an aggregate of interacting individuals socialized into cultural values and engaging in diverse communications and exchanges, especially in markets (Alford and Friedland 1985: 17). This interpretation rightly highlights the role pluralism allots to the civic culture in providing the subjective bonding in an atomistic and competitive market society. Yet the characteristic element which marks pluralism off from straightforward liberal individualism – the sociology and psychology of *group* formation – is glaringly absent from the sketch.

Another critical reviewer assimilates pluralism into the tradition of the theory of political elites (Graham 1986: 125ff.). The logic of this move is that pluralism's 'realistic' side is emphasized at the expense of its 'normative' elements. Thus, the pluralists' emphasis on competing groups, parties and organizations, plus its 'realism' about the necessary limitations of popular rule in a modern society, produces a somewhat cynical rationale for the long-favoured 'iron law of oligarchies'. This interpretation is also plausible, but it does tend to underestimate the normative aspect of pluralist theory. Although minority groups do compete for power under the banner of self-interest, pluralists believe (perhaps mistakenly) that a wide range of groups are able to exercise a democratic voice. From below, pluralist society emits a strong (and ever-changing) flow of citizen concerns. From above, the condition of democratic stability is that groups ensconced in the political system must show themselves to be sensitive to societal demands and to the expectations of the democratic culture generally.

This unstable amalgam of hard-headed realism about the imperfect democracy and a certain idealism about the virtues of pluralist market society came unstuck in the later 1960s. The notion that deep social polarity was a thing of the past and that an end to ideological politics was in the offing simply evaporated as serious strife re-entered the fabric of modern democracies. The complacency of the pluralist suggestion that minority voices can be heard without resort to conflict was rudely shattered by the racial and social violence which erupted in a spread of major US cities. The rediscovery of millions of free Americans living in poverty bluntly dented the feeling that democracy and affluence went hand in hand. The onset of economic recession spoiled the technocratic vision of smooth growth. The systematic questioning of the social order by students – the very sons and daughters of middle America – revealed that a concerned voice for internal change and for the rest of the world would not, it seemed, be listened to in the normal process of institutional democratic politics.

The impact of the political and cultural alternatives on respectable America was closely connected to the fact that, and the way in which, the strongest country in the world was conducting a war on one of the poorest peasant societies: Vietnam. Not the cosy picture of articulate pressure groups securing a response from a friendly local senator, but harrowing images of the bombing and napalming of peasant communities became part of the underbelly and substance of domestic western politics in the late 1960s. Nothing could more dramatic- ally reveal, radical critics felt, the coercion which lay behind consensus, the brutalization behind homilies on freedom, and the imperial interests which sustained an advanced economy upon which, according to pluralism, democratic norms depen- ded. In response to the emergent radicalism behind that disillusionment, middle America turned to the more openly disciplinary politics of the Nixon era. But the promise of trust and openness could no longer be maintained without question, and the Watergate bugging scandal of 1973–4 seemed the apotheosis of the transformation of democratic promise to a polyarchy which was imperfect indeed.

The impact of these events on pluralist thinking was profound. Some political theorists were moved by these and parallel European developments to separate further the question of democratic *stability* from that of societal pluralism. By the mid 1970s a strong anti-pluralist current was prominent in international political science: the 'crisis' of the democracies was asserted to lie in the expression of *too many* turbulent group voices, *too much* responsiveness on the part of in- creasingly 'overloaded' government (cf. Crozier et al. 1975). For several of the key conventional pluralists, notably Dahl and

Lindblom, a more apt response was to move in a self-critical direction. In their important 1976 Preface to *Politics, Economics and Welfare*, these authors argue that polyarchy has taken an adverse turn, due to the growth of an 'imperial presidency', the entrenched accumulations of private wealth in the face of public squalor, and a singular failure to combat social inequality. The remedy, if one is to be found, must involve a far greater degree of active popular participation.

One aspect of the development from conventional to critical pluralism is the questioning of the somewhat functionalist and 'technicist' account of social evolution it embodied. Pluralism did not, as is sometimes alleged, lack a sense of history, or even of historical *conflict* (cf. Beer 1969), but it did assume that economic growth was a steady, necessary foundation for democracy, and that such a process is relatively independent of the social conflict surrounding it. In the later phase of pluralism, an element of this equation of growth, pluralism and democracy remains (e.g. Dahl 1971: 78), but there is a newly perceived sense of ecological and democratic danger in any neutral and limitless conception of economic advance. The realization that global resources are finite and that the choice of sources is itself a matter for careful moral consideration is one part of the questioning of growth. Another is the sense that the waste and pollution spawned by the very industry which sustained modern society now threatens to engulf and poison it. Yet another is the awareness of chronic 'underdevelopment' in some lands as a *consequence*, and not just a contingent accompaniment, of advanced development in others. This seriously undermines the idea that the west's 'lead' in technology is ultimately the hope for the rest of the world. These issues are mentioned only in passing in the new introduction to *Politics, Economics and Welfare* (1976, xxii) but they are seen as involving a qualitatively new set of problems for classical pluralism. Above all, as Dahl and Lindblom recognize, political issues of this sort are essentially *collective* in nature: of necessity they posit the need for action towards a common good. The theoretical currency of competing interest-group bargaining is not well equipped to provide a positive appreciation of such increasingly important items on the sociopolitical agenda.

Another – by now obvious – source of pluralist revision is an enhanced awareness of distinctions amongst groups. There is a greater sense than before that the configuration of interests requires an emphasis on profound social *division* rather than overlapping commonalities. Cleavage and conflict are now as much at the centre of analysis as consensus and freely undertaken negotiations (Dahl 1980: 20). The very notion of social 'interests' appears to have been sharpened too. In the earlier texts, the political importance of those interests which could take the form of *organized* pressure groups already went against the idea of spontaneously achieved democratic balance. In the last work of his 'conventional' phase, Dahl indeed had moved away from any temptation to convene totally different entities under the label 'interest group'. Organized political lobbies constituted one group-type; but the sociologically rich notion of 'subcultures' (Dahl 1971: 203) indicates a rather different order of analytic concern. An interest in the distinction between local, societal and international dimensions of interest-formation is evident too. True, Dahl for one continues to keep a line open to small group psychology when he asserts that local solidarities might simply be *recalcitrant* in the face of the rather abstract identities produced by structural reflection. But it is taken for granted that the complexion of local campaigns and attachments is likely to stem from the way in which general societal patterns and interests are locally embodied (Dahl 1982: 62f.).

The privileged role of business interests, as we have seen, was recognized to an extent in conventional pluralism. In the critical variety business is uniquely charged with having an effective *veto* on the entire political system (Dahl and Lindblom 1976: xxxvi–xxxvii). As well as acknowledging the personal influence of entrepreneurs in decision-making circles, a more general structural imperative is sketched whereby the political system is driven by its concern for business interests.

> It becomes a major task of government to design and maintain an inducement system for businessmen, to be solicitous of business interests, and to grant them, for its value as an incentive, intimacy of participation in government itself. In all these respects the relation between

government and business is unlike the relation between government and any other interest group in society. (Dahl and Lindblom 1976: xxxvii)

A conventional pluralist thought was that in a polyarchy business privilege could be neutralized. Lindblom, however, has now broken with that proposition, disturbing the hitherto implicit link between democracy and free market society.

The mere possibility that business and property dominate polyarchy opens up the paradoxical possibility that polyarchy is tied to the market system not because it is democratic, but because it is not. (Lindblom 1977: 168–9)

In other words, Lindblom is asking whether democracy-as-we-know-it (polyarchy) works in favour of a capitalist system precisely by giving the *appearance* (but not the reality) of equal pluralist participation in decision-making. This suggestion bears surprising resemblance to Lenin's well-known phrase that (bourgeois) democracy provides capitalism with its 'best possible shell' by conceding to the working class a degree of political freedom while continuing to enslave them economically. In a similarly quasi-marxist vein, Lindblom reasons that labour cannot possibly have a tendentially equal influence in the polity since the state has no need to offer workers inducements in the same way as it has to placate employers. On the contrary, workers will continue to contribute to the system without inducements 'because they have no choice but to do so' (Lindblom 1977: 176).

One of the real-world features which has caused the pluralists to become less sanguine about their earlier propositions is the continued centralization of the economy in private hands, in spite of considerable state intervention in the free market. That process overturns the impression that economic development represents a public good and a vital public domain. The interests of the giant corporations, pluralists now think, are governed principally by the imperatives of global expansion and profit. Rather than, as before, trying to theorize the role of business *within* polyarchy, the very accountability of private assets to public criteria of utility is seen as a threat to democracy. Critical pluralists are persuaded that in effect a

systematic *rivalry* between business and polyarchy has developed, a contest between 'the voters' and 'the rich capitalists'
(Duverger 1974: 5).

In order to appraise this problem adequately, pluralists have
had to reverse exactly the terms of their analytical discourse.
Not only is the previous idea of parity between interest groups
now strictly 'unthinkable' (Lindblom, 1977: 193), the very
concept of pluralist politics as a market-place wherein groups
bargain for advantage must be rejected. The pluralists perhaps
did not embrace this free-enterprise terminology as openly as
Joseph Schumpeter (1943) or the 'economics of politics'
theorists who regarded political choice as a species of consumer
preference (Tomlinson 1981). And in an effort to emphasize the
purely political character of pluralist theory, Truman (1951: 48)
and Dahl and Lindblom (1953: 516–17) tried to theorize a 'third
way' between the 'grand alternatives' of individual enterprise
and state centralism, capitalism and socialism. Even so, the
earlier pluralist work is pervaded by images drawn from
'bourgeois' economics.

Lately, Dahl in particular has jettisoned this terminology and
its dominant paradigm. In an important switch of priorities, he
is now concerned to examine economic organization itself in
democratic terms, rather than the other way around, and he has
come up with some radical equations. If the assumption of
democracy is that binding collective decisions ought to be
made only by those persons subject to them, then why does
the principle not apply to a central arena of decision-making,
namely economic enterprises (Dahl 1985: 57)? Currently,
limited ownership and control of enterprises secures political
inequality through its adverse effect on equal access, resources
and life-chances. This is partly because capitalist enterprises
are themselves fundamentally undemocratic in structure and
decision-making. The democratization of capitalist firms is
therefore a major prerequisite if a genuine pluralist democracy
is to emerge. Here, much greater recognition is given by
pluralists to the substantive conditions of formal democracy
and participation. For full political liberty to be secured, the
argument goes, workers must become 'citizens of the enterprise'
(Dahl 1985: 92). And, in turn, for that to happen, there must be
a substantial equalization of ownership and control.

On political grounds, corporate capitalism is inimical to democracy ('I do not see how private ownership of corporate enterprise can be a fundamental moral right') (1985: 74). The implication that it is capitalist economic organization which supports the pluralism which in turn sustains democracy has, with these arguments, dramatically been turned around. Without economic democracy and a radical spread of effective collective control, the new view suggests, pluralist democracy will remain superficial at best.

Dahl lays down some fairly stringent conditions for democracy, and his list in *A Preface to Economic Democracy* looks considerably more substantive in character than the somewhat formal analogue in *A Preface to Democratic Theory* almost twenty years before. In addition to equal votes, Dahl specifies effective participation, enlightened understanding, inclusive membership of the polity, and final control of the political agenda by the *demos* (Dahl 1985: 59–60). These considerations are far from constituting a technical checklist; yet they reflect a renewed concern for the norms of classical democracy, however 'unrealistic' these might appear in our complex civilization.

Some of the specified items clearly derive from reflections on the state of the civic culture. If societal pluralism cannot of itself produce effective polyarchy, never mind democracy, then the criteria of citizen participation and subjective commitment to political norms are ever more important. We noted that some doubt was expressed in conventional pluralism about how freely formed any democratic consensus could be. But there seemed a degree of genuine optimism that the people were at least content with the workings of the political system and that the level of participation was acceptable. Such optimism – or perhaps it is sheer contradictoriness – now strikes the critical pluralists as problematic. They perceive a decisively causal relationship between the very restricted terms of the political consensus and general 'indoctrinated complacency' (Dahl and Lindblom 1976: xxxix). This is secured, it is asserted, through the uniquely powerful mass media and education system. The narrowness of the basis of political agreement reflects and sustains, according to Dahl, an 'irrational and deformed public consciousness' (Dahl 1980: 29). Consciousness is deformed, the argument now goes, because the

very legitimacy of the system itself is never placed before
intelligent democratic judgement. Thus the grand or primary
issues about the social system itself are removed from the
political agenda and indoctrination in the myth of balance
encourages passivity and homogeneity in the public mind. The
tones of a conspiracy theory in these sentiments involve no
extraneous imposition of vulgar marxism on these democratic
pluralist reflections. Lindblom especially sees the agencies of
ideology as actively promoting business interests, and in general
regards the 'core' beliefs of the polyarchies as 'the product of a
rigged, lopsided competition of ideas' where the appearance of
open belief-formation is secured mainly by the closed, circular
operation of propaganda (Lindblom 1977: 202–12).

A final aspect of the broadening of pluralism as a social
theory is its partial change in attitude to ostensibly non-
polyarchal countries ('hegemonic' societies, in Dahl's earlier
terms). In the old model, the *bête noire* of pluralist ideology was
Communism, a system whereby, it was alleged, no significant
social pluralism existed. Political competition was absent and a
uniform political culture was imposed by the centralist state on
an oppressed people. However, in the thaw following the Cold
War period, it became clear that serious sociological and
political questions of a pluralist sort could in fact be asked.
Which groups, exactly, are most influential in Eastern Europe?
What is their social basis? Even if there is no official party
competition, are there other channels of representation which
exhibit elements of popular control?

These interesting questions constitute a considerable research
agenda. Together with the recognition that pluralist democracy
itself might work to inhibit rather than enhance citizen
participation, the stark polarity between pluralism and totali-
tarianism begins visibly to crumble. Moreover, the inexact
status of 'interest groups' becomes compounded in the move
from pluralist theory to comparative empirical research
(Solomon 1983: 4–6). The latter actually reveals a multitude of
group-like entities in non-pluralist states like the USSR. Party
cadres, managers of enterprises, trade unions, soldiers, technicians, jurists, anti-pollution groups, anti-corruption watch-
dogs, welfare rights committees, and even 'public opinion'
generally have all been identified as holding some degree of

influence and each can be seen to an extent as 'relatively autonomous' of the state itself (Skilling and Griffiths 1971: 11–19, Brown 1974: 71–2, Lane 1985: 243–8). Sovietologists in the USA perhaps still prefer to regard these phenomena as signifying 'imperfect monism' rather than genuine pluralism. But the abstract idealism embodied in the notion that the latter points to a *fully* autonomous range of group interaction is apparent and ill-founded. Thus pluralists such as Dahl (1985) have returned to the question of how far socialism and pluralism are compatible, with no easy answers to reveal.

Let me summarize the current political contours of pluralist theory by reference to Steven Lukes's influential analysis of models of power (Lukes 1974). Lukes argued that a 'one-dimensional' view of power was evident in studies which restricted attention to the way in which political decisions and outcomes reflected the combined specific inputs of a number of relevant interest groups. This one-dimensional view, Lukes argues (1974: 12), can be seen as the 'central method' behind conventional pluralist analysis. It is an essentially limited analysis, because power relations are determined not merely by what decisions happen to be arrived at, but also by the efforts of groups and individuals to *prevent* certain issues arising (Bachrach and Baratz 1962). For example, a dispute amongst groups and parties about the best way to conduct a war (let's say in Vietnam) does not raise the issues of the purpose or legitimacy of the war itself. Indeed it may be that sharp disagreements about options within a system deflect critical attention away from the system as a whole. In a two-dimensional theory of power, the *legitimacy* of the political system itself and the social patterns of resource allocation which ground it would be precisely the sort of thing about which 'non-decisions' are made.

Lukes himself goes further. The one- and two-dimensional views share a focus on forums of decision-making and what does or does not appear on political agendas (1974: 21). For a deeper account still, we have to examine the way in which a whole socio-economic structure shapes the nature of people's wants, expectations and overt interests. In this model, conscious decisions and expectations are only one part of the wider political phenomenon to be analysed. The latter will include unconscious values, tendencies to apathy, overt manipulation and covert preferences. The adoption of a full critical analysis with respect to these variables involves a commitment to hypothesizing what people's real interests would be *outside* of a particular issue, forum or system. For example, people may not respond in the face of the threat of poisoning from pollution, but it can still be asserted that they have a profound *interest* in not being poisoned. It may well be that the very political system which is 'open' formally to their representations has somehow served perversely to silence people on an urgent human problem. Lukes allows that the relevant hypothetical argument about what people's real interests actually are cannot be decisively *proven* as such, but the three-dimensional analysis of power at least insists on a sociological examination of the material and ideological *conditions* of participation and decision-making.

The elaboration of this model represented an attempt to show the poverty of conventional pluralist theory. What is interesting for our purposes is that 'critical pluralism' as I have outlined its development now conforms to a large degree with the three-dimensional view. Lukes rightly noted Dahl's concern, in *Who Governs?*, to show how *indirect* were the influences on political decisions, thus in a way breaching the confines of the one-dimensional view. Phase two pluralism goes much further, revealing the strength of structural as well as personal influence by businessmen and corporations. It has sketched in greater detail the logic of non-participation in polyarchies and that of 'agenda-setting', thus enriching its understanding of popular democracy in the process. And it has openly asserted that inequalities of resources and responses, which themselves render the grand edifice of open government a façade, are systematically sustained by a *rhetoric* of consensus which is generated through the socialization process and the ideological institutions. Pluralist theory has always had two faces, one of which looked somewhat cynically towards the reality of elite rule in formally democratic nations. The other face was turned optimistically to the future in the hope that imperfect democracy could be steadily enhanced. On waking up from their American dream, the pluralists have attractively revised their previous, limited conception of democracy.

3

MARXISM AND 'THE QUESTION OF PLURALISM': HISTORICAL MATERIALISM

1. Introduction

In the scenario of historic opposition, the marxist conceptions of social structure and political agency depart substantially from those of the pluralists. Where the latter look to the variable influence of interest groups in the context of modern industrial society, marxism forefronts class struggle, stemming from inherent tendencies in the capitalist mode of production. The latter itself is held to form an integral part of a dynamic historical sequence of epochal changes. Marxism thus possesses a firm doctrinal basis for a political project aimed to usher in a higher phase of human civilization, one based not on inequality and exploitation but on co-operation and self-realization. For those reasons, marxists cannot accept the kind of epistemic and ideological pragmatism which marks the pluralist tradition.

Most marxists would probably recognize this outline of their theoretical heritage. However, in the late twentieth century, no comparative assessment can ignore the fact that disagreement among marxists about just how to interpret and exemplify these lines of theory and practice are quite as momentous as any consensus on basic aspirations. Marxism has thus witnessed its own proliferation of variants, ambiguities and silences. A roll-call of the kinds of urgent questions which have confronted every party or intellectual circle inspired by the classical marxist project indicates the depth of the problems of interpretation. What is it about capitalism (or history generally) that allows it to be regarded as 'progressive'? What is the balance between the 'objective' and 'subjective' dimensions of epochal change? Is the revolutionary process bound to be violent or peaceful; concerted or gradual? Is the labour theory of value tenable? In what sense do parties 'of' the working class 'represent' it? Can the proletariat ever act as a unitary political agent? What is the import of non-class-based movements and identities for socialist strategy? Do market exchanges have a role in a socialist economy? Does Marx's image of advanced communism represent a feasible or desirable political future?

A proper treatment of the way marxists have come to terms with these and similar questions would require a full developmental history of the tradition (cf. Hobsbawm 1982) and a dissection of the main theoretical offshoots (cf. Kolakowski 1978). My purpose is instead to approach some of the key issues from the point of view of the 'question of pluralism', conceived broadly to include sociological, political, and philosophical strands. Throughout its history, marxism has been attacked for its *monistic* forms of understanding and organization. This (disapproving) accusation has been expressed in a variety of registers, such as the charge of 'determinism' in the theory of history, of 'reductionism' in the analysis of politics, and of rigid cultural uniformity as the practical outcome of marxist principles. In turn, generations of marxists have expended much effort rebutting these charges – with considerable success, it should be said. Especially in the currents of 'western marxism', the classical theory has been sculpted to reflect the *complexity* which critics and adherents alike perceive in contemporary society. Yet in some ways, building 'complexity' into the 'basic' marxist considerations has resulted only in the *intensification* of queries about the scope and function of marxist concepts. Perhaps such complexity is not so much the saving of marxism as an expression of its inherently *contradictory* character? That sceptical note – and it is one which is increasingly struck by many marxists themselves – suggests that the oft-cited 'renaissance' of marxist thought since the 1960s has been so much gloss on what is by its nature a *limited* explanatory framework.

The question of pluralism is central here, first, because these interrogations reflect the pluralist temperament which pervades the intellectual culture today. Secondly, the monism/pluralism contrast appears to encapsulate the way in which the general sceptical query bears on specific problems in the different domains of marxist interpretation. Arguably, then, if there is a crisis in modern marxism, 'the question of pluralism' gets close to the heart of it. How far, we must ask, can marxism go towards the recognition of diversity without losing its distinctive grasp of substantive and theoretical issues? In the rest of this chapter, I pursue the implications of this challenge for arguments about the marxist theory of history. This is the dimension of theorizing that pluralism is supposed to lack; but pluralist concerns can be sharply expressed on this terrain as well as in the 'sociology of politics'. In the following chapter, I return to the marxist assessment of politics, which is connected to the theory of history through the crucial category of *class analysis*.

2. Primacy and development in history

Few marxist philosophers would today summon up the figure of Georgi Plekhanov, writing in 1895, as the most subtle or consistent exponent of historical materialism. On the question of pluralism, though, Plekhanov is interesting. He is virtually the only major marxist thinker to appeal directly to monism as the necessary basis for the marxist theory of history. Monism, on this account, is the attempt to explain the totality of social life in terms of 'one main principle' or motive force (Plekhanov 1956: 12). Plekhanov also made a sharp distinction between materialism and idealism, and polemically championed a fairly crude version of the former. But he was careful to say that monism as an explanatory ambition was independent of its embodiment in idealist or materialist terms. The logical opponents of the monist, he maintained (e.g. Plekhanov 1956: 212, 229), and marxism's main opponents in this regard, are not so much the idealists as the dualists and *eclectics*. The hallmark of eclecticism, in Plekhanov's terms, is the inability or refusal to see patterned, determinate change in history, and the tendency to treat the social whole as an indeterminate product of the 'interaction' between qualitatively different factors.

In my terms, Plekhanov is describing the conventional *pluralist* theoretical outlook. Two further points are worth noting. First, Plekhanov raises the possibility that a materialist approach to particular social phenomena is not sufficient to stand as historical materialism conceived as a theory of history in general. Second, he strives hard in his book to fend off the criticism that a monist understanding is equivalent to (economic) 'single-factor determinism'. Monism, he responds (e.g. 1956: 210), involves a sense of the complex, developing totality of social life; single-factor explanations, by contrast, already concede the grounds of eclecticism by admitting the existence of separate causal powers, thus inviting an eclectic retaliation in terms of the neglect of other important factors.

Plekhanov the marxist stands at an important juncture in the history of socialist thought. Unlike Karl Kautsky, he was never treated as a complete renegade by Lenin and the Bolsheviks, and in part this allowed his doctrines about marxism and history to contribute heavily to an orthodoxy which spans Second and Third International marxisms and their Soviet successors. Plekhanov the *thinker* by no means adequately resolves the issues he raises, but those issues – the suspicion of analytic pluralism, the distinction between determinate wholistic explanation and determinism, the question of marxism as a theory of history in contrast to merely a materialist perspective – continue to perplex. It is thus quite appropriate (if somewhat ironic) that the last decade of *Anglo-American* reflection on marxism and history should have been dominated by the systematization, by G. A. Cohen, of a position very like that of Plekhanov.

That position involves firming up Marx's distinction between the productive forces (materials, tools, techniques and knowledges) of a given social epoch, and its relations of production (forms of possession of the means of production and appropriation of surplus product). According to Cohen, who claims to be following Marx, it is the growth of the productive forces (PFs) which account for the pivotal changes in social relationships. The PFs are to be taken as primary over the relations of production (RPs) in the sense that successive sets of RPs come into being because they promote PFs development, and disappear when they cease to do so. For Cohen, the RPs exert considerable influence on PFs development, since they control the rate of change of the latter (Cohen 1978: 165). But a period in which the RPs 'fetter' PFs growth cannot persist for ever: a new set of RPs more conducive to PFs growth sooner or later emerges. This is a view of history as driven by the inherent tendency of human beings to enhance productive power, a dynamic in which PFs and RPs are alternately in a state of contradiction then correspondence.

The above picture can be said to be monistic in its conception of history as a developmental whole, and in its assertion of a single moving principle (the development of PFs). It is not, strictly speaking, a technological determinism (though this has often been assumed by readers of Cohen). This is because Cohen thinks of the distinction between PFs and RPs as analytic only. Consequently, the relationship between PFs and RPs is not straightforwardly causal. Departing decisively from Plekhanov in this respect, Cohen insists that only if we see the relationship between PFs and RPs as *functional* can the theory meet the dual requirements of PFs primacy and social complexity. The relations do not merely 'react back' on the forces, but supply the very context in which PFs growth is possible. So there should be no suggestion, in Cohen's view, that the RPs are either socially insignificant or that their composition is wholly determined. Still, they do flourish (or decline) insofar as they promote (or fetter) the growth of the forces. So, theoretically, it is the character of the latter which must be assigned explanatory priority (Cohen 1978: 162–4).

Cohen's theses, and the sophisticated philosophical apparatus deployed to defend them (not illustrated here) resurrected marxism's monistic credentials at a time when historical materialism, in western circles anyway, was rapidly shedding the burden of 'historicism'. It has been rightly observed that the structuralist current which dominated much of 1960s and 1970s marxism was essentially an attempt to steer a path between the largely discredited determinism of 'orthodox' historical materialism and a humanistic pluralism, with its 'congeries of discrete interacting elements' (Elliott 1987: 155).

As Cohen wrote, few of Louis Althusser's sympathizers would have claimed that his structuralist gambit had wholly succeeded (cf. Benton 1984). It can certainly be argued, a decade on, that Cohen's restatement of 'productive forces functionalism' constituted the major strike against any drift to non-marxist indeterminism in the wake of the tortuous compromises which marked Althusser's thought.

The problem is, that while no one has disputed the economy and elegance of Cohen's version of monistic orthodoxy (many admirers and critics alike come out of the engagement with his text *sounding* very like him), almost no one believes in the theory of history Cohen proposes. There are serious problems with Cohen's definitions of the basic concepts (PFs and RPs), with the theses of the primacy of the PFs and their autonomous development, with Cohen's claim to speak for Marx, with the nature of his empirical references, and with his defence of functional explanation. These problems are worth detailing, and some of them can be run together.

Take, for example, the very distinction between forces and relations of production and the postulated primacy of the former. Cohen shows that Marx declared such a view on many occasions, above all in the '1859 Preface' to the *Contribution to the Critique of Political Economy* (in Marx 1968). Indeed, as in other defences of orthodox historical materialism down the years, this short, brilliant text is taken by Cohen as the definitive statement of Marx's method. Yet, as Richard Miller comments, sceptically, it is quite remarkable that the general theory of such a major and productive thinker as Marx should be 'reconstructed, in large part, by a close reading of a brief formulation embedded in an autobiographical sketch in a preface to a book that [Marx] gladly allowed to out of print' (Miller 1984: 62). Accordingly, critical commentators (e.g. Sayer 1987: ch. 2, Rigby 1987: ch. 7) point out that Cohen omits to examine those many occasions on which Marx wrote (confusingly, in the light of Cohen's work) of the 'social forces of production', 'productive powers', and the like, with no apparent desire clearly to separate technologies and knowledge from social relations. Above all, this is true of the various forms of human co-operation in the labour process. Marx frequently referred to such work relations as the principal productive force, yet Cohen requires that these be placed definitively *outside* the PFs in order to preserve the latter's purely 'material' character. The critics conclude that Cohen is not true, at least not always, to the letter of Marx's texts, and hardly at all to their spirit.

Since this is not an exegetical work, I do not propose to press the issue of Marx's ultimate beliefs, other than to say that generally I accept the protest of Cohen's critics (cf. McLennan 1981: ch. 3). Their considerations on the historical evidence for the primacy of the PFs are also persuasive in showing that in Marx's detailed historical analysis, the primacy of the productive forces – in Cohen's sense – is seldom unambiguously asserted, and often (at least implicitly) denied (Miller 1984: 68f., Rigby 1987: 110f.). Paradigmatically, Marx explains the transition from feudalism to capitalism, and that from manufacture to machinofacture within the stages of capitalist productive growth, by reference to the prior appearance of new work relationships, themselves steeped in the conflictual social relations of the time. As long as Cohen excludes work relations from the PFs, he cannot comprehend this typically Marxian account. If he does admit them, his (necessarily) sharp distinction between PFs and RPs breaks down.

History is also invoked by Cohen's critics to counter the idea of the inherent *development* of the PFs, this time largely on the basis of evidence from historians other than Marx. This argument states that in regarding PFs growth as the inherent, leading factor in social change, Cohen defies the historical record, which reveals many instances of technological stagnation and even reversal (whether as a result of 'Mathusian' crises or, by contrast, ruling class sufficiency). It can be further pointed out that particular societies at similar levels of development have gone down *different* paths of social organization; and that 'advanced' technologies have been available to particular cultures which then failed to utilize them to significant effect. This suggests that the 'time' of each technology awaits the arrival of the appropriate stage of social relations. Either way, there is not much scope for the primacy of the PFs in these cases.

The historical evidence, then, can be ransacked without much effort for counter-instances to the primacy and development theses. The grounds for the development thesis are particularly important, since without it the primacy thesis, as a component of a general theory of history, could not survive. Other than as a logical requirement for the primacy thesis, the development thesis seems to rest on two very broad assumptions. One is that the _fact_ of overall productive growth in human history can be taken as indicative of an inherent driving tendency. The other is that human beings tend to reduce toil. Given the nature of things, and themselves, people will seek to enhance productivity. Cohen's opponents question any such transhistorical 'natural' tendencies. The assumption of rationality seems to reflect a very western image of instrumental conduct, while the assertion of an urge to overcome scarcity forgets that people have often proved to be extremely adaptable to given levels of need. Moreover, the anthropological literature alerts us to the rich symbolic and economic contexts in which productive improvement arises as a matter of social choice rather than necessity (cf. Diamond 1974, Sahlins 1974, Godelier 1986; ch. 1).

There are further questions to be asked about the exact nature of PFs development. For example: is it the current _level_ of the PFs which is fettered by the RPs, or their potential for further growth (van Parijs 1984: 89f.)? Or, different again, is the RPs demise supposed to occur only when they are _suboptimal_ for the PFs development (Elster 1985: 259–60)? As yet Cohen has not come back on these challenges, though (as with the historiographical material) he may yet do so. On the other hand, such a renewed defence of his position is unlikely given his _own_ serious reservation that the RPs may be better perceived as fettering the _use_ of the PFs rather than their development (Cohen 1983). This is a major withdrawal from orthodox historical materialism because the determination of the use of the PFs implies nothing about their inherent tendency to progress. Also, the revised proposition tends to reinforce the central role of the RPs and not the PFs, for it is social motives, power and conflict which decide the utilization of productive resources, whether or not the latter happen to be expanding or stagnating.

At this point, it is useful to pull out of the detail of criticism in order to try again to consider the overall character of Cohen's theory. In fact, many of the critics seem to clinch their objections by treating the 'productive forces' position as a deterministic theory. So if RPs can be shown to come first in history, or shown to 'dominate' the PFs; or if Marx 'in practice' is ◆revealed as incapable of holding to his own schematic distinctions, then the PFs are *not*, after all, the decisive factor in history. This critique, however, misses the possibility that Cohen's theory has the shape of explanatory monism rather than causal determinism. He perfectly well accepts, for example, that RPs often appear first – but they do so because they are conducive to (later) PFs growth. Cohen can accept too that RPs strongly dictate the *pace* of PFs growth – for, of course, in reality these are not separate causal entities, but part of a developing complex totality.

To pursue this line of analysis, the much-neglected first chapter of Cohen's book *Karl Marx's Theory of History: a defence* is worth examining. There, Cohen tries to make out what distinguishes a marxist *theory* of history from a Hegelian *reading* or image of history. The only passage in which this argument occurs is the following:

> [We] may attribute to Marx, as we cannot to Hegel, not only a *philosophy* of history, but also what deserves to be called a *theory* of history, which is not a reflective construal, from a distance, of what happens, but a contribution to understanding its inner dynamic. Hegel's reading of history as a whole and of particular societies is just that, a *reading*, which we may find more or less attractive. But Marx offers not only a reading but also the beginnings of something more rigorous. The concepts of productive power and economic structure (unlike those of consciousness and culture) do not serve only to express a vision. They also assert their candidacy as the leading concepts in a theory of history, a *theory* to the extent that history admits of theoretical treatment, which is neither entirely nor not at all. (Cohen 1978: 27)

This train of thought is slightly odd; it certainly lacks Cohen's customary clarity and finesse. The last sentence, for example, which seems set up to clinch the argument, actually leaves the epistemic relation between 'real' history and a theory of it quite unclear. Moreover, the idea that in and of themselves certain concepts (productive power and economic structure) 'assert themselves' as 'leading' candidates for such a theory is at best cryptic. Marx for his part is held to offer only the 'beginnings' of 'something' (?) more rigorous than a vision, though we are told that he also has such a vision. But we are not really told how *that* differs from his theory of history. Lastly, it can be noted (despite what Cohen implies) that *all* theories are, in a sense 'reflective construals, from a distance' of what concretely happens, and so are any number of candidates for the understanding of the inner dynamics of history. In short, Cohen fails to make his point, and leads the reader to wonder whether he has one. He does not persuasively demonstrate the asserted difference between a theory and a reading, and vacillates on how either of these notions can be seen as connecting to real history. Indeed, the lack of any specification of criteria for empirical adequacy is striking.

Perhaps, in the end, everything depends on what we make of all that follows in Cohen's text. Yet we have seen that what follows does not resolve the question as to just what *type* of 'reflective construal' productive forces functionalism is. Moreover, while in that first chapter Cohen is trying to say that marxism is *not* a philosophy of history in the speculative manner of Hegel, he also asserts and exhibits the 'common structure' shared, in his view, by Marx's and Hegel's outlooks. Cohen certainly emphasizes the important fact that one set of categories are materialist and the other idealist (1978: 26, 22), but Plekhanov's characterization of monism flickers in the background here. Cohen says that the form of Hegel's idealism is that of a 'non-empirical explanation' deriving from Hegel's general philosophy. All the same, it would be hoped that such an explanation could be vindicated in part 'by the study of history itself' (1978: 5). Confronted with the empirical diversity of nations and cultures, but also with their temporal succession, Hegel figured that *something* must account for the sequence as progressive and necessary, and himself 'could recommend the concept of the world spirit'. The proposition therefore emerges: 'It is because it reflects the world spirit that the history of humanity is characterized by progress' (Cohen 1978: 5–6). This is the structure of explanation which Cohen thinks Marx shares with Hegel. Had he justified a clear distinction between a theory and a reading, and also developed a criterion of empirical substantiation, this parallel may not have reached dangerous proportions. As it stands, though, it looks as if Cohen – after Plekhanov – is retaining a monistic formal structure and merely replacing the idealist categories by materialist ones. Instead of the world spirit, Cohen is 'recommending' the growth of the productive forces as the 'something' which accounts for historical progress. The hope here too is that history will support this candidate rather than Hegel's or anyone else's. However, since it is the bewildering empirical variety of history that stands in need of explanation, that cannot be decisive. Indeed, it is precisely the reflective distance which Cohen establishes between history-overall and history-as-it-happens which enables him to brush aside central historical cases (such as the decline of classical antiquity) as temporary 'stallings' and exceptions only (Cohen 1978: 156). More empirically minded marxists are bound to find this hard to take (e.g. Callinicos 1987: 60).

The general point here connects to the post-Cohen controversy over the legitimacy of functional explanation (e.g. Elster 1982, van Parijs 1982). Some reject functional explanation altogether (Giddens 1979: 16, Sayer 1987: 125). More sympathetic commentators would envisage accepting functional explanations only as long as they can be satisfactorily 'elaborated', i.e. that causal mechanisms are invoked and attested which show how it is that one factor/species/phenomenon serves to promote another. Cohen, though, hesitates over this: elaborations, he thinks, are not wholly necessary for an explanation to be a good one, though it may be desirable to provide them (Cohen 1978: 266, 1982). Actually, Cohen's theory involves not only that some set of factors (RPs) facilitates another (PFs), but that the RPs are *brought into existence* in order to promote potential PFs growth. But it is not obvious that such a claim *could* be fully satisfied by reference to the 'normal' mechanisms of human intention or independent 'Darwinian' adaptation. Perhaps for this reason, and the above considerations on historical 'readings', Cohen has acknowledged in another revisionary article (Cohen 1983a) that he is no longer sure how we could decide whether historical materialism is true or false.

This admission is of course crucial, for it seems to confirm that his account is monistic in just the sense I have been probing. Cohen's philosophical skills have certainly demonstrated that, with subtle logical adjustments and lapses of historical detail, orthodox historical materialism can be rendered *viable*. Its truth and credibility, though, are other matters entirely. The status of causal 'elaborations' very much depends on the prior issue of what sort of theory marxism involves. Cohen seems as perplexed about this as most other historical materialists.

3. The contingency of history?

Some modified version of the theory of the primacy of the PFs may yet prove to be empirically sustainable and informative. Meanwhile, Cohen's original challenge remains on the table: *if* historical materialism is a strong theory of history, it has to be of the type he advances. Anything less is not a theory of history in the strict sense. I have been suggesting that it is precisely the *type* of theory which has been quite as controversial as any particular content it prescribes. It follows that critics of orthodox historical materialism are under some pressure to give a coherent alternative construal of marxism's explanatory purpose, and a satisfactory recasting of its basic concepts. In tackling the many difficulties this task presents, another option insinuates itself: why not openly embrace empirical pluralism? One of the foremost commentators on Marx and marxism, Jon Elster, happily takes that road. Elster's commitment to marxism, he confesses, is mainly moral (1985: 531). What remains valuable in Marx, he thinks, involves no theory of history whatever and no reliance on explanations couched in terms of classes, forces, epochs or any other 'methodologically collectivist' categories. It is instructive to see how other critics of Cohen try to avoid these conclusions.

The starting point for a 'middle way' between Cohen's monism and Elster's pluralism is once more the PFs/RPs distinction. Some writers (e.g. Balibar 1970, Rigby 1987), in order to counteract productive forces determinism, argue that the RPs are primary. This allows considerable empirical flexibility, as the precise state of PFs and RPs 'belongs' to the theorization of the particular historical epoch under examination. However, the problem with conceiving historical epochs – the modes of production – as necessarily determined by their dominant relations of production (and all 'technical' features by 'social' ones), is that a general rationale for change is hard to sustain. Etienne Balibar's structuralist perspective, for example, makes transition between modes especially difficult to conceptualize. If modes of production are structured totalities, how does one develop into another? In effect, Balibar has to invent a 'special case' whereby in transitional modes of production a more dynamic tension is posited between PFs and RPs (Balibar 1970: 302f.). This lack of structural correspondence was *not* allowed in stable modes of production (the normal case), because of the logical dominance of social relations. It seems clear that some part of the impetus for a higher level resumption of normal correspondence between forces and relations must be ascribable to the particular character of the PFs themselves (suitably 'released', perhaps by an appropriate social context).

In a less structuralist mould, S. H. Rigby generates a similar theoretical dilemma. Rigby asserts the dominance of the RPs over PFs, and indeed advises that it is an error to restrict the definition of the RPs to 'economic' criteria. Exploitation, he argues, involves an inescapable 'subjective' element and the superstructural factors of ideology and politics enter into the very constitution of the RPs. Accordingly, there is simply no necessary technical or economic momentum which 'governs' historical change: the only motive force is the class struggle (Rigby 1987: Part 2).

In assessing this argument we should remember an important sideline in Cohen's position. He stated that the class struggle could only be considered a motive force if its outcome was firmly anchored to a historical dynamic which featured the PFs. Otherwise, this implies, references to 'class struggle' are merely rhetorical guises for indeterminacy (Cohen 1982: 495). That stricture is plausible when applied to the case where RPs are dominant over PFs, but where no Balibarian breach of correspondence is proposed to account for structural development. Certain class relations (which have a vital subjective dimension) are succeeded by others, but this is a product of the class struggle alone. There is arguably *no* theory of history here, because 'the class struggle' has no intrinsic logic: it all depends on the balance of factors (especially the subjective ones?) in particular times and places. Rigby thus appropriately describes his understanding of historical materialism as 'the empirical investigation of concrete hypotheses' (1987: 13).

If it is truly the lack of empirical concretion that makes us question strong historical materialism, then we must wonder whether the type of standpoint just described can be pushed further. For example, if the *rigidity* of the PF/RP distinction is a problem, then simply to reverse it creates its own difficulties. Similarly, if artificial distinctions between abstractions together with inflexible transhistorical essences pervade marxist orthodoxy, then to erect 'the class struggle' as the guarantor of concrete adequacy may be merely a categorical substitute, couched in activist terms. This line of thought can be pursued by reference to Derek Sayer's (1987) polemic against Cohen. For Sayer, *all* Marx's categories are internally related and 'empirically open-ended'. To engage in general theorizing about history as such is precisely, in his view, to undermine Marx's basic practice and insight. Indeed, Cohen's hypostatizations can reasonably be said to constitute a case of the 'reification' of the human understanding which Marx regarded as typical of bourgeois culture. All concepts, Sayer affirms, are instead to be assigned an essentially *historical* provenance and definition (1987: 22). With that injunction in mind, the 'empirically open' marxist is bound to question the fixity of the reference to class struggle as much as that of the productive forces. From a general position akin to that of Rigby, Sayer goes on to propose that a fully adequate historical materialism should be expanded *beyond* the struggle over the production of material goods. That is, it should now encompass the production and *re*production of real *life* (1987: 78). Consequently, gender, age and perhaps a number of other important spheres of social meaning are to be set alongside class as necessary and equal dimensions of empirical concern.

Sayer has not lost the traditional marxist worry about the danger of pluralism in this process of reasoning (1987: 114). As with other writers who favour models of internal, organic unity (e.g. Rader 1979), models which seem to dissolve distinctions, a 'minimum' of a priori theory is nevertheless retained by Sayer as necessary, and a back door is kept open to some sort of logical differentiation between base and super-structure, and between PFs and RPs – though supposedly not as 'conventionally drawn' (147, 73). Whether this latter phrase represents mere prevarication cannot be decided, owing to the relatively sparse 'positive' side of the critique of Cohen. Meantime, though, we should note Sayer's revised formulation of the nature of the domain of marxist interest ('the production and reproduction of real life') and of marxist method ('empirical history informed by critique') (148). Non-marxist historians and sociologists are unlikely to find anything controversial in this.

A further 'middle way' towards a controversial yet undogmatic marxist theory of history can be approached by trying to preserve *something* of the productive forces standpoint, but not determinism. If the PFs/RPs distinction must be retained, this argument runs, then let the definition of the PFs be suitably broadened to encompass the 'work relations' which pre-occupied Marx yet which Cohen excluded from the PFs in his narrow definition. This could enable a view of PFs development as having a qualitative as well as technical/quantitative aspect, the former being significantly governed by the RPs (Miller 1984: 76). The forces, however, remain important and will be particularly relevant when identifying the resources for, and consequences of, epochal change. Thus the PFs are not autonomous, but they can be seen as primary 'with respect to change' (Miller 1984). PFs development through history cannot, on this reckoning, be given a quasi-logical status. Historical unevenness is too palpable, and development too precarious, for that. All the same, in this position, PFs growth is more than happenstance: in spite of the counter-tendencies they confront, the PFs transmit a 'weak impulse' to growth, sufficient to 'trigger' serious periodic crisis (Callinicos 1987: 93, Larrain 1986), the outcome of which will then depend on class struggle and class capacities.

This attractive-sounding synthesis does away with the autonomy and optimality of PFs growth, and calculates its impact on two levels, quantitative and qualitative. The question needs to be posed, though: does weak, circumscribed PFs growth explain *all* epochal change? The answer must be that it does not. Richard Miller, who defends the middle way we are assessing, points out that the dominant theme in Marx's *Grundrisse* (Marx 1973) is the 'self-transformation' of the RPs. Variously, this could be accomplished by way of class struggle, or by the tendencies to self-destruction on the part of ruling classes, or by the 'exogenous' effects of trade on a mode of production (Miller 1984: 83). Consequently, there is once again a wide range of conditions of change: internal and external structural tendencies, objective and subjective class phenomena, qualitative and quantitative impulses from the PFs, and so on.

To summarize; marxists have laid great store by a theory of history in order to resist a headlong 'descent' into eclectism and pluralism. The only strong theory to persist through the generations has proved unsatisfactory on both historical and conceptual grounds (and possibly also on issues of Marxian exegesis). This monism in turn has regularly been challenged by more dialectical and empirical formulations. But these also seem unsatisfactory, tending to create a one-sided Marx of their own and sometimes glossing the near-absence of determinate propositions by quasi-activist rhetoric.

While that alternative will perhaps appeal to the proclivities of some marxist historians, the borderline between pluralist indeterminacy and historically specific marxist theory becomes hard to discern (cf. Gottlieb 1984, 1987). A third option suggests itself, one which manages to combine empirical sensitivity with some significant and determinate marxist propositions about history in general (cf. McLennan 1986). Yet, from the reflections of Marx himself through the dialectical-materialist heritage of marxism to the current crop of academic debates I have referenced, it is not clear that this can be consistently achieved. Indeed, each solution generates further uncertainty about what the explanatory objectives of historical materialism actually are.

Andrew Levine, who also makes this point, fails to follow it through in his interesting depiction of a sequence of stances which retreat by degrees from 'strong' historical materialism. Levine considers that *historical evidence* will ultimately decide between 'strong', 'weak' and 'restricted' historical materialisms, and between any variant of the marxist theory of history proper and marxist-sounding 'materialist sociologists' (Levine 1987: 102–5). However, Levine's own characterization of what is involved in the strong theory itself goes against this conception of arbitration. Full-blooded historical materialism, Levine proposes, requires that change be theorized as an internal, necessary pattern which 'exogenous' factors can only affect 'accidentally'. Moreover, it is the concepts of the privileged discourse that define the domain of 'history itself', a theoretical object of a different logical order from the 'irreducibly heterogeneous' course of historical-empirical micro-events. The empirical adjudication is inappropriate here, since, on Levine's own account, the higher level of the theory is simply not the sort of thing to be rendered tentative by its *explananda*. (This, incidentally, is precisely the view of an uncompromising defender of 'strong' historical materialism in the analysis of the transition from feudalism to capitalism (Laibman 1984).) It is therefore unconvincing to speculate that in spite of strong marxism's conception of change *as propelled by* internal necessity, historical materialism does not repeat 'the teleological structure of earlier philosophies of history' (1987: 101). On the other hand, no 'quasi-marxist' or serious reflective historian – far less a strong or weak historical materialist – would be wise to submit the labours of theory to the acid test of a 'historical record' conceived only as an uninterpreted assemblage of data and events.

4. Mode of production, social formation

In his influential characterization of marxism, Leszek Kolakowski refers to the way in which a 'single type of circumstance' determines the whole social superstructure. Against this 'monistic interpretation of social relationships', Kolakowski posits the pluralist alternative, namely that there are 'several independent types' of condition which help explain social phenomena (Kolakowski 1978: I. 351). Now many 'weak' historical materialists and 'empirically open' marxists make a similar critique of 'vulgar' marxism. The critics try themselves to give a corrective, 'complex' understanding of the central marxist category 'mode of production', avoiding where they can the notoriously mechanistic connotations of the 'base and superstructure' metaphor. One object of this move is to register where necessary the contingency of social causation and the relatively autonomous impact of 'non-economic' forces.

At the same time, few marxists are willing to accept outright causal pluralism; otherwise the very concept of a determining mode of *production* would be pointless. Indeed, right across the many variants of the tradition, the precise nature of the relationship between 'mode of production' and the concrete society it 'inhabits' is a source of difficulty in theorizing just how marxism is able to stave off sociological pluralism. Productive forces marxism, we have seen, does not straightforwardly single out a set of material 'circumstances' and assert a mechanical chain reaction which eventually takes in the outreaches of mental representation. Rather, strong historical materialism develops an explanatory framework which posits functional and causal interrelations between forces and relations of production, and between relations of production and the key institutional/cultural forms. In each case, it is true, the direction of causality goes unambiguously from the first reference to the second, sometimes without due 'elaboration' of the mechanisms involved. But there is nothing formally improper about such a hierarchy (cf. Hellman 1979).

More 'sophisticated' versions of marxism, moreover, do not (as often advertised) achieve a coherent or even very different solution. As Maurice Godelier – no vulgar materialist – has noted, marxists must be committed to identifying *which* of the countless local causal ways in which the superstructures affect the base are the decisive ones. In his formulation, only those superstructural phenomena are decisive which 'assume the functions of the social relations of production' (Godelier 1986: 21). Contrary to the use which is sometimes made of Godelier, this formulation does *not* encourage the view that there is simply no distinction to be made between base and superstructure; nor does it demonstrate that relations of production cease to be *economic* phenomena. Material production and the form of appropriation of the surplus are *inescapably* 'economic' activities. The point is rather that economic mechanisms simply cannot operate in a self-sufficient way in many modes of production. This is because, in pre-capitalist society (and arguably in capitalist society too), political, legal, familial and ideological forms control the access to, the organization of, and the allocation of the fruits of particular labour processes. Godelier concludes, then, that the distinction between base and superstructure is a division amongst functions, not amongst institutions as such (Godelier 1986: 29f.). That conclusion certainly goes against, for example, Cohen's tendency to restrict the designation 'superstructural' to institutions only (Cohen 1978: 216); but strong historical materialism does not demand this particular restriction, nor does Godelier's formula prohibit the analysis of institutions from the functional standpoint.

There are undoubtedly important differences between the varieties of historical materialism. But they all confront the problem of how to theorize the 'primacy' not only of the PFs or RPs with respect to the mode of production, but also of the latter in relation to concrete society. On the one hand, the mode of production is never simply a material substrate operating mechanistically; on the other, it cannot be altogether dissolved into an undifferentiated realm of cultural experience and interaction. Accordingly, marxism constructs mode of production as an abstract social totality, not a discrete causal sequence binding one *part* of the totality to another. This preferred conception builds into the abstract logic of the mode certain non-economic conditions.

In strong historical materialism, the functional connections bring together RPs and PFs, base and superstructure in a skeletal social totality. This goes beyond the strict definition of mode of production, but it is a legitimate extension, an assertion of the typical or appropriate conditions of existence and consequences of its operation. It is not yet, though, the level of the concrete social world, which is admitted to include all manner of other determinations. In weak historical materialism, a similar epistemic scenario operates. Here the broadly pitched mode of production actually *includes* the productive forces and any relevant superstructural specifications. Relations of production – the economic 'level' of the mode – already incorporate political and ideological features. In the (slightly different) terminology of structuralist marxism (e.g. Poulantzas

1973: 13), the 'global' mode of production is constituted by the articulation of the 'economic' level or instance *together with* the political and ideological – and perhaps other – instances as theorized in their own right. Clearly we are again dealing not with an economic form but with a social totality. However, we should not yet think of the latter as the concrete society, not even when the further articulation of *different* modes of production is conceived as constituting a 'social formation'. As Ted Benton points out (1984: 74–5), the move from mode of production to social formation, in structuralist marxism, is one which takes place *within* the idealizing procedures of 'theoretical practice'. The real-concrete is still a further jump away, once again involving a richer series of determinations.

The point in focus here is that vulgar and sophisticated marxisms alike seek to retain the determinate primacy of the 'economic' level or, more specifically, of the relations of production. Both species typically involve functional and causal determinations, but do not typically make clear the relations between these modalities. Each 'builds in' to the conception of the economic process some appropriate cultural implications, whether in the form of functional supports or by way of a multi-layered extension of the mode of production concept itself. For all marxists, though, the abstract social totality is conceived as somehow *representing* the core logic of the concrete society. Marxists do not at all deny that their idealizations select and abstract from the multiple causalities of concrete society; but the derivation (mode of production→social formation)→concrete society is intended all the same to be a scientific appropriation of the inner logic of the real-social.

However, marxists of all types have said relatively little about why their categories *should* be taken as representing the real-essence of societal relationships. The characteristic pattern of thought is twofold:

1 Life is indeed made up of a plurality of phenomena and causal relations.
2 There is nevertheless an inner structure or hierarchical functional logic to that multiplicity which is 'captured' by marxist theory.

In this discussion I have been showing only that marxists of all sorts are swayed to and fro by the contrary weightings of these principles, the first being a more pluralistic impulse, the second a monistic (but not necessarily deterministic) one. Moreover, in spite of a century of marxist philosophy after Marx, a satisfactory combination of both emphases seems to be achieved only by way of statutory assertion.

5. Unilinearism and transition

Much specialist marxist historiography is engaged on the task of how precisely to characterize the various particular modes of production. Traditional historical materialism specifies five main modes: primitive communism, ancient slavery, feudalism, capitalism and advanced communism. The historiographical debates centre around (1) the empirical and theoretical adequacy of the specified labels, (2) the nature of the transitions between modes, and (3) the strength of the candidacy of other modes of production for inclusion in the list – for example the 'Asiatic' mode, and socialism. While salient points in these debates will be picked up as we proceed, their precise details cannot be covered here, nor are they all relevant to the questions of pluralism that I am principally concerned with. (For useful summaries see Gandy 1979, Rigby 1987). However, some of the specialist questions *are* guided by, and react upon, a classical dilemma of monism/pluralism: is the sequence of modes, whatever the latter turn out to be, necessary and singular or by contrast contingent and diverse?

Two designations are commonly applied to marxism in this regard, usually with derogatory intent. One is that history is seen by marxists as a *teleological* process, that is, that everything in history is shaped according to its contribution towards a necessary end-stage, namely advanced communism. The other charge is that the stages of history form a singular path of development, that is, a *unilinear* process.

Even in this summary it is clear that the accusations of teleology and unilinearism are not quite the same, though critics often run them together in a somewhat catch-all way. Indeed, it tends to be assumed as self-evident both that marxists do exhibit these characteristics of a monist historical theory, and that the study of history can readily do without such impositions. On both counts, I would argue, the situation is more complex than that, though historical materialism certainly faces a number of near-intractable problems in this area. One of the most basic of these can be drawn from the preceding section: how are the concrete societies which are supposed to exemplify the progressive sequence of the modes of production to be described? Jon Elster formulates one interpretation of unilinearism as the thesis that all nations go through the same stages in the same order, possibly at different speeds (Elster 1985: 302). Whilst Elster rightly goes on to say that Marx himself probably did not hold to such a rigid version, he (Elster) fails to note that the very use of the category *nations* here is problematic. This is because formally-constituted nation states are a feature of modernity and cannot be 'retrojected' into the past. Accordingly, and unselfconsciously, Elster talks instead of 'countries' and then of 'communities' when he pursues the credibility of the unilinear sequence further back in time – though significantly he omits to mention what is perhaps the crucial mediation between community and nation, namely *empires* (cf. Kiernan 1987: 116). Since these various designations for the appropriate type of 'social formation' are not in any meaningful way equivalents, it is hard to see how *any* restricted empirical concept could fulfil the terms of the first unilinear formulation. No doubt it is for this kind of reason that Marx and marxists have resorted to a more abstract concept of the concrete social totality, such as social formation.

The alternative reading of unilinearism is to give a wider spatio-temporal reference to the evolutionary pattern. Thus, marxists speak of the modes of production as mapping on to particular historical *epochs* of humanity as a whole. In this conception, the relevant social entity can be nothing less than *global* in scope. This possibility most nearly accounts for marxists' proclivity to pronounce some empires or nations or communities within the global-epochal frame as more 'advanced' or more truly *representative* than others of the inner logic of history. Marx certainly took England to be the 'classic' capitalist case in this sense, whilst recognizing its empirical distinctiveness. However, the same kind of 'representation' becomes more controversial for pre-capitalist modes, since for marxists it is uniquely *capitalism* that has as one of its central developmental tendencies the very 'globalization' of production. On that logic, it could be considered illegitimate to treat 'humanity' before this epoch as any sort of unitary spatial and social entity. 'World history' as such is therefore little more satisfactory than 'nations' as the proposed carrier of the 'stages' of productive advance. Rather, it is a specific empirical outcome of the chequered and heterogeneous histories of particular peoples and regions.

One way of trying to build unevenness and specificity into this second type of unilinearism is to see historical development as taking place most rapidly, *first* in one time and place, then in another. In this conception (Semenov 1980), there is no mysteriously uniform progress; instead, there is a concrete hypothesis that some human collectivities, through a variety of natural and social advantages, develop superior technical and organizational resources than others. Through a social learning process, stimulated by trade and conquest, the relatively 'underdeveloped' collectivities can come to 'bypass' the kind of obstacles that the 'leading' society eventually comes to face. Protracted problems of one sort are thus quickly overcome by previously 'retarded' parts, which themselves then come in time to confront other difficulties. The 'torch' of historical progress is then once again passed on.

This theory evades some of the crasser objections to unilinearism. It also diminishes the charge of overt teleology, since there is no need to invoke communism as the specific and necessary terminus of the social learning process. Moreover 'humanity' need not be seen as a global purposive agency. Of course, as with any theory whatsoever, the overall process could be seen as morally and politically progressive, but this moral overview need not unduly influence the causal investigation of the empirical sequences.

For all that, the 'torch-relay' model still requires that a principal *source* of movement be specified (usually the productive forces' development), and that the 'external' causalities of inter-community relations be reinterpreted as 'internal' mechanisms within a holistically conceived spatio-temporal order. Non-marxists would dispute that this is an appropriate mode of analysis for social science generally; increasingly marxists too are declaring themselves to be 'multilinear'. Theoretically, there are doubts about the legitimacy of *any* global and transhistorical incarnations of humanity within historical theory. The very terminology of advance, setback, bypass and the like is intrinsically geared to the idea of a one-way ticket to a better, higher-level destination. Not only is this likely to prejudice from the start the treatment of diverse routes, it arguably inhibits full and adequate theorization. Both these points can be indicated by reflecting on the nature of the labels which are frequently given to the modes of production.

The 'primitive communist' mode, for example, seems to be logically connected to its counterpart at the other end of the historical progression, namely *advanced* communism. Many anthropologists may well protest that such an overtly teleological specification must involve ignoring the complexity and variety of societies coming under that head. The concept of an 'Asiatic' mode of production has also been criticized, this time for expressing a *geographical* essence rather than one couched in terms of the social relations of production (Hindess and Hirst 1975: 180). Recent interventions in this debate have put on the agenda the possibility that Asiatic-type societies actually form part of a wider principle of economic organization in pre-feudal times: the tributary or taxation mode of production (Amin 1978, Wickham 1984). This interesting contribution is 'heretical' in that the role of the *state* (a 'superstructural' phenomenon) is placed at the centre of the process of exploitation. As for the classification of antiquity, we should note that one popular designation relies on the (still controversial) assumption that such societies rested fundamentally upon a *slave* mode of production. Alternative descriptions are of a more temporal character (the 'ancient' mode), whilst others again are mainly cultural in orientation (the 'classical' mode). At the very least, critics could conclude, we should postpone judgement on unilinearism until a logically equivalent and substantiated set of stages is defined. It could be supposed that the marxist analysis of *feudalism* must fare better. But once more note that this term does not accurately specify a single set

of relations of production, and indeed has more than a whiff of
the political and cultural institutions of medieval Europe built
into it. As Victor Kiernan points out, this specific reference
often goes unheeded when marxists try to extrapolate to a
global epoch. The result is, from an empirical point of view,
that very different civilizations and their representative figures
'are all herded together like stray animals in a village pound'
(Kiernan 1983: 92). In all this, the most definite theorization,
and the one most likely to 'save' unilinearism is the development
of the productive forces. But this is the part of the picture
which modern marxist historians are least willing to encumber
themselves with (cf. Kaye 1984), especially when it comes to
the *transition* between modes. Certainly, in the classic case of
feudalism to capitalism, the consensus now clearly revolves
around the decisive impact of class struggle in the context of
broadly similar technical and demographic circumstances
amongst the European nations (Brenner 1985).

If there is a general marxist theory at all, it seems, it cannot
be unilinear. Marxist historians are extensively reworking the
concepts which demarcate pre-capitalist society. These are *not*
now envisaged as wholesale embodiments of unitary modes of
production. Nor is there any apparent difficulty in accepting
'dead-ends' of development. Moreover, a variety of communal
forms (classical, oriental, Germanic etc.) can be perceived as
unevenly and overlappingly emerging from the 'primitive'
commune. In other words these formations can be expressed
in a 'horizontal' plane rather than the 'vertical' one which
always occurs in unilinearism (Melotti 1977). Finally, multilinear
marxists put less doctrinal weight on the tenet that social
change is necessarily *internal*. It is on the basis of a severely
internalist model, for example, that those marxists who have
put forward ideas about the significance of trade, conquest, or
cultural influence as causal components of modal transitions
have been cast out of the temple as 'bourgeois' and unscientific.
But once the idea of the mode of production as the growth of
the PFs within a limited 'national' context is put on one side as
itself the 'unscientific' part of marxist historiography, the door
is open for a more considered empirical assessment of
'external' causality.

Clearly, this prospect of a multilinear historical materialism appears to overcome some residual traditional problems by moving closer towards a pluralist conception of change. All is not quite clear, however. R. J. Holton has provocatively and usefully indicated what would be involved in a new 'intellectual idiom' of pluralism, multilinearism and contingency with respect to the debate on the transition from feudalism to capitalism (Holton 1985: 145). Certainly, the implication is that there are, irreducibly, a *number* of diverse tracks down which societies can develop; that not all societies do in fact develop; and that the rationale for change within some social collectivities may be entirely different from that relevant to others. Now, marxists might be able to accept this, suitably reformulated. The logical necessity of strong marxist accounts of the transition, it can be agreed, has been effectively challenged. That there is only one prescribed pathway to modernity is also taken as in large part refuted. But Holton rightly indicates that two further steps are necessary before marxists can inherit the pluralist idiom, and neither, I think, could be embarked upon even by multilinear marxists without a rigorous search through their intellectual conscience and armoury.

The first step in adopting a 'post-evolutionary analysis' for historiography, is to begin to speak not of *the* transition from feudalism to capitalism, considered as modes of production, but rather of transitions (in the plural) to specific states of affairs. Similarly, talk of *non*-capitalist forms rather than *pre*-capitalist forms is necessary to keep teleology at bay. The second step involves reinforcing the distinction between a particular, contingent state of affairs (such as capitalism) and its construal within a preferred theoretical discourse (such as marxism) as a stage-outcome. This further step is necessary, for the pluralist, since the temptation to unilinearism begins precisely with the belief that a concrete society or process materially 'embodies' a particular conceptual essence, and the task of elaborating the *development* of that essence inevitably then gets under way. This problem, it is alleged, lies behind the eternal argument between theories of history as regards the 'prime mover' of social change. The pluralist resolution here is to treat all such general concepts as useful tools of analysis, but to treat them as *tools*, not as real outcomes. There might simply be no case for trying to establish which of the several available concepts of the transition from feudalism to capitalism is 'ultimately' more valid.

There is good reason to think that this general pattern of pluralist argument – and we will be returning to it several times in the rest of this book – would be strenuously refused even by multilinear historical materialists. The first step goes against the inclination to highlight the central aspects of earlier modes of production which give rise to processes of change leading to later modes. Further, it is not clear that multilinearism, of itself, rules out the ranking of modes of production as 'lower' and 'higher' according to some acceptable marxist criterion. Marxists of every stamp, moreover, are inclined to view modes of production not merely as useful concepts but as real structures. Accordingly, the notions of internal contradictions and systemic dynamics remain important. The centrality of the productive forces may require serious qualification, but the interface between PFs and RPs continues to generate powerful motives for change, especially in the structural logic of periodic crises (which indeed that interaction chiefly explains). This kind of allegiance to internalism and a (qualified) sense of material necessity applies even to those marxists who emphasize 'external' causation, since externality is usually asserted as a way of drawing attention to an unduly restricted conception of the relevant social totality. When that totality is reformulated as, for example, a global pattern of uneveness and contiguity, the logic of internalism can readily be restored.

From these considerations it follows that multilinear marxism is not after all coterminous with the kind of pluralist reworking of the modes of production debate that I have sketched. Marxists of all types retain from unilinearism the global 'necessity' of capitalism's development, and the real pressures this creates for the development of a new, higher stage in human history. Moreover, while the difficulty of finding a one-way route out of primitive society establishes a necessary complexity in the overall historical theory, it might also tend to encourage a *repackaging* of the stages into even broader categories in order to preserve a coherent pattern; for example: primitive communism, pre-capitalism, capitalism, socialism (Sawer 1977). Marxists, therefore, are likely to continue to defend the kind of 'universal' guidelines which historical materialism lays down, admittedly with significantly varying degrees of commitment. It is worth finally noting, though, that within marxism itself there is another powerful drive towards the historical relativization of any particular universal schema, and this leads once more to a pluralistic train of thought.

One source of relativization comes from the 1859 Preface: the (superstructural) realm of ideas always has a distinct basis in historically specific modes of production. Why, we might ask, should marxist ideas be any different? Another source for an explicitly historical epistemology is Marx's denser but subtler 1857 Introduction to the *Grundrisse* (Marx 1973, Hall 1975). In that text, Marx criticizes apologetic conceptions of history which contrive to treat the past as merely a number of steps leading up to the present form of society (Marx 1973: 106). Marx appears to condemn such 'one-sidedness' as unwarranted moral teleology. Nevertheless, Marx does not at that point attempt to offer an entirely context-free theoretical alternative. Rather, he argues that just as our knowledge of simian anatomy is inescapably conditioned by our concern with *human* anatomy, so the analysis of the structural anatomy of past societies can only be undertaken from a perspective which takes the current, bourgeois social structure as its point of departure. The implication here is that while categories such as mode of production are reaffirmed as central to the understanding of the stages of social development (1973: 107), the perceived value of that kind of category is itself a historical product, a bounded – not a literally universal – conceptual standpoint.

If this is so, there can be no a priori reason for accepting marxist reference points as timelessly true or even useful. It may be that other social relations – together with their own type of universal propositions – will develop and take root in changing historical conditions (Adamson 1981). Certainly, this possibility is what many empirical marxist critics of 'strong' historical materialism have in mind when they reject the latter's 'transhistorical' claims. As material and cultural structures change, so too do epistemic considerations. So whilst marxism, as essentially one of the products of high industrial capitalism in the nineteenth century, quite 'naturally' advances its own set of universalist categories (production, class etc.), other perspectives, often explicitly *post*-marxist in formation, will begin to advance other sets. Thus, for example, feminists and 'Third World' activists may not feel able to regard the prime movers specified by marxist theory as the central, objective historical tendencies. They may still take something from the marxist corpus of concepts, but these 'later' theoretical and political currents vigorously criticize, respectively, the male-centredness and Eurocentredness of classical marxist analysis. By a slightly different route, then, a pluralist conclusion re-surfaces: there are many ways of envisaging the phases of human development, none of which is more logically necessary than others. Indeed, since a great many factors evidently contribute to specific outcomes, there may be no reason to treat human development as a singular, overarching process at all, far less one governed by a particular type of intrinsic dynamic.

4

MARXISM: THE CLASS ANALYSIS OF POLITICS

1. Theoretical and historical context

We saw how empirically-minded marxists sometimes deployed references to the primacy of the class struggle in order to temper the monistic implications of strong historical materialism. In that sense, the assertion of 'class' as the major explanatory concept seems a more pluralistic analytical move than assertions of (for example) the primacy of the productive forces. However, 'classes' in marxist discourse are conceived as collectivities of agents sharing a common position within the specific relations of production of a mode of production. This concept suggests a firmly 'structural' account of historical agency, and one which – we also saw – is grounded in at least a nominal sequence of progressive modes of production. It should also be noted that when 'strong' historical materialists make the move down the ladder of abstraction from 'mode of production' to 'concrete society', the relations of production are just as central to their hypotheses as they are to those of 'weaker' historical materialists.

The purpose of class analysis in marxism is therefore to give a coherent and determinate account of social agency, behaviour and institutions, based on prevailing modes of production and their potential for epochal change. The contemporary mode of production and its prospects for change are, of course, especially important. In the historical sequence of modes, it is capitalism, according to the marxist tradition, that develops and socializes productive resources to the point where the global elimination of want and exploitation becomes possible. Then, Marx stated, humanity can enter into a phase in which its true potential as a co-operative society of free, creative individuals can be realized. The major obstacle to this developmental tendency, or at least this possibility, is the private appropriation of social wealth; and the main agency of change is the social class which produces that wealth, i.e. the working class or proletariat. Only in capitalism does commodity production become a generalized social phenomenon, within which the sale of labour power itself as a commodity on the market constitutes the mechanism of class exploitation. It follows, for marxists, that the proletariat has a profound interest in ending the reign of capitalist social relations, and it is held to be the first class in history which, in pursuing its own interests through class struggle, acts as the representative of all-round human emancipation. This is because capitalism is the first truly universal form of production; so advanced alternatives to it will also have to be universal. Class struggle is necessary to any process of emancipatory change, in that class antagonism is intrinsic to capitalism. And the process of change must be *revolutionary*, first in the sense that class exploitation has to be completely abolished, and second because those who benefit from the latter are unlikely – as a class – to be willing peacefully to throw in their lot with the claims and visions of the exploited. The concepts of class and class struggle, it can be seen, are the crucial mediating links between a formal delineation of modes of production and a sense of the social forces at work in the past and future making of history. Classes are not only structural *positions*, but also formations and movements of people in struggle. They are thus inevitably *political* phenomena, social forces.

I suggest that across all the varieties of marxism, few would dispute that summary of the inherited general concepts and aspirations of 'class analysis'. But serious disagreements do begin to emerge once the detail, purpose and validity of class analysis is delved into. As in the case of the wider historical materialism debate, of which this is probably the most vital part, the extent to which pluralist propositions can be inserted into the fabric of the class analysis of modern capitalism is a sensitive and crucial question for the understanding of marxism today. The theoretical issues revolve around three main axes: the definition of classes, the analysis of political and social forces in terms of class identity, and the political complexion of a classless society.

As a tradition forged in and sustained by political movements, it would be ironic and mistaken to treat changes in marxism, of all paradigms, as a purely intellectual matter. Before looking at the three dimensions of theoretical modification, therefore, it is important to give some indication of the living context of the pluralist challenge to, and within, modern marxism. Very generally, two things stand out. First, there has been no successful proletarian revolution in the advanced capitalist countries. Indeed, this prospect – at least in the literal sense of a violent and decisive replacement of capitalist relations of production and state power – has come to be seen by many on the left as increasingly remote. This is not merely a matter of reinterpreting the meaning of the terms and aspirations to 'fit' changing circumstances; rather, it means posing the possibility that the terms themselves and the very logic of the revolutionary marxist outlook need to be substantially repaired in the face of actual events.

Within the core capitalist nations, socialist agitation has involved a degree of acceptance of pluralist political conditions. The organizations of the left have had to compete openly and peacefully with 'bourgeois' parties for democratic endorsement. This practical acknowledgement that the *form* of politics is not immaterial prompts the further recognition that the working class in formal democracies has to be seriously addressed not as a class entity as such, but as a part of 'the people' and indeed as part of 'the electorate'. Furthermore, at least part of the state must be treated as a legitimate arena of struggle, and not merely as a closed shop for the interests of the capitalist class. The priority of winning the working class to a vision of socialism has thus involved coming to terms with the substantial if limited gains associated with representative democracy, and the need, under that system, to respect the prevailing interests or preferences of the people. Regard for the conditions of, and obstacles to, the attainment of popular *consent* as a precondition of socialist transformation becomes, with these practices, a crucial consideration. Overall, the traditional marxist and Leninist distinction between revolutionary parties and those considered to be essentially reformist, begins to blur.

An important (and suitably controversial) adjustment along these lines is the 'Eurocommunist' movement, prominent in western Communist Parties since the early 1970s. These Communist Parties, or factions within larger orthodox parties, have moved steadily away from a Leninist conception of class representation. In the latter, the Party is conceived as the advanced brigade of the working class, which itself stands as the vanguard of the masses. Electoral competition is only one possible move in the general Leninist strategy of decisively overthrowing the capitalist state apparatus. In severe qualification of this conception, Eurocommunism develops a respect for the predominantly non-socialist attitudes of the people; indeed the (diverse) modern proletariat is effectively treated as *coextensive* with 'the people'. There is therefore small role for a confrontationist vanguard politics: the 'advanced' task of the mature marxist party is by contrast to work to win a broad and progressive series of gains within capitalist democracy. These advances involve working with a range of ostensibly non-class movements (today, typically, women's movements, ethnic movements, ecology groups etc.) to develop a mass-based, participative socialist culture. Though not a product of minority direct action in the traditional sense, that kind of development is nevertheless held to be a qualitatively different – a revolutionary? – form of democratic collectivism.

The second major historical reality (and a related one of course) is the establishment first of all in relatively 'backward' countries of socialist nation states, dominated by ruling Communist Parties and self-designated as 'Marxist-Leninist' in inspiration. Under the hegemony of the USSR, these states have been taken to be the working examples of marxism in power, and as such are the sources of endless controversy as to whether they can be regarded as being 'genuinely' of marxist inspiration and whether, indeed, they represent any advance on capitalism.

In defence of 'actually existing socialism', it is sometimes said that the process of industrial and political centralization under Communism was necessary for those desperately 'backward' societies to move towards a more progressive, advanced economy and culture. The strong state of such socialist countries has in part, arguably, been the product of intense capitalist hostility and encirclement, just as the backward environment is due to the ravages of imperialism. Judged by the context rather than any speculative ideal, communist states have notably served to both release and constructively channel the energy of their peoples (and in the process enabled the defeat of fascism as an alternative global order). For all the problems encountered and remaining, this line might conclude, the reality of socialism continues to contrast favourably with the deep-seated illusions in the west about the ability of liberal capitalisms to deliver meaningful popular democracy. To clamour for extensive institutional pluralism in these circumstances, might be to run the costly risk of political disintegration.

Against this optimistic picture, libertarian socialists and critical marxists emphasize the massive and unacceptable costs in human and moral terms of the 'sacrifices' which Communist development has demanded. Moreover, the state socialist claim to constitute 'people's democracies' is challenged to a more or less radical extent. Liberal pluralists, for their part, tend to regard the visible lack of (western-style) democracy as intrinsic to Communism's tyrannical essence, rooting both its illusions and deceptions in the work of Marx and Engels themselves. Libertarian socialists counter this view by defending the democratic proposals of Marx against the distortions imposed in his name by the entire Bolshevik and other state-centred traditions. Trotskyist marxists place the deformation of the democratic workers' state further along the developmental sequence, at the point where Stalinist forces highjacked Lenin's valid embodiment of marxist popular revolution for their own repressive and elitist purposes. Eurocommunists (cf. Carillo 1977) – who for the Trotskyists represent the 'bourgeois' expression of Stalinist conservatism – hedge their bets on whether or not Soviet-style socialism is intrinsically flawed. In the meantime they urge that a process of deepening democracy be undertaken. Through all these different positions, though, a major common assumption is that any socialism worth the name must have independent democratic institutions.

Within orthodox Communism itself, some rethinking along these lines has been taking place. In the Soviet Union and China, for example, reforms have been introduced partly with a view to making their centralized economies more efficient. In smaller European states such as Hungary and Yugoslavia, a compromise between directive and market economic criteria has for many years been in operation. But moves towards greater democracy and pluralism are not exclusively to be seen as the means to *economic* ends. The prospect (a reality since the 1960s) of formally socialist states engaging in war with one another has punctured any cosy idea of spontaneous fraternity. The visible persistence of privilege in socialist countries wrecks the notion that the absence of private capital automatically secures equality. The pervasiveness of bureaucracy, together with distinct signs of cultural malaise, simply puts an end to the expectation that under socialism people will necessarily feel less *alienated* than under capitalism. Additionally, these ideas, and the facts which accompany them, are today debated within a common global medium of visual and ethical communication. The political legitimacy of state socialist politics depends increasingly on the type of demonstration that these forms entail. In all, a serious commitment to feasible democratic change and infrastructural reorganization in the Communist bloc requires a profound process of social pluralization.

The theory of socialist democracy in all these variants of marxist political strategy is manifestly more central to their credibility in the modern world than in days gone by. Yet the explicit acknowledgement within marxism that issues of social and political pluralism form an essential *part of* socialist democracy is still only tentative. Marxists have usually been concerned to point to the *limitations* of pluralism for democracy rather than its scope for enhancing socialist democracy. How far marxism can go in embracing political and cultural diversity largely depends on the extent to which class analysis and pluralist concerns are compatible, and it is here that vital questions of the definition of terms arise.

2. Defining classes

The appeal of the category of class, but also the source of much perplexity, lies in the combination it effects between an 'objective' and explanatory logic on the one hand, and a 'subjective' and descriptive purpose on the other. The objective features of class analysis stem from the high level of abstraction of the concept 'mode of production'. The relations of production, which define the distinctiveness of each mode, specify the central types of ownership and control of productive resources. The social classes, in this first approximation, are groups of people who share a common situation, of ownership/possession, or non-possession, of such resources.

One important set of issues within marxist theory is to do with the further characterization of this overall 'systemic' conception of class. It may be that the fact of ownership/ possession, or its absence, is only a minimal criterion and that, even at the level of the abstract mode of production, it is a potentially misleading one. Workers and slaves, for instance, share a common relationship to the means of production (non-ownership) but cannot be said to be part of a common class. Marx's well-known stipulation in *Capital*, vol. III (Marx 1909: 919) needs to be entered here: it is the precise way in which the surplus is 'pumped out' of the producers that defines specific sets of relations of production (which in turn enables the proper identification of the major classes).

Thus, the surplus in the capitalist mode, according to classical marxist theory, is derived from the difference between the value of the worker's labour power which the capitalist buys in the market-place, and the value of the product of labour actually performed. The slave, by contrast, is bought once and for all by the master, and the whole of his or her being becomes the master's property to do with as he will. In spite of eloquent passages in Marx where the worker's plight under capitalism is likened to slavery, the two mechanisms of surplus production are not after all the same.

This process of deduction seems to indicate a two-class logic for each mode of production: the owners of productive resources derive a surplus from the direct producers. The latter, in a sense, *have* to work for the former, and their product (including the surplus) is appropriated by the owning class. But even in establishing this outline of the workings of a distinct mode of production, Marx himself introduces the possibility of *intermediate* classes, and of different class *fractions*. In the case of capitalism, Marx allows, a third class – the petty bourgeoisie – owns and operates its own means of production. It neither exploits workers nor is itself exploited by capitalists. Moreover, while under capitalism all productive resources are commodified, capitalist profit can accrue from the control over different sorts of resources. Marx singles out the way in which profit is derived from rent on land, for example, as being qualitatively distinct from productive capital in manufacture. On that basis, he accepts that *landlords* can be viewed as a separate social class.

Another important dimension of class-definition, even at the relatively abstract level, is the sense in which the surplus is 'appropriated' by the owning class. As emerged in the previous chapter, the process of appropriation is one which appears inescapably to raise issues of *power*. Peasants, it is sometimes insisted, do in fact possess their means of production: they yield up part of their product to the feudal lords only because they are coerced into doing so. Such coercion, it follows, cannot be regarded as the automatic reflex of any pure economic logic, since the surplus itself in this view comes about through coercive domination. Only in capitalism is the production and sale of commodities universal enough to ensure the appropriation of the surplus product as part of the economic mechanism itself.

This argument is not altogether convincing, but it points to some theoretically consequential semantics, such as the relationship between 'ownership' and 'possession', and between 'appropriation' and 'exploitation'. As a way of opening up this array of definitional nuances, it can be suggested that feudal lords *do* effectively own or possess crucial productive resources (land, mills, ovens, and so forth). Their 'appropriation' of the surplus is thus not based on straightforward coercion, nor are peasants always typically in a position to produce autonomously. The picture of capitalism can be adjusted along similar lines, though this time in the other direction. For classical capitalists, it might be floated, do *not* themselves own and control all of the key resources and means of production. Materials, land, finance, and labour power at different times and in various degrees can be seen as being under the control of agents who are not capitalists, at least again as *typically* conceived. Capitalist appropriation, moreover, requires a tightly formulated set of legal entitlements and dispute procedures, and a stable social environment in which to operate if the general process of surplus value extraction is to prevail. Marx was of course exceptionally sensitive to the brutal aspects of ensuring social order in the formation of classes and in the establishment of modes of production. While his attempt to reveal the pure, logical anatomy of the systems which emerged can be respected as an intellectual exercise, the idea that capitalism is secured through the 'dull compulsion' of economic sale and return alone ignores the massive political apparatuses which sustain its 'logic'. In sum, 'appropriation' entails that marxists cannot hope to define classes exclusively at an abstract level. It suggests that the ownership of the means of production can be taken as the basis of a class understanding in social terms only in the sense of *effective possession*, not formal entitlement alone. But possession and control are, manifestly, modalities of conflict which a narrow conception of economic relations cannot readily embrace.

This kind of argument, however, does not of itself discount the need for an initial, skeletal definition of classes as places set by the logic of the process of production. 'Appropriation' is less technically suited to that task than another prominent marxist concept: exploitation. Traditionally, it is the theory of surplus value which has stood as the canonical explication of 'exploitation'. In the pure capitalist economy, Marx believed, goods exchange in relation to the amount of 'abstract socially necessary labour time' which they embody. The commodity labour-power is no different in that respect: capitalists purchase it by paying the going rate sufficient for its reproduction. However, the peculiarity of labour-power lies in its ability to produce a value greater than its cost of reproduction. Accordingly, out on the other side of the production process, the commodities so produced sell in the market for a price which reflects the enhanced value which labour has supplied. The sale price of the end product, though higher than the compound cost price, is nevertheless a *fair* price in market terms, because it continues faithfully to reflect the amount of human labour time it embodies.

The Marxian theory of value has a crucial effect on class definitions. For example, some marxists adopt a narrow definition of the modern 'working class' such that the proletariat consists solely of those labourers who directly create surplus value in the process of production (Poulantzas 1975). This position has the merits of concentrating attention on the ultimate source of capitalist profit and accumulation, and reaffirms the primacy of production over circulation (market transactions) in understanding the root cause of social division. However, it is not clear either that Marx held to this restrictive definition, or that it can be clearly sustained as a social classification (cf. Hunt 1977). The *source* of profit may well be surplus value, but wage labourers are every bit as necessary for the *realization* of surplus value and indeed for the *reproduction* of labour and capital alike. It is only analytically, not socially, that the distinction between formally 'productive' and 'unproductive' labour is significant. A more inclusive definition of the working class is thus appropriate, one which draws in all those workers who sell their labour power for a wage.

The argument about broad and narrow definitions tends to presuppose the validity of Marx's labour theory of value. However, value-theory has come under systematic attack within as well as outside the marxist tradition, and the question is posed: if value-theory *cannot* be upheld, is there *any* basis for a 'pure' theory of class using the concept of exploitation?

One line of critique in the debate about value-theory (cf. Steedman et al. 1981) is that, contrary to Marx's assumption, labour is not the only commodity which serves as the basis upon which to theorize what stands as the common denominator in the exchange of goods on the market. Corn or oil, for example, could just as well serve this purpose in capitalist calculation. A second point is that when capitalists do calculate realistically (as Marx concedes they do, in *Capital*, vol. III (Marx 1909)), they do so in terms of aggregate market *prices*, a calculation in which it has been asserted, 'values have no role whatsoever' (Elster 1985: 137). This is because the macro-level of the real economy involves (amongst other things) the heterogeneous character of labour tasks, the widespread existence of joint production processes, and the need for average rates of profit across different sectors. Yet none of this, it is held, can be derived from the abstract notion of embodied labour time. Indeed the very idea of 'socially necessary abstract labour' is something of a conundrum, something ritually asserted to be necessary but which cannot be observed in any of its supposed manifestations. From this critical standpoint, the traditional marxist economist can only defend the proposition that the movement of prices will reveal a 'tendential' approximation to the level of labour values as a metaphysical act of faith. This is a charge which has been strenuously countered by exponents of value theory (cf. Fine and Harris 1979), and the debate cannot be pursued further in this context.

The debate on the validity of value theory, for all that, need not monopolize the marxist search for a defensible and intuitive generic meaning of exploitation as forming the basis of class identification. One such general formula might be: the forcible extraction by non-producers, from the direct producers, of an economic surplus, i.e. an amount above that required to reproduce labour. Yet, there is a danger of considerable imprecision in all pocket formulae of this kind. For example, exploitation is often *willingly* complied with; the specification of a 'surplus' as merely anything above that required for reproduction is quite a limited way of picturing the struggle over social resources; and the idea of unitary classes as defined by the touchstone of 'direct production' could be regarded as unduly restrictive. As a way of getting round issues of this kind, and as a *via media* between intuition and the (allegedly) murky depths of value-theory, an alternative concept of exploitation has been developed by modern 'analytical' marxists (Roemer 1986, Wright 1985: ch. 3).

According to this school of thought, exploitation should be conceived in terms deriving from game theory. In this vein, we can reflect on the balance of gain and loss among a connected pair of 'coalitions' or groups once the currently worse-off group 'withdraws' from the initial arrangement. If a scenario of feasible withdrawal rules can be specified such that the worse-off group improves its situation at the same time as that of the currently better-off group worsens, then the latter must be held to (currently) exploit the former. This simple-seeming formulation has three main advantages. First, the nature of the exploitative relationship does not appear to depend on the broader, non-economic concept of domination. The latter may well be important in considering why exploited groups do not engage in withdrawal, and for detailed descriptions of the powers at work within the labour process. But, in this perspective, exploitation itself consists only in the material content of relative benefits. The theory thus keeps open the possibility of a 'pure' definition of class in the (supposed) classic marxist manner.

Second, it is a definition which requires that for any given type of exploitation, there are only two main class categories – the owners and non-owners of productive assets. Again, this is designed to conform to Marx's rigorous logic at the highest level of abstraction. Orthodoxy is reaffirmed in a third way in the conception of communism as a society without exploitation, i.e. without inequalities in any type of asset-ownership, and therefore as a *classless* society. However, the analytical marxists depart considerably from tradition when they extend the idea of productive assets to include not only ownership of the means of production and labour power, but also organizational position and the possession of skills. These latter sources of exploitation are regarded as the chief characteristic of, respectively, the 'statist' class structure, now asserted to come *after* capitalism in the sequence of modes of production; and of 'socialism', the next form of class society and the one which precedes communism. Communism is, as ever, defined as the classless society, that is, one without inequalities in any sort of asset-ownership.

This innovative contribution facilitates a serious estimation of whether post-capitalist societies are *class* societies, without having to force them into a strait-jacket, whether capitalist or communist. The analytic reworking also tries to preserve some way of making initial theoretical distinctions at a high level of abstraction without overly 'complexifying' class identification.

But whatever the advantages gained here, we should be clear as to what is being lost from Marx's original enterprise. Certainly, value theory is rejected. Although an alternative general theory of exploitation is offered, in which capitalist exploitation figures as a sub-type, a suitably *dynamic* conception of capitalist accumulation and crisis – a dynamism Marx himself definitively perceives in value terms – is missing in the analytic alternative. Instead, a formal model based on static equilibrium notions is preferred (Callinicos 1987: 72).

John Roemer, in developing his theory of exploitation, tends to refer to historical materialism as the (undefended) premiss for his theoretical labours. So it is possible that he takes the growth of the productive forces as the dynamic factor in capitalism, as in history generally (Przeworski 1982: 305). Roemer has himself, though, expressed reservations about Cohen's version of the theory of history (Roemer 1982: 513), and in any case, the difficulties with this theory have already been explored. The charge of 'stasis' in the models preferred by analytic marxists still sticks. What is additionally interesting here is the analytic marxists' self-image as constructors of theoretical rationalizations for essentially *pre-existing* beliefs. Thus, Roemer writes:

> There is nothing objectively correct about the labour theory of exploitation in the sense of its being deducible from economic data. It is rather a particular theory of exploitation that corresponds to the interpretation of capitalism as a class struggle between poor workers and rich capitalists, which, according to historical materialism is the most informative historical interpretation of capitalism. (Roemer 1986: 101)

For this reason, Roemer's text is scattered with references to the effect that a particular formal analytic device, say the 'withdrawal rules' under feudalism, is 'correct' only in so far as it 'gives the result' we are after, in this case that 'serfs are exploited and lords are exploiters' (Roemer 1986: 104). This deductive procedure can, it is true, be independently supported by the valid contention that we learn a great deal when we choose to 'make true' some particular theorem which derives from a 'deep theory' that we intuitively support (1986: 111).

And the deep theory itself may well deserve reconsideration as a consequence. All the same, *Marx's* account of exploitation was undeniably put forward as 'objectively correct', in that it claimed to *explain* the 'economic data'. Indeed, intuition, in Marx's view, was a source of much illusion and his developed theories of exploitation, he hoped, would make intuition redundant. Roemer's promotion of theory-construction as pedagogy plus his intuitive starting point, can legitimately be questioned as constituting a distinct 'ethical' marxism which substantially departs from Marx's own goals. Exploitation, from this angle, is the unfair or unjust unequal exchange which occurs as a result of differential asset ownership. For Marx, exploitation was indeed unjust when seen from the long-term perspective of human emancipation. But as a matter of the workings of capitalism, exploitation was simply the inner logic of the system, to be analysed as such (cf. Lukes 1985). For Roemer, the perceived injustice of exploitation is what motivates a coherent theorization of it; but how far that theorization captures the objective logic of the system does not appear to be the right sort of question to pose.

The ethical marxist bent of the analytic account finds a suitable expression in the terms of game theory, because subjective evaluation is crucial to the reasoning of the posited actors and coalitions in that style of exposition. Exploitation is said to exist only when the withdrawal of the worse-off group could feasibly result in an improved situation. That formula implies that if withdrawal was likely to produce, realistically, a *worsening* of the exploited coalition's plight, then there would be grounds for rejecting the idea that they are currently exploited. This, indeed, is the logic behind frequently heard claims that capitalism is *not* exploitative, since it involves voluntary and mutually beneficial exchanges of services between capital and labour. Similarly, if no feasible alternative to feudal exploitation was available in which peasants became better off, the relation between lord and peasant could be seen as a (necessary) trade-off between, for example, rent and protection (Roemer 1986: 102, Rigby 1987: 210). Here, though, the ethical assessment of the fairness of 'unequal exchange' depends in turn upon the estimation of just how *feasible* a given alternative is in the circumstances. That this condition is potentially unrevolutionary is obvious: convincing-sounding reasons for thinking that a radical alteration of dominant social relationships is *not* feasible are always easy to come by. More germane to the current discussion is that the very estimation of feasibility must bear directly on the subjective perceptions of the agents themselves. In this respect too, the strenuously 'objectivist' purpose behind Marx's notion of exploitation has been discarded.

Distinctive though it is, the analytic marxist enterprise is governed by the same sort of rationale as that of other idioms of western marxism: the felt need to render basic marxist concepts more flexible in order the better to comprehend the complexities of modern social relations. In trying to meet that need, analytic marxism has managed to preserve, technically, a two-class logic of exploitation. But a final noteworthy point at this stage is that the place of the classically conceived 'mode of production' consequently looks less secure. In the terminology I have already introduced, analytic marxists have difficulties in seeing how the abstract relations of the mode of production 'map' on to the concrete society. They prefer to theorize exploitation as logical types of class structure which may then be considered in various combinations until the mix seems appropriate for the concrete society under consideration. Thus, they do not see social formations as the 'expressions' of modes of production (as in the Hegelian marxist vein), or even as the combination and articulation of different modes (after the structuralist marxist manner). Rather, societies will tend to combine, in an ordered and weighted way, some or all of the abstract types of class-exploitation relations. There is thus no need here to introduce the mode of production considered as a 'social totality'. The concept of a mode of production can certainly be accepted by analytic marxists as heuristic or informative in certain ways. But that it has been nudged out of its central position is indicated by Erik Olin Wright's glaring omission of the term in his analytically redrawn tables of the sequence of social formations (Wright 1985: 67, 83).

3. Marx's class analysis

The rationale for the kind of extensive revisions the 'analytic marxists' put forward is well encapsulated by Wright. Wright says that Marx produced two types of class analysis, namely, 'abstract structural maps of class relations, and the analysis of concrete conjunctural maps of classes-as-actors.' Wright also says that Marx did not provide a 'systematic linkage' between the two levels of analysis (Wright 1985: 6–7). However, it is also noted that Marx posited as a central historical tendency of capitalism the increasing polarization of groups into two principal classes or 'camps'. This, in my view, just *is* the 'systematic linkage' in Marx, and the one which ensures, in Wright's terms, an 'effective correspondence between the abstract and the concrete categories of class analysis' (1985: 8). The point is that Wright, like many other marxists one hundred years after Marx, does not quite believe in the polarization thesis, and only barely in the prospect of a classless society. The issue is not entirely squared up to, however, because such commentators are tempted to find in Marx himself reflections of their own ambivalence. One of the most important of these is held to be the apparent difference in style and purpose between Marx's abstract theoretical treatises, above all, *Capital* and his more subtle historical analyses represented best by the *Eighteenth Brumaire of Louis Bonaparte* (Marx 1973a). The latter text has certainly been subject to many helpful 'readings' which partly bear out what Wright says (e.g. Hall 1977). That is, Marx has a brilliant eye for the rich empirical details of social divisions when classes take to the stage of real history.

It is nevertheless worth briefly reflecting on these key texts, because it is arguable that the tendency to see such a 'gap' as a debilitating problem is a hallmark of the *modern* marxist temperament, not of Marx's own. The most relevant theoretical statement is Marx's unfinished final chapter in *Capital* volume III. Most commentators have regarded this text as an ironic and enigmatic way to break off the manuscript of his major work. Marx was doubtless about to embark on a characteristically full account of the 'three great classes of modern society' (Marx

1909: 1031). However, this incompleteness in the text gives no reason for despair, since the pattern of argument of the paragraphs that Marx *did* leave behind is fairly clear.

Marx notes how, even in the 'classic' case (i.e. England), class stratification does not emerge in the concrete society in its pure form. Rather, clear-cut class boundaries are 'obliterated' by the various 'middle and transition stages' which can become especially prominent in an urban setting. One way *not* to conduct fundamental class analysis, Marx warns, is to derive the class position of individuals from their precise form of *revenue*. This move could, he thought, trigger off a damaging proliferation of categories, serving to reproduce in theory 'the infinite dissipation of interests and positions created by the social division of labour among labourers, capitalists and landlords' (Marx 1909: 1032). In other words, just as there are possibly many intermediate or overlapping positions between the two principal classes, so there are innumerable divisions of interests *within* them. Even so, Marx goes on, 'this is immaterial for our analysis', because:

> We have seen that the continual tendency and law of development of capitalist production is to separate the means of production more and more from labour, and to concentrate the scattered means of production more and more in large groups, thereby transforming labour into wage labour and the means of production into capital. (1909: 1031)

When Marx follows this preamble by asking 'what constitutes a class?' and answering as a first approximation, 'not revenue', his manner is more didactic than puzzled, for the basis of a definitional answer is already given. It is the extent of a group's ownership/possession of the major means of production which constitutes it as a class. The answer is also, significantly, *developmental*: the historic tendencies of capital lead to the steady empirical confirmation of the abstract logic of class identification.

So much is perhaps uncontroversial. More contentious is the view that in spite of the descriptive-theoretical refinements on display when Marx looks at the class content of French politics in his *Eighteenth Brumaire*, the pattern of explanation is in effect the same. This work (Marx 1973a) is generally taken to show how seriously Marx regarded the 'relative autonomy' of the state and politics with respect to the class structure. Marx seems to be taking as his analytic problem a period where class conflict reaches a sort of stalemate, and in which cross-class or déclassé groups can come to wield state power, often against the interests of the ruling class itself. A slightly different interpretation is that this process could be seen as the *abdication* of overt class power on the part of the bourgeoisie in favour of an authoritarian state clique to whom the capitalists entrust (perhaps foolishly) their essential interests.

Under these theoretical headings, Marx proceeds to describe a complex web of class fractions and their political 'representatives' on the French political scene. Even at this sub-class level there is no easy correspondence between class forces and political movements or phases of state organization. Marx additionally conjures up the immense power of traditional ideologies and the call for social order as ways of offsetting class perceptions. Marx freely acknowledges that we are dealing here with a period containing 'the most variegated mixture of crying contradictions', one whose murky shades are painted 'grey on grey'. But he insists that 'common delusions' about the overall character of the epoch must nevertheless be avoided (1973a: 170–2). Marx's purpose, in short, remains rigorously explanatory, and this requires keeping the *epochal* significance of events in mind as he recounts the 'peculiar physiognomy of the period' (173). The latter resides not in a superficial analysis of the collective actors in party political terms (republicans, royalists), but rather in terms of the 'class struggle'.

Applying this dictum, Marx identifies as the main issue the failure of nerve on the part of the bourgeois class as a whole, just at the point when they could (and should) have consolidated the 'pure conditions of their own class rule' (175). The insurgent working class had been brutally crushed after the June days, and subsequently formed an alliance with the petty bourgeoisie in the person of the social-democratic party. This alliance, for Marx, could not emerge as a decisive political force precisely because as a coalition it represented an impossible 'harmony' of interests 'between the two extremes of capital and wage-labour' (176). Since the petty bourgeoisie is essentially a 'transitional' class, one in which true class interests become 'blurred', its rhetorical prominence betrayed a total lack of real substance.

The bourgeoisie, however, chose not to perceive this demise of the fundamental challenge after the June days, when the proletariat passed into the background of the revolutionary stage (154). The bourgeois parties accepted and fuelled the fear of a continuing communist/anarchist threat, to the point where an organized force which promised tranquillity could intercede and take the initiative, even from the ruling class itself. For Marx, the constitutional republic is the bourgeois state form *par excellence*, where the fractions of capital are able to rule 'jointly' (165). The French bourgeois republic, though, degenerated into intra-capitalist squabbles. Legitimists vied with Orleanists, a struggle which Marx refuses to think of in terms of differences of 'so-called principles'. In reality these parties represented, respectively, 'big landed property' and capital, 'the bourgeois parvenus' (173).

Unable to forge a positive class unity, the bourgeoisie passed ever greater powers over to the state machine itself. Initially, Marx projects an image of 'the social revolution of the nineteenth century' as being more mature, bold and progressive than its 'superstitious' and half-baked predecessors of the eighteenth (149). The 'farce' of the period 1849–51, for Marx, was twofold. In the first place, the bourgeoisie despicably failed to respond to the tasks modernity had set for it. Secondly, the ghost of the first Napoleon, who had decisively paved the way for an 'appropriate modern environment for the bourgeois society in France' (147), took the shape of his nephew, a mere 'adventurer' and 'cardsharper'.

At this point Marx's class-analytical thrust begins to weaken, because it seems as though the vast power accumulating in the state did not have a clear class basis – unless Bonaparte himself can be assigned a representative role. Marx reserves some of his most excoriating prose for the sections in which Louis Napoleon is depicted as in one guise the embodiment of the 'lumpen-proletariat' (197); in another the shield of a state breed of parasites (243); and, most emphatically in *class* terms, as the representative of the peasantry (238–9). But in spite of the ideological resonance of traditional peasant concerns, and in spite of their continuing political weight as a mass, Marx concludes that the peasant smallholding 'has outlived its day' (244). Ironically, every day under Bonaparte the objective economic basis of peasant interests was disintegrating, as rural assets became transformed into forms of capital. Bonaparte had thus little option but to try on top of everything else to represent the middle-class interest, thus sustaining some of the central economic tendencies of the capitalist mode. The material source of bourgeois dominance was thus 'kept alive', even if its political effects were suppressed (245).

Consequently, Marx identifies Bonaparte's rule as structurally contradictory, reflecting no single set of class interests (246–7). Precisely because of this, it was bound to be a temporary phenomenon. State power, it is implied, cannot for long be left unanchored to either of the basic class forces in the modern mode of production. The Second Empire could simply not afford simultaneously to sustain aspects of the bourgeois economy and yet also bring it constantly to a state of 'confusion' (248).

Whilst Marx does not finally resolve the riddle of the bourgeoisie's failure of nerve, he sets in motion some ideas which serve to qualify his initial idea that the modern mode had indeed reached sufficient maturity for the capitalist class to step out boldly on to the historical stage. The importance of the peasantry, for example, is carefully recorded, even though its demise is certain. This indicates that there are still powerful 'transitional' forces at work. The bourgeois factions, moreover, are perhaps too finely balanced to confirm the necessary predominance of manufacturing capital. Thus Marx notes the lack of clarity in the bourgeois ranks about economic trends (225) and the genuine mutual 'incomprehension' amongst its stubbornly 'heterogeneous' components (214, 221). The state, finally, does not, as it seems to, 'hover in mid air'. The full development of capitalism in fact requires the assertion of strong centralizing impulses which will clear out the 'debris' of old state forms and transitional formations (244–5).

With this rationalization of the stage reached by the bourgeois revolution, Marx's rigorous class logic is about complete. The fact that he operates a *two*-class logic, however, should not be forgotten. Though it has been defeated, Marx reflects, the proletarian revolution can afford to take to the background for a spell in order to engage in self-criticism, thence to return to the fore (repeatedly if necessary) until it finally faces a situation in which 'retreat is impossible' (150). From Marx's analysis, two interim developments are necessary. One is proletarian understanding of the futility of class-alliances (for example, of the workers with the petty bourgeoisie). By their nature, these hybrids cannot result in a historically decisive politics (194). The other is the 'perfection' of executive power, in the refinement of which Bonaparte unwittingly bestows a long-term benefit on the bourgeoisie. However, in turn, this concentration of social command serves to focus the energies and objectives of those engaged in the longer-term revolution. When this 'thorough' and 'methodical' process is completed, Marx hopes and imagines, then Europe will indeed 'leap from its seat and exultantly exclaim: "Well worked, old mole!"' (237).

4. Class as a social and political formation

Marx was well aware of the difference between classes conceived as abstract types and understood as collective actors. He pondered over the mismatch of class position and class behaviour in the case of both the bourgeoisie and the peasantry. In describing the latter, he notes how a class is *formed* by dint of its distinctive material conditions. However, in order to *assert* the interests which stem from those common conditions, it is necessary for a class to develop 'a feeling of community, national links, or a political organization' (239). In *The Poverty of Philosophy*, Marx (1975: 159–60) extended this distinction to the proletariat. He stated that the latter's common situation and common interest already defined it as a 'class against capital'; but in order to become a 'class for itself' the proletariat must unite in a *political* class struggle.

As my commentary indicates, Marx was only troubled in a *political* sense by the discrepancy between class positions and class actions. It was not an *epistemological* problem for him. Marx's long-term evolutionary and revolutionary framework served constantly to resolve any such uncertainties in clarifying the meaning of class 'representation' in the cultural and political spheres. Modern marxists, however, do not share either Marx's confident political anticipations or his unconcern with epistemology. They tend to doubt whether class interests or class unity ever can be directly 'transferred' from the ethereal domain of abstract concepts to the dense fabric of social interaction – a domain which reveals, as Marx put it in his *Grundrisse*, 'a rich totality of many determinations and relations' (Marx 1973: 100). Marx somewhat heroically expected his own method of political economy precisely to establish a coherent order of determination, a 'unity of the diverse' (1973: 101). Nowadays, by contrast, marxists cannot take this promise on trust. If class definitions are intrinsically simplifying, abstract categories, the plurality of determinations cannot be reflected in them. If they are applied without extensive mediation, they are likely to impose an unrealistic degree of coherence on the empirical world. But by the same token, the source of necessary mediation must be derived from elsewhere, from *outside* the abstract class logic. Whichever way the issue is turned, it seems, there is a tension, not a unity, between class coherence and multiple determinations in the analysis of social forces.

Whilst Marx's belief in a class polarization thesis is in-controvertible, he did *not* – at least by the time of the writing of *Capital* – seem to view this process as requiring the reduction of the many forms of non-capitalist labour to one homogeneous type, that of 'productive' manual work. On the contrary, Marx pointed to many of the mechanisms by which capitalism itself calls into being as its necessary effect an extensive array of financial, commercial and service occupations. In the century since Marx this diversification of functions has proceeded apace, and the classic cultural image of the factory worker is generally agreed to be no longer typical of working-class life. This, however, only intensifies the dilemmas marxists face in 'reading' the cultural and political springs of action in abstract class terms.

One resolution to the problem is to build a political and/or ideological component into the very definition of class. This move can have two opposite effects. First, it can lead to a very narrow concept of the proletariat; secondly, it can be asserted in such a way as to render impossible any 'objective' notion of class structure. Following the first strand of thought, it has sometimes been argued that the class struggle is political from the outset in that the process of surplus value extraction is inextricably one of domination in the labour process. From this standpoint, workers who perform a supervisory function can be seen as the 'agents' of capitalist domination, and thus should be legitimately 'excluded' from the ranks of the proletariat. Moreover, since the production of surplus value is pre-eminently a *material* process, class divisions are sustained in part by the generalized separation of manual from mental labour. Accordingly, those workers who are engaged in designing the work process contribute substantially to that 'ideological' precondition of capital's domination of labour, and on that basis they too should be disqualified as part of the working class.

Writers who take this kind of line face three major problems. The first is that once the class criterion is allowed to contain an ideological element, the way is clear to define 'class interest' – and therefore those who are to be collated as 'genuine' proletarians – in controversial and subjective ways. Poulantzas, for example, excludes engineers from the working class on these grounds (Poulantzas 1975: 241), whilst Carchedi (1977: 8–9) almost requires that true proletarians be card-carrying members of the revolutionary party. Taking the 'surplus value' definition alone, the contemporary working class would appear to make up only about twenty per cent of the working population in some advanced capitalist countries (Wright 1975: 55, Therborn 1983: 171). It follows that if the aspiration behind the revised class concept was to encompass the social reality of classes in struggle, it must be deemed unsuccessful. Thirdly, 'domination' is not suited to serve as a basis for *marxist* theory, since the classical claim of the latter is that it helps to *explain* the phenomenon of power. Indeed, without a prior commitment to 'economic' notions such as exploitation, power is a concept which is *particularly* prone to generalized application across diverse social spheres. This subordination of economic class criteria to those of (disparate) control and decision-making mechanisms is, paradoxically, one of the main contentions of conventional pluralism (Wright 1985: 57).

The other way of trying to highlight a politico-cultural definition is to assert that classes are *constituted* by a range of social and political considerations. Interpreted *liberally*, this claim could mean that, regarded as social actors, classes cannot be adequately described by reference to economistic 'objective' criteria. This view certainly poses a problem for the ultimate adequacy of class analysis, but its exponents are often still prepared to reaffirm a version of Marx's class in itself/class for itself contrast – probably with the weight more on the second foot (e.g. Hall 1977: 50).

Interpreted *literally*, the thesis of the political constitution of class is rather more heterodox. It asserts that there is only, ever, 'class for itself', even at the starting point of definitions. This view, sometimes encapsulated as 'class as a social process', has been suggested by a number of neo-marxist writers (e.g. Thompson 1968: 9–10), but most extensively in a theoretical vein by Adam Przeworski (1985). Przeworski's theoretical baseline for the radical interpretation is that the supposedly objective 'economic' level is itself in many key ways – particularly in the very idea of its *separateness* – the product of political and ideological practices. Taking that angle further, the only reasonable way of looking at class is as an active and ongoing process of class *formation*, governed by human struggle and comprising a totality of economic, political and ideological aspects. Przeworski goes on:

> Positions within the relations of production, or any other relations for that matter, are thus no longer viewed as objective in the sense of being prior to class struggles. They are objective only to the extent to which they validate or invalidate the practices of class formation, to the extent to which they make the particular projects historically realizable or not. And here the mechanism of determination is not unique: several projects may be feasible at a particular conjuncture. (1985: 67)

The very concept of class, in this version, is the product of practices of class formation, which in turn are conceived by Przeworski as being the outcome of political projects. Accordingly, he states that the very questions 'What are the

classes?' and 'Are interests of classes antagonistic?' are determined by politics and ideology: 'the ideological struggle is a
struggle *about* class before it is a struggle *among* classes' (1985:
70). To support this, Przeworski examines the way in which
the concept and expectations of class have been moulded into a
shape suitable for *electoral* reasoning in accordance with the
goals and practices of social democratic parties. The logic of
class struggle here turns out to be the way in which *any*
struggle (for example, party politics) has an effect on 'class
organization or disorganization' (1985: 80). The latter is in turn
not to be viewed as the organization (or disorganization) of
pre-positioned agents. Rather, the ideologies and practices
which are *about* class actively construct individuals in their
very self-image as agents involved in class struggle.

This challenging conception of class formation acknowledges
explicitly the effect of practical politics on theoretical debates.
As indicated towards the beginning of this chapter, the
theoretical trajectory of marxism in the twentieth century
cannot be envisaged beyond the concrete experiences of
socialist politics. But Przeworski's view implies something
more, and it is this extension of the valid stress on historical
context which renders his views somewhat contradictory. For
Przeworski is effectively saying that the very notion of an
objective class position, and indeed of *any* objective social
relation, is the creation of particular political projects and
ideologies. Without any objective anchorage, however, there is
no special reason to favour a *marxist* version of the social
project as against others. As he rightly remarks, 'several
projects may be feasible', since socialist movements themselves
are not class products *per se*, but the outcome of 'multiple
determinations' (73).

Trying to hold on to marxism in the face of the prospect of
pluralism which opens up in these propositions, Przeworski
throws out a series of questions for the reader, who must feel
that they come from the author's heart as well as his pen. 'Are
all struggles class struggles? How can we recognise class
struggles?' Why should any of the very many important
'struggles between sexes, races, religious groups, regions,
ethnic groups, and so on . . . be analysed in class terms' (79–
81)? To ask the questions in this vein, of course, is more or less

to answer them: there seems to be *no* particular reason, in classical marxist terms, to look at these things under the auspices of class theory if the latter is conceived as only one ideology/political project amongst several. Perhaps this conclusion has startled Przeworski, for he begins to back off again, first by suggesting a minimal 'methodological postulate': '. . . all conflicts that occur at any moment of history can be understood in historical terms if and only if they are viewed as effects of and in turn having an effect on class formation (1985: 80). But this rather bizarre formulation solves very little. It seems to imply, in a notably circular and essentialist manner, that the only genuinely 'historic' forms of conflict are ones which bear directly on class formation. But class formation, in Przeworski's terms, is still tied up, not with something so privileged as the real movement of history, but rather with the twists and turns of discourses about class, projects of social interpretation. He tries again: 'The theoretical function of class analysis is . . . to identify the objective conditions and the objective consequences of concrete struggles' (81). This more orthodox-sounding formula in fact still harbours the idea that 'objective' conditions cover more than economic relations. Moreover, the adumbration of objective conditions, whilst necessary, is not sufficient for proper class-formation analysis. Even so, Przeworski has chosen not in the end to propose a wholly radical alternative to Marx's distinctions, and so leaves in place the conundrums he generates. He accepts after all that 'individuals occupy places within the system of production', and that such 'rudimentary' propositions as this can begin to answer, if anything can, the pluralist challenge: why not some other focus of struggle?

5. The democratic state

The first major move in the marxist analysis of politics – the treatment of (crucial) social movements as essentially class movements – is, I have indicated, a far from straightforward or convincing operation, whether in the hands of Marx himself or a modern western academic such as Przeworski. Classes do not usually appear on the historical stage as unified collective agencies, and social struggles or conflicts, whilst often class-related, are usually strongly characterized by social, political or ideological features which are not reducible to the effects of class position alone.

Thus, for example, it is now widely accepted that if there is a sense in which the French Revolution of 1789 was a *bourgeois* revolution, i: is not because that series of movements was led by significant owners of capital acting as such. Nor is it satisfactory to argue that prominent groups (lawyers, the 'sans culottes', the Jacobins) somehow served as typical cultural representatives of the elements of the post-feudal society (cf. Furet 1981, Doyle 1980). It *can* I think still be successfully argued that the upheavals of the French Revolution had significant class *conditions* and eventual class *outcomes*, in that capitalist relations emerged in and through the kind of cultural and economic processes that the Revolution initiated or accelerated (Kemp 1971). Yet it is clear that the viability of marxist explanation here depends upon an analytic 'retreat' up the levels of abstraction from the heat of political motives and the clash of social forces to the relative calm of a retrospective standpoint, one designed to identify epochal structural con-sequences which may not have been intended as such by the agents themselves. This level of explanation is indeed central to the business of critical social science, but it does not license the 'class analysis' of political forces in any strong or detailed sense.

The second move in the class analysis of politics is the depiction of forms of state, particularly the democratic state, as determined by class interests. This operation is revealed in many of the key terms of marxist debate, terms which tend to run the political and economic dimensions together: ruling class, capitalist state, bourgeois republic, dictatorship of the proletariat. The Leninist strand within marxism has been the chief advocate of this kind of rigorously 'expressive' class analysis. Basically, state forms, and the regimes they sustain, are perceived as the embodiment or reflection of class relations in society generally. To be sure, the Leninist theory of the state accepts *ab initio* that the state as such has a specific character which sets it apart from other social relations and institutions: it is the main concentration of coercive power. But Lenin (1970) goes on to argue that the coercive and representative forms of all states have their underlying rationale in being expressive of particular class powers.

Thus, for Lenin, there should be no need for moralistic arguments about the inherent political value of, say, democracy as against other forms of regime. Parliamentary democracy, like other species of political domination, is a class phenomenon, providing in this case the 'best possible shell' for advancing and stabilizing the interests of the bourgeoisie. Parliaments can uniquely secure capitalist legitimacy by offering the appearance of participation and representation to subordinate class forces, though the coercive essence of the democratic state form sometimes has to assert itself beneath and beyond these institutional trappings (as for example in the 1914–18 war) (cf. Harding 1981: 203).

Just as, for Lenin, the bourgeois republic at bottom is a form of class dictatorship, so the organized socialist state, the necessary vehicle of proletarian ascendancy, is the 'dictatorship of the proletariat'. In this context, a developed political pluralism cannot be countenanced. Since official parties are regarded as necessarily class-based, to allow party competition for any length of time would be effectively to postpone the advent of a classless society. By definition, the existence of multiple organized groupings has no basis in the latter. Accordingly, Lenin's merely tactical and partial dealings with democratic procedures are logical enough. When the Bolsheviks gained only 25 per cent in the Constituent Assembly of 1917, the latter was disbanded; voting rights in the Soviets were heavily weighted in favour of industrial workers; and the desired political profile of key committees was established by appointment where it could not be achieved by election (Medvedev 1981: 92, Polan 1984: 150–1).

That elements in Leninist thought, notably the relative unconcern for democracy – except as a tactic – served as a source for further moves towards arbitrary rule under Stalin seems undeniable. This does not entail the view that Stalin is the logical consequence of Lenin any more than Lenin's political thinking is directly entailed in Marx's writings. However, the stringency of the connections between the analysis of class position, a sense of historical progress, and political action in the marxist tradition as a whole is notable. Many writers, by no means all attached to Bolshevik political strategy, are committed to similar class-representational tenets.

Thus, Rudolph Bahro, for example, an 'eastern' critic of the Stalinist legacy, maintains that parties are always representations of classes, and it follows that to advocate political pluralism as a part of genuine socialism is to run the risk of perpetuating social division (Bahro 1978: 350–1). It can also be pointed out that Trotsky and Luxemburg, who were arguably more concerned than most revolutionaries with the issue of mass democracy, could not bring themselves to propose party pluralism in the establishment of the socialist state (Geras 1981: 85). More recently, the standard Trotskyist complaint against Eurocommunist revisionism has been precisely the latter's overturning of the doctrine of the state as essentially a machine for class oppression (Mandel 1978).

One conclusion which suggests itself is that the very structure and purpose of marxist categories involves class 'reductionism'. However well intentioned marxists are nowadays about the need to value democracy, the latter simply cannot play a significant *theoretical* role in the class analysis of politics. This line of thought (Mayo 1955: 308, Pierson 1986: ch. 3) clearly makes a mark against overly 'expressive' versions of class politics such as those already mentioned. Indeed, we have seen too that Marx's own concrete analysis is beset with the same kind of *problem*, if not quite the same *degree* of class expressiveness.

However, the charge of 'reductionism' is too often a matter of dismissal by definition: the assertion that fundamental structural constraints operate on what can be said and done in the dominant institutions is interpreted semantically as effectively exhausting the meaning of the political. The conclusion ('reductionism'!) follows as a matter of necessity. But the identification of pervasive and effective constraints on politics, while it *can* lead to determinism and reductionism, need not. To imply, as some critics do, that the citing of a specific type of constraint *must* lead to reductionism is itself a reductionist mode of argument, one that virtually puts an end to any reasonable quest (marxist or otherwise) to ascertain the determinate character of political life.

That kind of rebuttal, together with the more sympathetic attitude of marxists towards multiple determinations, has led modern marxists (e.g. Isaac 1987: 205) to more or less take it for granted that marxism possesses a coherent *non-reductionist* theory of the political sphere. This is not obviously the case. Indeed, the problem here is that if marxists allow that class analysis must be 'supplemented' by all manner of non-class factors in order properly to understand the political sphere, the original 'explanatory promise' (Hindess 1987: 1–2) of class analysis has not been fulfilled.

Accordingly, once more we can identify a certain tension between the specific determinacy (but not necessarily determinism) set by class and the mode of production, and the extent to which supplementary concerns can be admitted by marxists. The term 'relative autonomy' has been identified with the structuralist marxist way of trying to resolve this tension, and so to preserve the 'scientific' aspirations of marxist theory; but in truth it applies to almost all contemporary variants. This includes the 'instrumentalist' approach of Ralph Miliband which received such a sharp structuralist counter-blast from Nicos Poulantzas in their now celebrated 1970s debate. It is often asserted that the former (Miliband 1969) emphasized only the way in which ruling class personnel and 'establishment' cultural networks influenced key decisions and appointments in the extended state. The latter, by contrast, highlighted the functional role of the state in acting as the 'factor of cohesion' for capital as a whole. The contrast is held to reveal the quite different marxist ways of showing how the state 'expresses' the interests of capital: the former by way of contingent personal control by the ruling class; the latter by means of the 'relative autonomy' of state tasks from particular classes or class fractions.

In fact, this debate has been considerably overdrawn. Poulantzas, we have seen, builds the autonomy and contingency of political and ideological relations into the very conception of the mode of production. Moreover, his general functional claim about the state's role in reproducing structures rather than individual rulers meshes well with Miliband's many assertions about the systemic ideological effects of the education system and the mass media – neither of which appear to

sustain any kind of 'conspiracy' thesis of the classic instrumentalist sort. The important contrast, visible *within* the
confines of most contemporary texts, is really between the kind
of causal or functional assertions *all* marxists tend to make
about the state in capitalist society, and the increasing
acceptance of political heterogeneity. That contrast can find
starkly contradictory expression in the most sophisticated
theorists. Göran Therborn, for example, in his book on state
power, summarizes: 'What then does the ruling class do when
it rules? Essentially, it ensures its dominant positions in the
economy, state apparatus, and ideological superstructures are
reproduced by the state' (Therborn 1978: 242).

In this odd and almost tautological formulation, the role of the
state as essentially functional for the dominant class is confirmed.
Indeed it is only if the dominant class *does* effectively
manipulate the state, or directly populate it, that it can be
called the 'ruling' (i.e. governing) class from the outset. There
seems little room here for division within dominant classes, or
for discrepancies between dominant social position and ruling
(i.e. governing) offices of state, or for mismatches of class
meanings across the different social 'levels'. The ruling
(dominant) class rules (governs) because in capitalism social
(class) power expresses itself transparently at the political
level, rendering the latter devoid of independent powers of
rule (dominance).

That this position is seriously overschematic can readily be
shown by the fact that dominant classes, defined structurally,
seldom do articulate their class interests in a unified or
elaborate political way, and that the state often *happens to*
reproduce the interests of capital by following its *own*
interests, or by simply trying to ensure social stability and
the continuity of economic expectations. In that sense, the
state's actions can be functional for the reproduction of
capital without entailing that the ruling (dominant) class
actually rules (governs) (Block 1977). In fact, within a page
or so of the sentence just quoted, Therborn returns to his
generally pluralistic stance by maintaining that state power is
always 'exercised within a contradictory and complex totality
which is in constant flux and development' (Therborn 1978:
243). Taken together, the drift of these assertions looks

distinctly contradictory. On the one hand, distinct types of class relations generate 'corresponding forms of state organization'. On the other hand, 'significant disjunctures' can appear between social relations and political forms 'at any given moment' (35).

Dissatisfaction with the general functionalist and determinist cast of the general propositions of the class analysis of the democratic state has led marxists in the 1980s further in the direction of historical specificity and contingency. Drawing extensively on the work of Gramsci, these currents have attempted to push anti-reductionist marxism as far as it will go. In Gramsci's (1971) prison writings, the very understanding of civil society, and the role of parties and movements in relation to it, is considered from the point of view of the political task of winning 'hegemony'. There is arguably less general theory in Gramsci than in any other major marxist theorist: his principal concern is to assess and reorder the political and ideological configuration of socio-cultural values. The problem of political organization begins from the nature of this cultural-political nexus and its expression in specific 'national-popular' contexts. The emphasis here is decisively on the complexity and autonomy of the various elements which comprise particular historical 'moments' and political projects. All the same, it should be noted that, for Gramsci, there is always a crucial 'moment' of analysis which is based on an 'organic' conception of the underlying historical tendencies, and these, as in all marxism, stem from the nature of the mode of production (Gramsci 1971: 210f.). Also, Gramsci's highly coded text still contains enough explicit references to the way in which hegemony revolves around the mobilization of the 'fundamental social groups' (183) to counter any temptation to dilute his principled marxism into a *supra-class* concern with national-popular movements and values. In particular, Gramsci accepts aspects of the 'expressive' theory of political parties, arguing that 'every party is only the nomenclature for a class' (1971: 152) and that 'every class has a single party' (157). Moreover, Gramsci's general tendency to see the relation between classes in terms of military metaphors and his recognition of the importance of 'relations of force' in the resolution of epochal conflicts (185) cannot permit his legacy to be interpreted (as it sometimes is) as that of theorist of ideology and consent above all else.

This latter construal (e.g. Simon 1982) is designed to serve the political ends of a more open and 'creative' marxism, such that a genuine dialogue can be established between class politics and the 'new social movements' which have emerged in the post-war era. To assume in advance, it is argued, that marxism alone holds the key to the productive development of radical politics, or to take it as given that the state is in every way an oppressive class instrument, is effectively to impose an impossibly pure and historically outmoded model of fundamental political change on the increasingly *diverse* experience of cultural and political life. How much better (from an activist point of view) to see the nature of civil society as an 'arena of struggle', open in at least some ways to progressive and popular democratic change? Lest the radical reformist optimism which emerges from this perspective be thought to follow as an intrinsic consequence of a non-reductionist theory of politics, the mood and content of Poulantzas's last work (1980) needs to be emphasized. For if the 'relative autonomy' of the state indicates an essential openness in the field of political struggle, it also holds the possibility of an authoritarian state solution to the burgeoning of pluralist claims. Democratic political states have shown some marked tendencies towards such authoritarianism in the last decade or so, Poulantzas rightly noted, and this could forever stifle the progress of a broad-based democratic road to socialism.

In sum, the tendency of the marxist analysis of politics has been to move sharply away from a general class theory of the democratic state to the point where the latter is regarded almost as an impossibility and certainly as a hindrance to further theoretical development (Jessop 1982: 111). Instead, it is asserted, the adequacy of marxism depends on its recognition of the *contingency* of the forms in which political exchange and social relations interact, and on its acceptance of the multiplicity of class and non-class influences on the state. However, the other point I have been making is equally important. Marxists can readily *recognize* plurality and to a considerable extent embrace it politically and descriptively; but marxism will always encounter great difficulty in attempting to *theorize* non-class constraints, because this involves the kind of causal and ontological *equivalence* amongst factors, which virtually dissolves marxism as an explanatory project. Of course, that route (as we will see in the next chapter) is attractive to those who wish to see 'non-reductionism' pushed to the limit, and who now agree with non-marxist critics that there is something inherently reductionist about *any* application of marxism.

For those non-reductionists who endeavour to hold on to a theoretical marxist perspective, though, the position is rather more awkward, since *both* reductionism and the assertion of the 'autonomy' of the political are viewed as unsatisfactory. As indicated before, the result of this sensitive holding operation is sometimes a somewhat contradictory amalgam. Thus Jessop, for example, concludes his comprehensive review of marxist state theory by firmly accepting the historical contingency and specificity of connections between social phenomena. This leads him vehemently to reject the idea of a *general* marxist theory of the state (Jessop 1982: 212). Nevertheless, he is still intent on seeking an adequate marxist *account*, if not a full-blown theory, and inevitably, this possibility will have to be couched initially in terms of capital accumulation, the reproduction of modes of production, and the centrality of class forces. For an adequate *marxist* account, it does indeed appear that some such general points of reference are indispensable. And they can moreover be supported by a number of macro-historical 'facts' about modern society: the concurrent development of democracy with capitalism; the role of law as a superstructural support for bourgeois private property; the role of the state in developing the productive forces and maintaining 'reserve armies of labour' within capitalism and in sustaining and reorganizing capitalist markets, and so on (Therborn 1977, 1978: 167f.). Such propositions, it might be suggested, do indeed involve some kind of general theory, albeit in the form of a research agenda.

The problem for pluralistic marxists is that the more 'adequate' a marxist account is in the terms of its own categorical priorities, the *less* adequate it appears to be in relation to the rich multiplicity of concrete social causality. Accordingly, Jessop offers 'guidelines' for an adequate marxist account which include some surprisingly unorthodox features, such as a neutral, institutional definition of the state, and the possibility that state power in modern democratic society does *not* follow a 'capitalist' rationale (1982: 221). Perhaps this move is only to accept the challenge that marxism will survive precisely as a provisional research agenda rather than as a priori theory. This idea would seem to involve a long-term *empirical* assessment of marxism's adequacy. However, this concept of assessment is itself problematic, since contemporary pluralistic marxist writers tend to follow the 'rationalism' of the classical tradition in holding that empirical criteria are themselves the *product* and not the judges of theoretical discourses (cf. Jessop 1982: 219). The conclusion suggests itself that marxism is best regarded not so much as 'falsifiable' but rather as one of *many* possible coherent discourses on the state. It would then follow that the search for a wholly 'adequate' account of any sort is but a chimera. The best bet for marxists in this predicament might be simply to ensure that non-class factors at the lower levels of abstraction are given due credit as causally effective, while at higher levels the possibility of other viable theoretical angles is endorsed. The situation is therefore that marxist propositions can be defended, but they must also be relativized and integrated with *other* points of reference, despite the fact that the logic of marxism usually pushes towards a privileged 'totalization' of its own analytic precepts (Jessop 1982: 228).

6. Prognosis for the future society

With the array of changes in marxist sociological categories and political analysis comes a rather dramatic shift in marxists' sense of what the socialist character of the future society involves. Notably, there has been a steady promotion of the concept of democracy as a constitutive, not an incidental, part of socialism. The classical marxist observation that there are several possible forms of democracy and that these are visibly tied to class relations (bourgeois democracy, proletarian democracy) might still stand as historical insights into the development of political structures. But many marxists have come to see that arguments for democracy generally, for particular *types* of democracy (direct, representative, plebiscitary), and for a range of institutional *mechanisms* of democracy (proportional representation, frequency of elections, status of representatives) all have a specific and irreducible moral resonance over and above their class connotations. Thus, while the direction and content of democratic progress may well depend upon the constellation of class forces, the logic of socialist argumentation is to recognize democracy as a goal in itself, and not as a means to an end specifiable in other terms (for example, the removal of class exploitation). Democracy, in that sense, becomes a central *test* of socialism's viability and worth. Marxists are therefore reluctant nowadays to posit a sharp break between 'bourgeois' and 'proletarian' democracy, or to characterize socialism as literally the 'dictatorship of the proletariat'. This terminology, of course, is apart from anything else *tactically* disadvantageous in conditions where much propaganda value is derived from the parliamentary character of democratic procedures. More profoundly, the marxist procedure of attaching significance to democratic forms in accordance with their supposed class nature dubiously assumes that the intrinsic value of a form of economic organization can be more or less established *prior* to the specification of its framework of political institutions. This indeed was part of the disastrous logic which enabled several state socialist countries to postpone the effective embodiment of democratic rights until the advanced industrial and ideological basis of socialism could be set in place. Similarly, it has taken some decades of political and theoretical engagement for marxists to recognize, in their practical attitudes, that 'bourgeois democratic' sentiments and movements are frequently progressive.

Part of the marxist concern to forefront the democratic complexion of socialism is bound up with the realization that the vocal pursuit of a *scientific* analysis can actively discourage a developed and convincing political *morality*. Of course, the claim to lay an objective foundation for political thinking is precisely what differentiates the marxist tradition from non-marxist socialism. But the idea of a scientific, non-sentimental and historically 'correct' perspective on human values and institutions carries formidable dangers. Most importantly, it severely underestimates the normative character of all politics and struggle: people are motivated by immediate issues of justice rather than by their sense of being on the march of history.

The renewed prominence of democracy and the rehabilitation of political morality as an independent force within marxist argument join together to demand a rethinking of the subjective conditions of socialist democracy. And here, in spite of all the sharp radical scorn thrown at conventional pluralism in this respect, the notion of a civic culture re-emerges as a substantial issue. That is, the formation of attitudes towards deep political questions cannot be assumed by marxists to be the product of ideological saturation by the capitalist system. For how then could people be expected to adopt, and argue, for socialist opinions? The new emphasis on democracy, moreover, casts doubt upon the Leninist concept that the transition to socialism requires, in the first instance, only a proletarian vanguard to be committed to marxist positions. With the Gramscian stress on the mass character of cultural and intellectual class leadership, and on its moral and democratic substance, the notion that socialism will require and stimulate majority *consent* becomes centrally important.

In order to develop a necessary concept of a civic culture of advanced socialist democracy, the democratic civic culture under capitalism must also be taken seriously. Sociological studies of workers' attitudes tend to show that a capitalist 'consensus' is far more pragmatic than it is ideally normative (Held 1984). However, elements of normative consensus, where they do exist, should not be put down wholly to the effect of propaganda. People's ostensible views, in other words, whatever the effect of ideology, have to be treated as the rational choices of morally autonomous agents. Public opinion, therefore, is a useful (if always slippery) concept which arguably marxists have been mistaken to treat as a smokescreen conjured up by the requirements of class manipulation. Rather, public opinion refers to the composite climate of personal, group and class experiences, and to the urgent political reference points of the citizenry. For marxists to ignore this level of persuasion and debate, it could be reasoned, is profoundly in error.

The concept of democratic citizenship is particularly important here. If marxists are more concerned now to 'take democracy seriously' they must allow that working-class people do have a voice as citizens of the public sphere. It is perhaps true that citizenship under capitalism often works to 'individualize' the members of the working class, thus hindering collective political action and encouraging a moral identification with the capitalist social order. All the same, the weakness of class politics has been the inclination to dismiss non-class sources of political identity as merely superficial, as if under socialism there will be no need for public opinion and a civic consensus around moral and social issues. Moreover, a class-politics line severely underestimates the radical potential in deploying the status of citizenship to show the political *failures* of capitalism in enhancing the democratic rights of its people.

The adaptation of the civic culture argument for socialist purposes is one way of recognizing that difficult problems of social order and public priorities are unlikely to disappear with the demise of capitalist exploitation, and that public opinion and consensus will have to play a part in coming to terms with them. However, some contemporary marxists aver that there is a kind of moral traditionalism lying in wait here, and point to the danger of an overly rationalist conception of the responsible individual socialist citizen. The progressive unity of social identity which is bequeathed by a class essence seems to have been replaced, in other words, by an unrealistic expectation of moral rationalism, with connotations of excessive social control and cultural conservatism, if you happen to deviate from the norm. Either way, there seems no proper recognition of the multiple forces which construct, work upon, and necessarily 'fracture' the individual self. Socialists influenced by psychoanalysis and semiotics, indeed, go further, taking it as established that there is probably no such thing (under any mode of production) as coherent subjective identity; rather, the latter is a complex site of competing forces and symbolic economies, massaged this way and that perhaps by overall discourses of essential meaning, but ultimately unstable and polycentric. In this context, the management of deviance in the name of higher socialist rationality, or even in the name of the consensual civic culture, must again involve the systematic repression of diversity.

Clearly, in some senses, these assertions about inherent

psychic instability can be pushed to the point whereby any conception of a socialist democratic social order must appear as involving the imposition of an illusory coherence on an ontology of necessary turmoil. At that point, once again, a determinate marxist perspective diverges, and sharply, from a quasi-politics of sheer diversity. For all that, such contributions re-emphasize that assumptions about a guaranteed and uniform democratic or socialist consciousness are problematical. The socialist task thus requires the very difficult welding together of inherited democratic values and new ways of ensuring diversity for individuals and groups. Whether such a prospect is feasible or not remains to be seen; but its development seems to rest as much in the sphere of the contemporary moral and political imagination than in oft-repeated assumptions about the virtues of post-class humanity.

One of the latter expectations which looks particularly vulnerable is the doctrine of the withering away of the state. This slogan suggests that Marx envisaged the future society as one wholly without public institutions or dispute-resolving mechanisms: a global federation of autonomous units, 'spontaneously' meshing together in fraternal exchange. Without denying the utopian inclination in Marx, it is equally clear that Marx's own scathing critique of the utopian socialists, his classicist image of vigorous public discourse and action, and his commitment to socially organized science and technology, entails a considerable socialist public sphere in which decision-making organs would have to play a significant part. Marx's apparent anarchism is more likely due to the idea that the state, as such, is by definition a class phenomenon. Public bodies, in *non*-class society, should, this implies, be called something else.

However, the implicit proposal for a new nomenclature for public institutions, together with Lenin's unequivocal strictures to the effect that the pre-condition of socialist society is the complete 'smashing' of the bourgeois state (Lenin 1970: 33), indicates a serious lacuna in marxist political theory. At the very least, the conception of a global socialist community based on direct democracy rather than representative institutions is unrealistic by current standards – though it is not by that token merely fanciful (cf. Graham 1986: 191). Marx's theory, for one thing, seemed to carry a somewhat naively benign view of technology and abundance as the prerequisite of communism, a view which ecological movements have rendered extremely problematic. Moreover, local and regional factors are bound to figure prominently in the formation of political and cultural identity, in communism as in capitalism, possessing the continuing potential to undercut any abstractly 'human' basis for general solidarity. Thirdly, there is no realistic foundation for assuming that everyone will want, or be able, to directly contribute to and determine all the decision-making processes which profoundly affect their lives. Of course, socialism should be marked by a far greater degree of participation and accountability than capitalist democracy. But the image of a polity without representative institutions and without significant variation in citizen motivation for things political seems to verge on fantasy.

Finally, the probability of the need for extensive regulation of economic and cultural life in a complex and diverse democratic society is very high. Relative divisions of experience, interests and skills in a context of limited freedom of action and movement (whatever the improvement in these respects over capitalism) is another likely constitutive feature of modern society. This feature suggests extensive opportunities for conflicts over loyalties, for group differentiation, and perhaps even for the persistence of systemic tendencies towards serious inequality. In that light, the marxist, and above all the Leninist (Polan 1984), conception of the 'transparency' of political life under communism, together with the speculation that the socialist state will be categorically unlike the capitalist state, amounts to a failure of theoretical and political nerve.

In all this, a sense of the necessary variety and complexity of post-class society is demanded. Marx of course had an admirable vision of the vast human potential for diversity in communist self-realization. But he did not provide much in the way of concepts towards the organizational, political contexts in which such life-choices are likely to be made. Marx, that is, was strong on diversity but weak on institutional pluralism. He, and the tradition which bears his name, tends to assume a quasi-natural, spontaneous medium for the realization of human projects, needs and exchanges. Marx's own estimation was that such developments would only occur after an intermediate or 'lower' phase of communism, customarily known as socialism. In spite of the canonical significance attached to these terms, their exact import remains unclear to this day. Above all, the theoretical status of socialism as 'transitional' between capitalism and communism leads to a number of political and conceptual ambiguities (as indeed is reflected in the way I have oscillated from one term to the other in the preceding discussion).

For example, there is the question, raised earlier, of whether such terms refer mainly to the mode of economic organization in a given society. In a sense, 'socialism' ought to refer to the *society* or political system which embarks on the possibly lengthy road that leads from capitalism to (advanced) communism. The latter is defined in terms of the opposite of capitalism: no classes, no state, human fulfilment, economic co-operation, rational allocation of (abundant) resources. We have seen that on the level of moral and political expectations it may be advisable to draw a much greater continuity between these two contrasting societies than the traditional sketch allows.

In terms of economic and political organization, marxists become endlessly embroiled in arguments about how far actual socialist states are progressing 'towards' advanced communism. Sometimes, indeed, this movement is reinterpreted as being towards *socialism* itself, partly to remove the stigma of sheer utopianism in the idea of 'higher communism' being just around the corner, partly to disallow existing post-capitalist societies the moral claim to be 'genuinely' socialist. After all, how can a socialist society possess a coercive *state* at all?

The problem in all this is to project the logical and moral dichotomy between Marx's notion of communism (itself perhaps excessively utopian) and capitalism, on to the political assessment of post-capitalist states. Only recently is it being (heretically) put forward that there may in fact be any number of variations on post-capitalism, *none* of which are likely to be 'leading to' a problem-free realm of human fulfilment and harmony. Faced with this suggestion, marxists will undoubtedly find it hard to break out of their holistic categories. The modes of production continue to be perceived as self-contained wholes, jointly comprising a total process for global human development. In this view, the transitions between modes are necessarily limited, revolutionary, and unidirectional. The idea of a reasonably stable 'mixture' of modes is not something that easily fits such a holistic logic. Thus the hostile reaction of 'fundamentalist' marxists (e.g. Mandel 1986) to the suggestion that 'feasible' socialism requires the sophisticated and whole-hearted use of market criteria to establish consumer preferences and to help decide the use of scarce productive resources (Nove 1983). That sceptical reaction is based on the persistent idea of an irreconcilable logical and moral difference between socialist-communist calculation and capitalist rationality (to which markets are unambiguously assigned). Pluralistic marxists, by contrast, are less and less convinced of the political value or theoretical credibility of the idea that communist civilization will represent an entirely new start to human history, blessed (if only we are vigilant enough in avoiding class collaboration) with unprecedented resources and a new type of 'socialist man'. This debate, undoubtedly, will continue; but an array of practical developments in the world today tends to suggest that the 'reformist' and pluralist orientation will become dominant. Indeed, one paradoxical possibility is that after a considerable period of diverse and problematical socialist experimentation with 'mixed' social forms, it will be the remaining *liberal-capitalist* societies who will be able to take advantage of the social learning process in order to inaugurate a 'capitalist road to communism' (van der Veen and van Parijs 1987). The *manner* of such a speculative transition, however, may not show much resemblance to the classical marxist image of revolutionary change.

5

MODALITIES OF ANTAGONISM AND CONVERGENCE

Up to now, my chief purpose has been to *characterize* the development of marxism and pluralism as I see it. The story-line has been, basically, that some central theoretical tensions in each tradition stem from the growing presence, within each 'home' discourse, of conceptual and substantive reference points more usually associated with the other paradigm. At various points in these interpretive profiles, arguments were marshalled for or against particular theoretical variants or conceptual gambits. Generally, though, I have been concerned so far to establish the terms and problems which constitute the 'debate'. As I proceed now to consider possible resolutions to · the dilemmas sketched, some themes will reappear which require more emphatic evaluation. Even so, to present an overall characterization or scenario for theoretical comparison itself constitutes a form of argument, and the critical responses of students and afficionados alike are inevitably triggered by the way in which the balance of debate is achieved. For example, I have evidently chosen to delve rather more deeply into the way in which pluralist questions can be squared with marxist principles than the other way round.

One response to any reservations about that kind of weighting is to say that the portrayal and assessment of two such politically charged traditions as marxism and pluralism is bound to reflect the specialist knowledge and intellectual commitments of the overviewer. There is nothing peculiar about this; indeed the conscious disavowal of spurious even-handedness is often the main source of theoretical stimulation in comparative social theory. That said, there is another rationale for my (relative) concentration on the details of marxist argumentation.

Firstly, marxism offers, as pluralism does not, a detailed theory of history as the necessary backdrop for its sociology of politics. The exploration of the current state of this background theory was an essential part of the history of the debate. Secondly, conventional pluralism was pronounced dead by sociologists at just the time (and for connected reasons) when marxism was being resurrected as an academically respectable perspective. Now that marxism has once again come under fire, from several directions, aspects of the pluralist critique and alternative have begun once again to look attractive as a specific type of resolution to the 'crisis of marxism'.

Indeed – and here we are moving into the ostensible concerns of this chapter – some of the most forthright reassertions of pluralism have emerged from writers hitherto firmly of a *marxist* inclination. By contrast, key figures in the critical pluralist camp seem unable at present to decide their theoretical allegiances. Lindblom, for example, regards himself now as (at best) a 'point five' pluralist (Lindblom 1983: 384), and estimates that American empirical democratic theory lags some years behind marxist-influenced continental currents in the sociology of politics (Lindblom 1982: 11).

An overview, then, contains an argument and a shape within which new statements can be considered as potential resolutions to identified tensions. The context also goes a considerable way towards judging the *credibility* of proposed resolutions. To see this, it is convenient to refer to a presentation of the marxism-pluralism debate which, though similar in some ways to my own, lends itself to a resolution of the debate which I would want to sharply criticize.

1. The fundamentalist marxist resolution

As illustrated in chapter 2, there can be little doubt that the basis of pluralist theory has been reshaped by the process of radical critique. The latter, in turn, while not always explicitly marxist in allegiance, has certainly drawn upon the resources of marxist theory. Accordingly, critical pluralism brings the question of economic ownership and class power back into the centre of political analysis, and, indeed, is sensitive to the possibility that conventional pluralism itself has ideologically assisted in concealing injustices and stabilizing inequalities. Such critical sensitivity, according to one commentator, John Manley, suggests that pluralism has been taken 'far towards a reconciliation with marxist theory' (Manley 1983: 372).

However, in this version of the debate, such a reconciliation does not amount to a compromise. Instead, all the key questions are asserted to have been resolved in favour of class analysis, with which pluralism is said to remain 'profoundly at odds' (Manley 1983: 372). Thus, what Manley usefully terms 'pluralism II' retains from 'pluralism I' a conception of the economy as predominantly a *public* domain, not a regime of private accumulation. This partial blockage in their thinking leads pluralists to continue to overestimate the power of public opinion to constrain business interests. On the question of inequality also, pluralists tend to opt for reformist measures of regulation rather than outright redistribution. Pluralist change is still, ultimately, a matter of bringing pressure to bear on public institutions rather than the struggle to restructure class relations. In the end, pluralism II, like its more complacent predecessor, is best seen as an 'implacable opponent' of marxism, and the two are not after all 'potential partners for a merger' (1983: 379).

That there is some substance in what I will call this 'fundamentalist' marxist resolution of the debate is undeniable. Even in Dahl's *Preface to Economic Democracy* (1985), the precise mechanisms of establishing and sustaining the system of democratic and co-operative economic institutions that he morally favours are barely elaborated. Against this, the marxist tradition has always distinguished itself from such 'petty bourgeois' socialisms by its insistence that only class struggle and revolutionary transformation – not an appeal to democratic good sense – are necessary and sufficient for such effective changes as even Dahl's morality envisages. It is perhaps not then surprising to find that the newly radicalized Dahl notably equivocates over the use and endorsement of terms such as 'socialism' (Dahl 1985: 50–1).

It is clear even from this one instance that there is still some distance between critical pluralism and classical marxist analysis. But Manley's mode of critique and his assumptions about the strengths of 'class analysis' are themselves open to objection, not least because of their lack of any self-critical dimension. The progressive developments within pluralism are first of all declared quite substantial, only to be deemed 'merely' apparent. The two traditions shape up for a reconciliation, only to part again as implacable opponents. The approach here is thus one of decisively damning with faint praise, of concluding the story-line well in advance, and of erecting a platonic notion of marxist wisdom. It is a style of argument which is frequently encountered in sectarian and dogmatic versions of marxist political orthodoxy. Apparent allies are disclosed as 'in reality' class enemies, and nothing appears to lie between their total defeat and pusillanimous class collaboration.

Manley's swashbuckling conception of the debate with pluralism is that of the prosecution of class struggle in the intellectual sphere. Perhaps the most thoroughgoing attempt in post-war times to revive the idea of philosophy as a means of theoretical class struggle was that of Louis Althusser (1971). Althusser was himself a very contradictory defender of 'classical' positions, since under the guise of militant rhetoric he tended to elevate 'theoretical practice' itself to the status of an autonomous level of the social formation. Yet in some respects Althusser was merely recognizing the inevitable concomitant of any claims for the 'scientific' character of a discourse: the acceptance of serious and self-critical intellectual exchanges with alternative perspectives. In Manley's case, however, this condition of effective critique is absent, since almost no reference is made to the catalogue of problems and shifts *within marxism* that I have been at pains to analyse. He also fails fully to appreciate the *positive* aspects of the apparent confusion in contemporary pluralism, once the parallel difficulties with monistic competitors are acknowledged. In their responses to Manley, Dahl and Lindblom take up just these points with considerable effect. Lindblom reiterates that his retreat from first-phase pluralism, whilst substantial, is only partial. He accepts the impact that issues of 'class hegemony' have made upon him (Lindblom 1983: 385), but defends 'pluralism I' against undue caricature. Dahl (1983) comes back in a somewhat bolder manner: *how* exactly, he asks, is class analysis superior to critical pluralism? Are not marxism and socialism increasingly plagued with questions about reform *versus* revolution; about the social conditions of pluralist democracy under socialism; about the fact that class analysis *per se* does not entail a developed political morality? Consequently, whilst the pertinence of class critique is better appreciated than before, Dahl and Lindblom object, validly, to being classified as irredeemably contradictory simply by dint of not going the whole way with class analysis. In spite of his useful (and often correct) summary of why there can be no easy merger between marxism and pluralism, Manley's substantive and stylistic approach wrongly conceives the debate *sub specie aeternitatis*. Each perspective is assumed to constitute a sealed and logically complete paradigm, such that the existence of any areas of overlap, uncertainty or 'contradiction' is anathema to the comparative logician. Such an approach was popular in the 1970s under the influence of Althusser's concept of scientific versus ideological problematics, and in Paul Feyerabend's (1975) idea of strictly incommensurable paradigms in science. The least we should require of a position which sees traditions as indivisible blocs of theory and practice is a restatement of such a philosophical underpinning. Manley does not oblige, and it has to be said that in the 1980s, the appeal of that kind of watertight 'paradigm' analysis has with good reason weakened considerably, both in the philosophy of science and in social theory generally.

Part of the problem, then, for a commentator such as Manley is, paradoxically, that he does attempt to take the debate with pluralism seriously, but then fails to be sufficiently self-critical. A more uncompromising marxist approach is to mount a renewed defence of class analysis precisely in order to put a halt to the creeping pluralism within the marxist movement. For example, Ellen Wood attacks several *soi-disant* marxists in just this way:

The modern world, we are told, no longer consists of clearly opposed social interests . . . Where have we heard this before? After much theoretical huffing and puffing, has not the mountain laboured and brought forth – pluralism? (Wood 1986: 63)

Ben Fine and his co-authors take the 'newer left' to task in similar terms:

It is perhaps no accident that this conception of politics has close affinities with positions within bourgeois social science. Just as the Fabians rejected laissez-faire and endowed control of the economy to an efficient bureaucracy, so the newer left's rejection of the state as a controller of the economy leaves it without an attitude on economic organization. . . . In terms of the politics of the newer left, their model is little more than one of a pluralism of conflicting and co-operating interest groups. (Fine et al. 1984: 9)

In these passages, the predominant mode of demonstration is guilt by association. Contemporary marxists who are considered to have abandoned the ground of economic determination are characterized as ending up in the company of pluralists and Fabians. Marxism is implied as representing a 'proletarian social science', just as the disfavoured perspectives are said to represent 'bourgeois social science'. These rival class sciences form a necessary theoretical disjunction, such that the very idea of a 'mixed' economy of knowledge must appear inadmissable, since it conflates aspects of two incompatible logics at the level of the mode of production. Yet in their haste to clinch a common identity between political opponents on the left and the class enemy, a number of serious issues are simply ignored by the defenders of class politics. For example, the analogy between the newer left and the Fabians is, as stated, a non sequitur, since the former vacates the role of the state while the latter emphatically occupy it. Also, the political dangers of parading the banner of a 'proletarian science' have been recognized even by orthodox marxists since the Lysenko affair (Lecourt 1977). It is further ignored that the idea of a 'socialist mode of production' is relatively undeveloped in marxist economics, partly because it is far from clear whether socialism itself should be seen as a mode of production, or a social formation, or a transitional form of state. To posit this concept as a clear resolution to confused ideas about 'mixes' of elements of different modes is accordingly very problematic. Finally, it is accepted (reluctantly) that a pluralistic marxism might add a 'little' to the conventional pluralist theory of interest groups, but no attempt is made to say what this supplement consists in, or how the theoretical rankings might be adjusted in line with the observation.

While some of the complaints about pluralism (as we have already noted) are indeed valid, the kind of fundamentalist rhetoric instanced here does nothing in itself to secure the cogency of the marxist critique. Indeed, 'fundamentalism', with its quasi-religious connotations, is not an inappropriate term to describe the overly moralistic polemical mode in operation here. The revisionist marxists' subjective lack of will-power and clarity is portrayed as the issue as much as the substantive 'errors' of their analysis. Putting both together, the sign that something serious is amiss is the visible contamination by the trace of the ancient enemy. How *can* marxists, of all people, be saying the same thing as pluralists, of all people?! In order to ground the view that the new left *is* essentially tainted in that way, an objective relation is further posited: revisionism reflects the petty-bourgeois class position of these academics (Fine et al. 1984: 9–10; Wood 1986: 10). Considered in that light, the temptation which bourgeois pluralism represents for the newer left is 'no accident'.

Throughout this polemic it is taken for granted that no significant changes in pluralist positions have occurred: pluralism remains the ideological adversary of the Cold War period. Secondly, the fundamentalist condemnation assumes that any developed attempt to theorise non-class divisions, and any challenge to the picture of social interests as definitively cut into opposing class camps is nothing more than 'huffing and puffing', an exercise in 'bourgeois' apologetics. So before we even learn much about what the issues are, such concerns are deemed to be so much wasted breath.

I have pressed this point about the rhetoric of fundamentalist reconciliation, not because Marx himself was free from polemical vitriol – far from it – but because that mode strikes me as the opposite of what is most admirable in Marx and the classical tradition that fundamentalism seeks to represent. These rhetorical pitfalls, and the associated caricatures to which they give rise, should be seen as themselves providing some grounds for scepticism about a marxist reconciliation even before the positions of fundamentalism are considered in derhetoricized form.

Nevertheless, the fundamentalist case cannot be dismissed solely in terms of the debilitating moralism which often attends it. The basic argument is twofold, and can again be best illustrated from Ellen Wood's broadside against the revisionists. First, the centrality of class to marxism and socialism:

> Class struggle is the nucleus of Marxism. This is so in two inseparable senses: it is class struggle that for Marxism explains the dynamic of history, and it is the abolition of classes, the obverse or end product of class struggle, that is the ultimate objective of the revolutionary process. (Wood 1986: 12)

In fact, this assertion *can* be questioned, as was indicated in the last chapter. Arguably, for historical materialism, it is the productive forces-relations dynamic which explains history, including the role of class struggle. And the *ultimate* objective of revolutionary politics is surely the attainment of a free, equal and prosperous society, the main obstacle to which is class division and exploitation. These qualifications may seem to be no more than pedantry, but close attention to formulation is vital if the exact force and credibility of contemporary marxism is to be ascertained.

Wood goes on to argue for the privileged role of the working class today:

> (1) the working class is the social group with the most direct objective interest in bringing about the transition to socialism; (2) the working class, as the direct object of the most fundamental and determinative – though certainly not the only – form of oppression, and the one class whose interests do not rest on the oppression of other classes,

can create the conditions for liberating all human beings in the struggle to liberate itelf; (3) given the fundamental and ultimately unresolvable opposition between exploiting and exploited classes which lies at the heart of the structure of oppression, *class struggle* must be the principal motor of this emancipatory transformation; and (4) the working class is the one social force that has a strategic social power sufficient to permit its development into a revolutionary force. Underlying this analysis is an emancipatory vision which looks forward to the *disalienation of power* at every level of human endeavour, from the creative power of labour to the political power of the state. (Wood 1986: 14–15)

This forcefully stated manifesto certainly reminds us of the logic of classical marxism. The problem is not that the propositions and their connecting logic are obviously false. Rather, it is that since Marx's time, even defenders of the theory (whatever they may say in theoretical hustings) have become aware of the *hypothetical* nature of the component theses. Wood's proposition (1), for example, assumes that the notion of 'objective interest' is viable and that 'the transition to socialism' refers to a definite, unitary stage in the historical process. In fact, both assumptions are questionable, particularly the latter, which many committed marxists will view as neither necessary nor perhaps even likely. Some concept of post-capitalist society seems at least worth exploring in order to capture the complexity and haltingness of the 'road to socialism'. Proposition (4) too, even if adhered to in a nominal way, can be rephrased so that the analytic potential (the strategic social power of the working class) contrasts rather starkly with its *failure* to act as a unitary revolutionary force in the modern world. This is not to 'blame' working-class people; rather it is to raise doubts about the categories used, and about the modalities of collective conflict. As has been pointed out by marxist historians as well as 'revisionist' theorists, classes seldom if ever constitute political agencies as such.

Proposition (2) in Ellen Wood's summary acknowledges that there are several sources of oppression and accepts that class analysis may not be able fully to account for them. This is actually a substantial concession to 'pluralist' criticisms of marxism, for it is certainly open to fundamentalists to deny *any* autonomy to non-class divisions. But once offered, that concession carries some worrying implications for fundamentalists. It could easily be argued, for example, that an oppressed ethnic group's interests do not rest, any more than those of the working class, on the oppression of other groups, and that in liberating itself, such a non-class group also helps to create the conditions for more general human liberation. The point here is simply to say that once serious oppression is accepted as existing in multiple forms, then specifically *class* action for emancipation cannot exhaust the claims of the socialist or humanist project. Additionally, proposition (3) questionably implies that class struggle *as such* is emancipatory. This serves conveniently to pass over a persistent thorn in the flesh of marxist analysis: the partial and defensive nature of many aspects of class struggle by comparison with the universal aspirations of the general emancipatory vision. It is no counter-revolutionary proposition to suggest that in a world where all the evidence indicates the unlikelihood of total and unitary global class action, all-purpose talk of *the* working class as *the* agent of *the* revolutionary-emancipatory project can serve to obscure rather than fulfil the connection between working class struggles (in the plural) and socialist transformation.

Finally, I have suggested that power is likely to remain an issue in any conceivable socialism. This is often read, and intended, as meaning that power will remain a problem and a danger. This is certainly true; but it is not all. Aspects of *authority*, and the necessary power which authority must carry, are also positive, that is, *enabling* features, and moreover features which appear to be *necessary* in some form for the attainment of any orderly social co-operation. To speak, as Wood does, in rather vague terms about the 'disalienation of power' at every level, is not a very precise or useful indication of the character of ideal socialist relations. 'Emancipation' and 'liberation' are motifs which are often better used in combating known forms of coercion than in heralding the future content of co-operation, since they inevitably introduce some dubious millenarian threads.

One overall difficulty with many fundamentalist 'refutations' of pluralist encroachments into marxism is the lack of any clear definitional discussion of class. Neither of the main explicit defences of 'class politics', for example, take the trouble to tell us *who* precisely is in the working class today (Wood 1986, Fine et al. 1984). I suspect this is partly because even to ask the question is to open up some serious ambiguities or political choices within marxism, and only revisionists (it is implied) are the sort of people who would relish this prospect. In her fourth proposition cited above, Wood states that exploitation is the clear-cut basis for understanding class division. From our earlier discussions, however, we can add that this proposition is by no means straightforward, and that legal ownership, effective control of the means of production, and the buying and selling of labour power are also candidates for deciding class identity. More generally, the real problem for class analysis is to move from propositions about class *identity* to specifying the conditions of class *action*. Let us take these two areas of discussion in turn.

In fact, fundamentalists do not have a clear-cut definition of class, nor is exploitation sufficient to deliver one. At one time it was common for marxists to assume the existence of a core working class, namely those whose sale of labour power directly supplies the surplus value upon which capitalism as a system depends. The appropriateness of this criterion is apparent in social formations where manual manufacturing and extractive work is the predominant form which labour takes. However, with the composition of the workforce (in the 'advanced' countries) becoming less 'manual' in form, Marx's wider notion of the working class as all those workers who directly *or* indirectly contribute to capitalist surplus becomes attractive. 'Indirect' exploitation allows us to include in the proletariat, for instance, workers in the services sector or state employment. Instead of a core of productive manual workers, therefore, the tendency has been to define as working class all those who have to sell their labour power for a wage/salary. Such a move appears to reconstitute the working class, once more ensuring that it comprises the vast majority of the population.

The scenario gets more complicated, though, if we consider

the criterion of effective *control* of the means of production. Formal legal ownership of property has not always satisfied marxists as the grounds of capitalist possession. Corporate trusts and humble individuals, after all, have shares in productive assets, but neither are capitalists *per se*. Similarly, top managers do not always legally own such assets, but certainly direct parts of the process of production, and effectively control the lives and work regimes of the collective labour force. However, as endless variations upon the theme of where the 'boundary' between classes actually lies, it is not clear that the criteria of control and asset ownership go together. A manager sells her labour power but may also control the production process. Which class does she belong to? Similar identity crises have been constructed in the past for specialist technicians, professional groups, skilled 'labour aristocrats', and even clerical female labour.

Another important recent move, we noted, has been to define classes in terms of 'asset exploitation'. Possession of the means of production is clearly one major asset-related criterion of class membership. Yet authors who work in this theoretical vein argue that asset ownership in fact goes much wider than this. The ownership of 'organizational credentials' or of 'skills' may, for example, serve as the basis of class divisions in post-capitalist society. But these forms of asset-exploitation are present in capitalist society too. Thus a top doctor, perhaps, can be said to 'organizationally exploit' less privileged groups in spite of himself being a seller of labour power. This conception allows a variety of positions in the stratification of society to be characterized according to more than one sense of exploitation, or in terms of 'net' exploitation when the possibly cross-cutting effects of multiple asset ownership relations have been added up.

Whatever the merits of each of these definitional ploys, no single criterion seems obviously 'correct', and the range of concepts of exploitation, productive and unproductive labour, ownership and control, are likely to be drawn upon to try to square the search for a stable marxist foundation with changing subjective perceptions of who 'ought' to be included in the proletariat at any one time and who should be excluded. All marxists, that is to say, are confronted with an empirical reality which reveals as much diversity and intra-class antagonism among working people as it does homogeneity and unity. And yet over the long term of capitalism, Marx maintained, classes would become objectively polarized, with more and more people sharing the subordinate and exploited condition of the proletariat.

The idea of the working class as productive manual labourers clearly gives little substance to the proletarianization thesis, since ever fewer workers fill that description. The cultural traits of contemporary proletarianization are also in key respects at odds with the classical revolutionary image. Common membership of the (broad) working class today does not necessarily imply, for example, a shared experience of labour task, or a shared focus on capitalist individuals as the exploiting employer. More commonly, the 'boss' will be a distant corporation or a state agency. In terms of class organization, a great variety of workers have come to join trade unions, and this is some limited confirmation of 'proletarianization'. But unionization *per se* does not enhance political unity, nor does it automatically meet the needs of the increasing proportion of part-time workers, home workers, and 'flexible workers' in the diverse fabric of the modern labour process. Within the unions, for example, a 'professional' ethic, or male chauvinism, can help reinforce rather than undermine the sense that the working class is fragmented. Amalgamation and mergers between unions are often as much about saving the financial and organizational framework than about advancing to a new-found class unity. Indeed, all-purpose unions with considerable administrative apparatuses and hierarchies can alienate especially low paid and specifically located workers as being unable to respond to and represent their needs, which may be perceived by marginalized workers as different to those in the same union on higher pay and conditions.

The 'classical' notion of proletarianization assumes a shared experience of life in the wider sense. Work, in many respects, *was* life – at least in the theory. Workers lived close to their place of work in similar housing conditions, with a developed sense of community identity born of direct mutual contact. Whether or not this picture is entirely realistic for any period (and I suspect it is not) is irrelevant here, because in any event today's urban environment manifestly does not match that image of a vital oral culture and spontaneous social solidarity. There are certainly major pockets of the advanced countries where this is true, pockets which (as with the British coalmining communities) are all the time being systematically dismantled by the workings of international markets and government policies. Solidarity and community amongst working class people is certainly not rare. But shared experience is now mediated by a sharper sense of differences, and by the global effects of electronic media as a factor in the formation of experiences and aspirations. These media, of course, often have a manipulative purpose and effect, but to see advanced communications systems as merely the apparatus of ideology is to hold out false hope for the resuscitation of a romanticized past which is gone. It is thus increasingly difficult to sustain the idea that beneath the phenomena of fractured markets, cultural difference, and media manipulation there subsists a purely class-defined nexus of need, expectation and potential revolution.

Marxist class theory has some difficulty, therefore, in assimilating such features of modern economic life as substantial intra-class differentials and income sources, status and authority relations within the workforce, part-time and flexi-time work, homeworkers, and various *degrees* of reliance on the sale of one's labour power for a living. Relatedly, the very role of material production and work – while still enormously important – has become less central to culture and experience in the modern capitalist phase of mobile resources, technical advance and the 'information society'. The role of the state too as an unambiguous prop of capitalism can be questioned. As Claus Offe has pointed out (Offe 1984; 1985) the state's necessary interventionist capacity effectively de-commodifies large amounts of capital and labour. Undoubtedly, all these things can continue to be 'read' using the grid of the labour theory of value and consequently as confirming the capitalist character of all 'mixed economies' and 'advanced technological' labour processes. But to persist with such a reading seems to require an increasingly broad or formal account of class location and value realization. Just how broad remains a matter of debate.

Ralph Miliband, for one, states that the working class today is still the class of the great majority, 'in terms of its location in the productive process, its very limited or non-existent power and responsibility in that process, its near-exclusive reliance on the sale of its labour power for its income, and the level of its income' (Miliband 1985: 9). John Westergaard similarly thinks of the working class in terms of those placed by necessity in routine jobs without much authority, and estimates that it comprises at least 60 per cent of the population (Westergaard 1984).

Both these writers supplement their positive categorization by a valuable 'negative' point about the history of capitalism. If the proportion of classical 'core' proletarians in the workforce was once much greater, so too – and vastly so – was the proportion of rural and service workers. Moreover, sectionalism and diversity have *always* been obstacles to class unity, as the most superficial acquaintance with the richness of, say, Victorian lower-class subcultures reveals. The project of turning objective homogeneity into political identity is thus not significantly harder to accomplish today; it might even be easier. Marxists are *not*, after all, required to be romantic about the past.

As for the present, though, Miliband's and Westergaard's definitions of the modern proletariat could in fact be seen as somewhat woolly and descriptive rather than strictly theoretical. Peter Meiksins grasps the nettle more firmly in asserting that in spite of – perhaps because of – the apparent complexities of intra-class differentiation, marxists must resort to the very basic view that all those in waged work are 'objectively' part of the collective labourer. Meiksins posits that there is indeed an identifiable 'general staff' of capitalism comprising specifically those who both own *and* control. Everyone else except the self-employed are working class, and the former can be designated 'petty bourgeois'. Meiksins in fact disrupts the logic of this position by allowing for one 'ambiguous' class location: those top managers who do not presently own substantial holdings, but who are in a position to be 'upwardly mobile' and thus to enter the ranks of the capitalists proper (Meiksins 1986: 113).

This local amendment is, unfortunately for Meiksins, in-coherent and strictly unnecessary, since it is only once such people *do* actually enter the ranks of capital that they can properly be classed as capitalists. Erecting a category of 'potential' capitalists opens up a great hole in the schema. Similarly, the working class must surely be regarded in the terms of the theory as the *currently* non-owning collective labourer. Otherwise, it could reasonably be hypothesised that literally millions of workers *could* make this same step up, even if most do not. The attraction to Meiksins of this 'deviant' move is itself interesting, in that it indicates the reluctance that marxists have always shown in receiving *all* workers into the ranks of the objective proletariat. Arguably this is due to the powerful political and cultural connotations of the term 'proletarian', evoking expectations of low status, oppression, collective struggle and monetary hardship. In round numbers, it is manifest that many members of the working class do in fact share these conditions of life. The point remains, however: in the broad fundamentalist definition, there appears to be no way of excluding from the structural position of the proletariat those relatively large numbers of workers who do *not* readily fit that series of traditional attributes. The problem here is essentially that any modern rendering of the proletarianization thesis requires some subjective potential for class action to be common to members of the broad working class. But, sceptical socialists will ask, can that really be expected of the likes of dentists, sales directors of multinational corporations, or leaders of Conservative local governments? In order to sustain the proletarianization thesis as a definitive tendency throughout society, an extremely loose criterion of working class membership is required, so that a considerable majority of working people are embraced. However, *either* this leads to some unlikely categories being admitted, with rather indeterminate political consequences; *or* secondary and often artificial criteria are invoked in order to exclude those who seem unlikely to develop the requisite subjective consciousness for revolutionary action. As Poulantzas (1975) saw, at least with the (shrinking) core definition (i.e. producers of surplus value), the working class knew its allies and enemies.

Miliband tries to stem the kind of sceptical train of thought I have been treating in the following way: '[there is no] good reason to believe that this recomposed working class is less

capable of developing the commitments and 'class consciousness which socialists have always hoped to see emerge
(Miliband 1985: 9). However, this claim is little more than
hopeful assertion. In view of the 'negative' history lesson
mentioned earlier, and in view of the difficulties with
definitions, there *is* good reason to question whether the broad
working class can become the agent of revolutionary change –
at least in the classical image. The demise of the conception of
classes as single entities which act as such; the question of
whether socialism can have an unproblematically assumed
'end'; the breaking down of the polarity between reform and
revolution: these developments strike harsh blows against
traditional political expectations. In this light, the broad
definition of class has the merit of consistency and inclusive-
ness, and preserves the logical integrity of the classical vision;
but it would be foolish to exaggerate what it is capable of
delivering in terms of political 'lessons'.

For example, an important locus of the alleged mismatch
between structural definitions and political experience is the
relation between class identity and other social sources of
identity and action (ethnic group, gender, parenthood, ecological
consciousness, or whatever). To conceive class narrowly and to
declare class determination to be more important than these
'peripheral' or 'diversionary' movements is certainly one
strategy open to fundamentalists. In this case, non-class
divisions would be deemed to be strictly deviations from
marxist politics. In fact, comparatively few marxists do hold
this view, partly because most of the conscious political
actions known to history would have to be dismissed as so
much deviation from history's ineffable and inexorable course.
But the alternative – a broad view of class – only allows the
relatively weak claim that since these groups are themselves
(mostly) working-class people, the specific problems which
face blacks, women, homosexuals, parents, ecologists and the
rest are *also* likely to have significant class-related dimensions.
This is, to be sure, an important statement of the continued
promise of class analysis, but it does not amount to a denial of
the plural sources of political motivation. As Jon Elster points
out (1985: 394), the non-class element of a political claim or

experience may be more important than the class aspect even in cases where the latter *is* obvious.

Perhaps the most plausible marxist way of resolving this kind of question is to say, first, that the class dimension of social conflict tends to become paramount in decisive, epochal moments of social transformation; and, secondly, that non-class forms of oppression are considerably exacerbated by capital's tendency to use and abuse already or potentially stigmatized social groups. The latter part of the response is an urgent issue for reflection and research, which cannot be foreclosed in advance by assuming class centrality. The problem with the first part is that because the primary inclination in marxism is to theorize epochal shifts in precise class terms, many instances of non-class conflict or quasi-class conflict become, almost by virtue of theoretical stipulation alone, secondary and sub-epochal in significance. A classic example of the attempt to reveal the underlying essence of class struggle within complex circumstances where other social identities are clearly present is G. E. M. de Sainte Croix's monumental *The Class Struggle in the Ancient Greek World*. Ste Croix's overarching aim in this work is to vindicate class analysis, and plainly he takes class relations to be the fundamental objective mechanisms of political and social conflict. However, this very purpose behind the work tends to foreclose other possible angles on the variety of conflicts in the Graeco-Roman era. Ste Croix understands that relations between, say, plebeians and patricians, or more usually between poor and rich, generally take the *form* of non-class conflict. Underneath, however, and in spite of the agents' subjective understanding of their actions, they are held to be expressions of class relations (Ste Croix, 1981: 45, 336). This enables a further interpretation of popular disturbances, brigandage and circus factions, amongst other things, as essentially class struggles. On the other side, long-lasting and bitter conflicts which might *look like* class conflicts (notably, the rivalries between the Roman Equestrians and Senators) are designated by Ste Croix as sub-class conflicts, a matter of status only, of 'superficial disagreement' (1981: 340). Consequently certain shifts in forms of state which might *appear* to be of epochal political import (the advent of first the Principate, then the Dominate – shifts denoting many decades of social reorganization) are considered not to be truly significant. From the class standpoint, these changes represent only the intensification of basic ongoing forms of exploitation (Ste Croix 1981: 373). To take this standpoint as a general protocol of 'class analysis' is bound to result – even in the context of an admirable scholarly specialism – in an implausibly heavy-handed 'reading out' of supposedly 'superficial' factors. To apply the method directly to contemporary politics is to risk creating a permanent gulf between most people's experience of struggle and marxism's redescription of that struggle.

2. The radical-democratic resolution

One response to the 'essentialist' rhetoric of the fundamentalist resolution is to insist that marxists accept as necessarily hypothetical the status of the broad claims of historical materialism. To take this amendment literally is to accept further that marxism is not really in the business of providing detailed guidance on the weightings of the balance between non-class and class-based movements and conflicts. In turn, such a broad understanding of 'class analysis' can be accused of effectively *withdrawing* from central marxist ambitions. For was it not precisely the scientific boast of Marx and marxism to supply the root causes behind the shifting details of social change? If so, how can marxists remain satisfied with a set of high-level quasi-objective categories which are nevertheless bound not to engage with the reality of specific political movements? That kind of profound questioning has led many erstwhile marxists down a path which leads to a major reconsideration of the supposed 'errors' of pluralism. The latter, in the fundamentalist marxist appraisal, consist in the evacuation of serious causal theory. But what if the supposed marxist superiority, delivered by way of a class essentialist analysis, turns out to be little more than a permanent failure to fulfil an explanatory promise (Hindess 1987)? The implication here is that the whole marxist enterprise, and not just one variant of it, is fundamentalist in character, and so those marxists who attempt to shore up a more flexible (because less definite) variant are in effect engaged in a doomed contradictory exercise. Take the following 'compromise' statement: 'Once the class forces appear as political forces, they have consequent political results: they generate 'solutions' which cannot be *translated back* into their original terms' (Hall 1977: 47). The post-marxist critic of class analysis would judge this attempt both to preserve a marxist baseline *and* to allow for the 'relative autonomy' of politics, as simply unsustainable. For if, at the moment of the very first appearance of political 'class' forces, there is no translation of the central new features *back* into positional class terms, then arguably no causal translation *forwards* could have possibly occurred at any stage. These 'moments' of class translation, which are openly accepted by 'broad' marxists to be problematical, are not 'translations' at all, but entirely discontinuous and discrepant elements. If socialists are to take the political conditions of democracy seriously, it follows, the class logic of political forms – a logic which has deprived the socialist project of a genuinely democratic dimension – must be dismantled. Rather than see democracy as in essence a class form of state, or even as something valuable which can only be 'fulfilled' by socialism, the post-marxist left should reverse this evaluative equation. What remains valid in socialist ideas becomes but a part of the more general struggle for the radical expansion of democracy.

Many of the strategic reservations involved in this 'radical democratic' rejection of class as the touchstone of politics are bound up with a philosophical dismissal of the predominant monistic and organic terms in which strategic marxist discourse has been couched. The impulse to view economic categories as being directly 'translatable' into cultural and political spheres, for example, stems from that kind of prior metaphysical commitment. Moreover, the 'totalizing' conception of society reflects, it can be argued, a typically Enlightenment approach to the question of social knowledge: in reproducing within knowledge (theory) the essence of the social whole, mankind can in turn shape the world according to its own inner aspirations. But these constructions of society and history as totalities are merely potent fictions, according to the radical-democratic view. They are meta-narratives (theoretical storylines) of a necessarily figurative or metaphorical sort which may well sustain us in our quasi-religious search for the meaning of life, but which cannot be independently proven as such. Nor are they ever likely to be acted upon in specific political contexts. The fallacy of this kind of meta-narrative construct is that it supplies a privileged criterion of the relationship between reality and theory, such that it is always a foregone conclusion that the privileged categories will turn out to be 'objectively' vindicated in the face of alternative views of social significance.

For the radical democrats, who in such arguments are drawing on 'post-modernist' philosophical themes, the permanent search for the *grounds* of the 'representation' of reality is merely the expression of an over-cognitive and over-foundationalist metaphysic. The problem with this, they argue, is that too high a priority is given to *knowledge* as the spring of social action, thus severely underestimating the non-cognitive forces of pleasure, risk, rhetoric, will, desire, and the like in constituting symbolic significance and subjective interaction. Marxism and other sociologies always seem to be 'gutting' the richness and uncertainty of existence in order to lay bare the supposedly rational abstract core of the social totality. If that kind of core is however regarded not as a necessary foundation but as an impossible quest, such rationalism is misguided. Purely cognitive modes of appraisal may be one form, but only one form, of gauging social relations and the social totality can always be carved up in any number of ways – or indeed none at all. Fragmentation and disconnection are thus probably more 'adequate to reality' as categories of being than unity and totality. What passes as the 'scientific' explanatory quest is in fact little more than a chain of optional *metaphors*. The crucial thing, for post-modernists, is to see that all representational claims are made within particular frameworks and sets of cultural assumptions: we cannot somehow leap 'beyond' these to a context-free vantage point. In the metaphorical structure of marxism, for example, we find, not a universally valid pattern of explanation, but a kind of romantic idyll of material production and labour, where the moral darkness of toil and oppression is relieved by the mission of the working class acting as a kind of avenging angel (Baudrillard

1975). The point is not that a modern parable like this is illegitimate or worthless; rather it is to recognize that its significance lies not in some grey realm of objective epistemic truth, but in its galvanizing role within particular social movements, principally in the self-assertion of labour movements, as having access to democratic rights. Marxism has been pivotal in this sense in extending the meaning and practice of democracy from the institutional-political sphere to wider social relationships. But in a new era where the identity of the classical proletariat and labour movement has dissolved into more general social meanings, the theory which sustained the earlier movements must be radically reshaped, and indeed perhaps better abandoned altogether, if the contemporary moment of the democratic struggle is to be properly seized.

In this train of radical democratic thought, the drift away from marxism rapidly returns as a tide of critique. The general epistemic reconsiderations just outlined carry concomitant propositions about society and political engagement. Above all, the relatively fixed relationship in marxism between positional or structural categories and the terms of political agency is overthrown. Social movements, far from 'reflecting' the categories of a positional discourse, are now seen as the very source of any meanings which the latter entails. However, social movements are active assertions and formations of political identity, expressing a mode of 'becoming' rather than a pregiven social 'being' (Touraine 1981: 1, Bowles and Gintis 1986: 22). It follows that the very conception of social relations as 'positions' cannot any longer be accepted. On the contrary, social relations are the unstable *products* of inter-group interaction, interactions constituted by political and symbolic struggles.

Without the notion of society as an *order* (Touraine 1981: 55), neither social being nor political conflict can be seen as representing a stable and homogeneous essence. Instead, social identity and the sources of political power have to be recognized as radically heterogeneous (Bowles and Gintis 1986: 94), so that any claims to political hegemony involve a 'precarious articulation among a number of subject positions' (Laclau and Mouffe 1985: 58). The *discursive* character of social relations and social movements is therefore central to the radical democratic conception, for if there is no intrinsic coherence to social positions as such, then the goals and logic of political struggle must be achieved through the coherence imparted by contingent political discourses. Above all, in the wake of the demise of the marxist 'positional' discourse, it is the discourses of democratic advance which supply the most potent sources by means of which a variety of subject orientations can be 'articulated' into a purposive, hegemonic political force (Laclau and Mouffe 1985: 145f.).

It can be seen from this account of 'post-marxism' that the radical democratic current is also, theoretically, radically pluralistic. As Ernesto Laclau and Chantal Mouffe openly assert, the problems confronted by marxism can only be resolved by taking plurality as the political and methodological starting point (Laclau and Mouffe 1985: 140). Two interesting questions arise. The first is whether radical democracy re-presents the convergence of some marxist themes with those of pluralism, or whether it embodies the 'victory' of the latter over the former in the inevitable antagonism of the debate. Secondly, we need to consider how persuasive the post-marxist democratic position is.

That the new post-marxism reflects many of the concerns of the old pluralist anti-marxism seems self-evident. The inter-actions between groups, groups involved in the self-definition of their political interests, is central to both. Democracy rather than class politics is seen as the more inclusive, and therefore the more fundamental, category. The subject positions amongst the social constituencies of democracy are conceived as overlapping, and the democratic identity of social subjects cross-cuts (at least in principle) any number of more specific positional structures. In some formulations, post-marxism rehabilitates the liberal pluralist notion of politics as the medium of social exchange (Bobbio 1987: 129). Competing claims and identities are swapped about and bargained over in the political market-place, and the very content of democracy is the notion of a voluntary political *contract*, symbolizing mutual tolerance of the rich diversity of strategic discourses. Socialists, to be worthy inheritors of the lineage of expanding democratic forms, must accept that the identity established .

through discourses of *citizenship* cannot be displaced as primary by those focusing on productive labour (Bobbio 1987a: 45). In some hands, then, the radical democratic transformation of socialism does seem to shade off into a somewhat naive restatement of liberal pluralism.

A number of differences between even critical pluralism and other aspects of the new radical democratic pluralism should however be noticed. The dimension of philosophical critique tends to be shadowy in liberal and conventional pluralism, but more explicit in 'post-modernist' currents. The purpose of this change of emphasis is not to highlight the primacy of philosophy but precisely to purge strategic political discourse of philosophy's all-too-shadowy influence. Here, it is possible that marxism and pluralism can be seen actually to *share* one chief effect of a metaphysical theory of politics: the interpretation of political interests as stemming from a sociological domain, conceived as having an intrinsic nature prior to all political articulation. In marxism, class positions within the mode of production are the a priori reference point, whilst for conventional pluralists interests stemming from modern industrial society form the constant core around which political variables circulate. These perspectives, far from being deadly rivals, can thus be seen as variants of a general, and fallacious, explanatory ambition: the sociology of politics.

In the terms of a writer working within the post-marxist British left, to analyse attitudes and interests 'as if they could be treated independently of the political work of parties, the media and other organizations' is inadequate and absurd; it is nothing less than 'sociological reductionism with a vengeance' (Hindess 1983: 4). In similar terms, a post-pluralist US political scientist argues that the pervasive grip of 'society-centred' explanations of politics, which marxism and pluralism pre-eminently embody, 'has resulted in a conception of the state as little more than an arena in which societal conflicts are fought out, interests mediated, and the ensuing results authoritatively confirmed' (Nordlinger 1981: 5). These two theorists in fact differ about how to go on to characterize autonomous political forces and decisions; but, strikingly, they share the conviction that the general 'sociological' approach to politics is unsupportable. The trouble with marxism is that it is not at all pluralistic, and the trouble with (conventional) pluralism is that it is not pluralist enough.

For Nordlinger, the solution to this impasse is to pay attention to the autonomous interests of political elites. For Hindess, the argument points to a close analysis of the organizational forms in which interests are constructed. For Alain Touraine, as for Laclau and Mouffe, the point is to examine social movements and their potential for radical democracy as an unstable process of antagonism and articulation, one which admits of no political or intellectual 'closure' whatsoever. Even critical pluralism is left behind in this sequence of reasoning. Interests are considered as *discursive* in a way that the pluralists omitted to analyse; individual subjectivities are seen as *intrinsically* fractured and unstable in a way the pluralists would hardly begin to fathom; and the overlapping social identities of pluralism are more a source of difference and antagonism than of stability in the radical democratic construal. Finally, where pluralism posited an emergent equilibrium among the social interests (including those stemming from class positions), many of the radical democratic theorists have adopted themes taken from game theory as a way of emphasizing the *calculative constitution* of such positionalities. Each set of identities can accordingly be seen as the effect of the subject entering into a number of recursive, rule-governed social games, amongst which, for those new democrats anxious to retain some link with marxism, the *class* game remains important (Bowles and Gintis 1986: 118–20). Unlike conventional pluralism, this view considers social games to be asymmetrical in terms of their benefits to the players, and potentially cumulative in their concentration of advantages. No equilibrium, in other words, need emerge.

It is not easy to say what the ultimate aim of radical democratic theory is. Some of its propositions can certainly be used to undermine class essentialism, leading to a more pluralistic marxism. Alternatively, it might be regarded as the *vindication* of critical pluralism as finally more acceptable than any variant of the marxist tradition. A third option is that radical democracy amounts to an attempt to go *beyond* the confines of the marxism-pluralism debate altogether in search of a non-essentialist approach to social relations and the political future. In the second part of this book I consider this third option further, drawing in other theorists whose starting point has been less obviously oriented to the marxist tradition than some of the authors referenced here.

In the meantime, the following points can be made in counter-criticism of post-marxism. In the first place, the radical democratic abandonment of marxism involves a condemnation of the rationalism and determinism of class analysis. Yet that very assessment, it should be noted, itself tends to display theoretically essentialist or 'logicist' features. Thus, in spite of the variety of marxisms, and the notable differences of subtlety in different marxist authors' handling of the perspective, all marxism is portrayed as inherently reductionist. The very logic of the class/production matrix of analysis, it is argued, cannot possibly allow a genuine recognition of non-class determinations. If a social phenomenon is to be *explained* by class, its own effective identity and other determinations of its character are necessarily obliterated in the logical space which the *explanans* establishes. The critique therefore ignores empirical variety in the *use* of marxist categories; it is the logic of the concepts which alone counts, and which condemns marxism, in its essence, to reductionism. Thus, Laclau and Mouffe say that the very meaning of the concept 'autonomy' ensures that no determinations can be firmly asserted. Marxists cannot, logically, invoke the *relative* autonomy of politics as something class analysis can embrace, for such a notion is inherently contradictory (1987: 92–3). The first point to make here is that for a perspective which prizes its new-found epistemic emphasis on contingency and relationism, and which (quite uncritically) endorses Wittgenstein's abandonment of invariant meanings (1987: 83), this is a suspiciously rationalist construal of the theoretical problem which marxism faces. A general logical definition is profferred, and the case is considered proven.

The *content* of the logical dismissal of marxism, as well as the form it takes, is also debatable, since it appeals to the time-honoured opposition of freedom and determinism, with the latter being conceived in a dubiously absolutist manner. Laclau and Mouffe brush aside any notion that marxist determination could mean, for example, the 'limitation' or 'constraint' which one set of properties entails for another. Marxist determination, they say, works according to the image of the shadow of a hand on the wall, which moves whenever the hand moves, and in exactly the same way. A more flexible metaphor, such as that of the restricted movements of the chained prisoner who cannot run but can still sing, is held to be inappropriate (Laclau and Mouffe, 1987: 92, Geras 1987: 49). But Laclau and Mouffe are quite mistaken in this argument. If we examine the scientific theory of mechanics – the paradigm of determinism – in neo-positivist terms (following Nagel 1961: 278–85), determinism can at most be regarded as the abstract, theoretically-defined causal relationships entailed by the state of a system. The unique and exhaustive logical determination of the state of the system occurs *only* at the level of abstraction appropriate to the scientific theory. That logic is operative with respect to *some* specified properties (amongst very many); it requires that the system be viewed as an instantaneous time-slice with theoretically established class-values rather than actual magnitudes; and it has no bearing on the way in which the relevant phenomena may be affected by *other* causal systems (e.g. chemical changes). The neo-positivist account can, of course, be challenged as tending to provide a 'purer' image of science and its (supposed) objects than is warranted either by scientific history or by the logic of concept formation and proof as construed in conventionalist or realist discourses of scientific reasoning. But this is just the point. The neo-empiricist summary of science is the one in which most effort is expended in trying to preserve an approximation to determinism as involving something like the complete and unique 'mirroring' of the constant by the dependent variable in a causal system. Even here, though, it is clear that there is nothing which could allow us, a priori, to prefer the shadow metaphor over the prisoner metaphor as an encapsulation of the typical explanatory problem for natural or social science.

Moreover, no philosopher of science, positivist or otherwise, comes to mind who would argue that the concept of determinism in theoretical mechanics can be mapped on to social enquiry point for point. The *scope* of the explanatory situation (whether to do with psychic events or epochal changes in political structure) depends wholly on the goals of the social theory in question. Likewise, the nature of the causal relationships involved – whether connections of general boundary-limitation, functional constraint or invariant mechanical chain reactions – cannot be established by mere stipulation. Lastly, in drawing attention to the 'primacy' of the relationship established in a given theory, the proponents of that theory are not at all compelled to ignore or deny a range of significant factors which counteract or diminish the proposed primacy. Such elementary general considerations suggest that the interesting and conspicuous revulsion from structural claims in some variants of post-marxism is founded on very slender theoretical argument. Consequently, it is quite legitimate for proponents of 'strong' social theories to consider the dependent phenomena within the theory as 'relatively autonomous' with respect to the fundamental structures. Where the social theory is fairly 'weak' or broad (as I have suggested marxism is), that conceptual designation is apter still.

If marxism faces explanatory problems, then, they tend to lie not in the form of the analysis but in its substance. And here it is possible that the general conditions of constraint and enablement established by the mode of production and its typical class relations are of necessity limited. Moreover, it could be doubted whether, as has sometimes been proposed (e.g. Mouzelis 1988), marxism as such contains in embryo the kind of supplementary concepts (such as 'mode of domination') which would serve as the basis for political analysis in a way analagous to the relation of 'mode of production' to the societal totality. In other words, the formal legitimacy of 'relative autonomy' does not guarantee its explanatory value. That will depend on 'the concrete analysis of the concrete situation', to quote one of Lenin's still-admired emphases. The overall point in hand, though, is that it is the legitimacy of the concept of relative autonomy, and not its variable explanatory value, that post-marxists tend to object to on logical grounds. This objection fails. There *are* interesting and unresolved issues for marxists around functional explanation, science, and the concept of causality; but the all-purpose charge of determinism and reductionism often blurs the distinctions necessary to address them.

A third reservation about the logic of post-marxism concerns its assertion of the discursive constitution of social relations, and of the heterogeneous, fractured and unstable character of discursive identities. If 'discourse' is taken in a narrow literal sense, the first part of this claim is that social relations are linguistic in character. Now while, as J. L. Austin (1962) made clear, linguistic performances certainly constitute social doings, it is equally plain that a great many social relations are not reducible to the linguistic features they involve.

A wider usage of the notion of discourse seems appropriate, then, one which usually involves the observation that all theoretical references to 'objective' relations are culture-specific and therefore inescapably embroiled in symbolic processes which do not have a 'universal', i.e. context-free, nature. Such an expansive notion of the discursive constitution of objects, when presented as an argument, is difficult to assess. In one form, it appears uncontroversial: we see stones as 'stones' and capitalists as 'capitalists' because of the kind of conceptual scheme we adopt. These objects are therefore discursively constituted (i.e. categorically specified and appre-hended) (Laclau and Mouffe 1987: 84). In social science, of course, all social relations must be regarded as constituted and reconstituted in and through discourse, because human beings are meaning-making creatures. In that sense too, it is hard to disagree with the view that interaction is discursively constituted. But equally, nothing prevents us viewing one kind of discursive constitution as more adequate than another to the nature of the relations in question. It is a further and more controversial claim altogether to say that objects and relations are discursively constituted in the sense of being the *products* of particular frameworks of apprehension and specification. This is a move which brings in its wake perennial issues of epistemic agnosticism and cognitive relativism. In other words, nothing in the supposed 'nature' of the phenomena specified could be cited which would adjudicate contrary discursive specifications. 'Stones' might in some discourses constitute spiritual packages, and 'capitalist profit' could shift its connotations to signify the fair exchange of services. It all depends on which discourse we choose to adopt. That 'idealist' conclusion will be considered further in the next

chapter, but for the moment it is sufficient to point out that
post-marxists are often reluctant to embrace it wholeheartedly
either in general philosophical terms, or more especially, in
positive assertions about contemporary society. A tension is
consequently set up between the remnants of 'positional'
propositions and the full-blown critique of them.

This can best be illustrated by the fact that the post-marxist
theorists do not quite intend (or manage) to dissolve 'socialism'
into pluralist 'democracy'. Whether or not socialism needs a
life-giving transfusion of pluralism or democracy, its characteristic logic is to posit central conditions for the abolition of
exploitation and the full realization of human talents. Whatever
their other merits, pluralism and democracy do not entail, as
part of their very rationale, that kind of substantive vision.
Moreover, the analysis of the obstacles to a substantively
egalitarian and democratic society inescapably requires the
citation of 'objective' social relations and the use of 'totalizing'
categories. So, when pushed to consider the persistent attraction
of a socialist (if not specifically marxist) orientation, radical
democrats can be discovered slipping back into the condemned
holistic mode.

Sam Bowles and Herbert Gintis (1986), for instance, having
made a theoretical case for regarding all interests as discursive
identities and all identities as unstable, clearly perceive the
development of capitalist property relations as conferring
stable (regressive) identities upon potentially democratic
human subjects. The democratic struggle for personal rights,
they say, is geared around this structural feature of modernity
(Wright 1987). It follows that if socialism is a means towards
the achievement of radical democracy, then the latter must
involve the universal abolition of capitalist power. The
possibility of multiple social identities does not, it seems, give
rise to infinite discursive complexity after all. The politics of
'becoming' can only be assessed in relation to the nature of the
typical and enduring subject positions which socio-political
systems impose.

Paul Hirst, for his part, reaffirms his belief in a project which
aims 'to provide the theoretical basis for a non-utopian
socialist politics which would ultimately lead the people of the
earth to make a human condition without famine, ignorance,

war and oppression' (Hirst 1985: 9). However broad and flexible this declaration may be, there can be little doubt of the importance of the cognitive connection it affirms between the analysis of global ignorance and repression and their practical elimination. The references to a singular human condition and a universal subject must similarly seek cross-discursive validity in order to have any plausibility whatsoever. Barry Hindess, for his part, says: 'Socialism is a political ideology based on the objective of constructing planned and non-commodity forms of production and distribution' (Hindess 1983: 10). The ideology, it follows, must be organized around translating a theory of global commodity production into the universal goal of its abolition. Nothing in this discourse requires its object to be itself primarily discursive, and a clearly rationalist connection between theory and practice is posited.

Laclau and Mouffe are more vigilant about the possibility that even such broad definitions of socialism as the ones cited are likely to catapult some of the discredited elements of totality and rationalism back into the centre of their project. For this reason, perhaps, there are few substantive formulations about the desirable society in thier book. But these theorists' methodological pluralism also only goes so far. They deny, for example, that the inevitable consequence of post-marxism is the 'logical pulverization of the social' (1985: 104). Moreover, they do not deny that the open-ended practice of articulation must have an 'anchorage' in a particular type of 'social imaginary', or that discourse itself is a kind of structured totality arising out of definite articulatory practices (3, 105). While 'society' as such is seen as an impossible object for this theoretical tendency, the very project of articulation does involve attempting to 'arrest the flow' of ideological differences, thus constructing a meaningful 'centre' which will 'dominate the field of discursivity' (111–12). This now appears to be the only available sense of hegemony. Class categories cannot serve *alone* as the centre or anchorage for articulation, but even yet they might form one part of a radical democratic hegemonic construction (141–2).

Socialism here is thus more or less equated with a 'radical, libertarian and plural democracy' (1985: 4), and *any* construction of a hegemonic discourse or 'political imaginary' is thought to be unable to cope with the necessary 'surplus' of the social, which overspills discursive attempts to 'fix' its heterogeneity. But we must surely ask, in that case: why bother? Does not pluralism *already* exist, given that all societies (and every individual) must, for Laclau and Mouffe, be seen as radically multiple and decentred? If all symbolic systems are *necessarily* 'polysemic' (168), why even attempt to introduce the relative fixity which, it is conceded, all hegemonic articulations seek to establish? These points are put as serious *questions*, because post-marxists tend to repeat, quite uncritically, some highly contentious propositions about the psychic fragility of human individuals as put forward in some strands of psychoanalytic and semiotic theory. Equally importantly, the relentlessly negative character of this style of arcane socialist pluralism puts the onus firmly on the exponents to produce something other than the rather simplistic celebration of endless diversity. To repeat, do we not already have a rich diversity? Why is there a need for specifically *socialist* democratic change?

This switch to a more urgent register of political questioning does, in fact, find a muted response in *Hegemony and Socialist Strategy*. It turns out that really radical pluralism, in the sense of perceiving a 'total diffusion of power within the social', would effectively conceal the existence of those 'partial concentrations of power' that are noticed as present in every social formation (142). Similarly, in the kind of pluralism 'proper to a radical democracy', simple 'diversification' of social identities would be transformed into something more meaningful, a genuine 'diversity' of groups of rationally autonomous agents (191). Finally, the libertarianism Laclau and Mouffe have in mind is explicitly argued *not* to be that proposed by Hayek and his associates on the Right, since the latter merely bolsters the kind of rampant capitalism which stifles autonomous diversity (171–2).

The upshot of this slim series of concessions to 'conventional' Left thinking is actually devastating. Radical democracy is manifestly something other and something altogether more than 'mere' pluralism, and the discourse which sustains it cannot after all be only one among others, with no substantive claims about the constitution of society as a whole. The process of radical democracy is therefore acknowledged to require collective forms of struggle against inequality and the primary relations of subordination (153). At length, it is even accepted, that 'of course', 'every project for radical democracy implies a socialist dimension, as it is necessary to put an end to capitalist relations of production, which are at the root of numerous relations of subordination' (178). Here, socialism is not after all coterminous with radical democracy, and it requires both a specific account of the pervasive sources of inequality and a collective means of transforming 'society' towards some better, more rational and autonomous, state of affairs for humanity.

I have somewhat relentlessly pursued the idea that for good or ill *socialist* versions of pluralism must eventually bring a halt to the logic of the post-marxist critique. A last illustration of this is to be found in perhaps the most determined effort explicitly to eliminate by declaration all traces of the 'incoherence' which marxist categories impart to socialist pluralism. On the one hand, Les Johnston flatly asserts that 'there is no essential constituency of interests or objectives that can be deemed socialist' (Johnston 1986: 140). This remarkable suggestion implies that there is nothing to prevent, for example, Hayekian libertarianism or a capitalist ethic being part of a socialist-pluralist construction. It also begs the question of how a political tradition can hope to have a positive vision if it is necessarily shorn of the appeal to interests and objectives. Very quickly, though, we discover that no such propositions can be upheld, for Johnston goes on to confirm the definition of socialism which Hindess offers, cited above, one which forefronts definite objectives of a non-capitalist sort. None of these authors, it can be summarized, either concludes, or succeeds in establishing, that the content of socialism can be satisfactorily regarded as a subsidiary moment of democracy *per se* (which, incidentally, both Hindess (1983: 48) and Johnston (1986: 139) stress amounts to no more than a set of formal mechanisms for arriving at collective decisions). Nor has the pluralism which consists in multiple, indeterminate and formal identities of 'difference' been persuasively developed as an analytic perspective, far less shown to be vital for socialist transformation. Perhaps in the light of this we can see why many post-marxists, somewhat inconsistently, hold on to the kind of rationalism they otherwise condemn in marxism itself, encapsulated in statements like 'rigorous socialist theory is the precondition of any effective socialist practice' (Johnston 1986: 141). While the serious weaknesses of class 'essentialism' rule out any aspirations to a unique and precise marxist 'science of politics', no coherent or convincing radical democratic *alternative* has yet emerged, and in particular the conclusion that 'class has no real place in socialist politics' (Johnston 1986: 124) has not finally been sustained.

PART II

Beyond the Debate?

6

THE CONUNDRUMS OF PHILOSOPHICAL PLURALISM

1. The state of the argument

Through Part I, the progression of the marxism-pluralism relationship was depicted as one in which the traditional scenario of mutual antagonism has been steadily undermined. It was also suggested (in the last chapter) that neither of the two main alternative construals of the state of the debate is persuasive. The fundamentalist marxist resolution certainly acknowledges that there has been some movement away from sheer opposition between the paradigms, but the extent of the explanatory difficulties created by the various shifts and concessions is minimized and dealt with one-sidedly. In its characteristic rhetoric, fundamentalism does not grant that critical pluralism is a credible stance which has overcome some of the principal weaknesses of pluralism's earlier conventional incarnation. Nor is it sufficiently recognized that the most defensible claims of class analysis are broad enough to allow considerable scope for the analysis of politics and social movements in terms other than those of class determination.

The second strong resolution I examined presented a reassertion of pluralist political and theoretical themes from the standpoint of a radical democratic project. This position was seen to be more than just another version of conventional sociological pluralism. Indeed, its representative statements have emerged from within the marxist tradition itself as attempts seriously to address the nature of the latter's contemporary crisis. All the same, some of the dubious aspects of pluralism which can be found across its variants tend also to reappear in the post-marxist tendency. Particularly questionable is the precipitous move from justified dissatisfaction with single-factor determinism to the conclusion that we confront an unstable social mosaic made up of infinitely heterogeneous identities and positions. Interestingly, the residual place of this option at one end of the pluralist spectrum, and the temptation it holds for radical pluralists, was clearly noted by commentators on both the original European current (Hsiao 1927: ch. 8) and US empirical democratic theory (McFarland 1969: 53f.). In the case of the modern writers I have been discussing the affirmation of irreducible plurality is ultimately compromised. This is because some degree of analytic or substantive 'closure' is necessitated in retaining any sense of dynamic structural tendencies within society, or any firm moral statement of the general benefits for humankind which socialism might offer. A completely open-ended approach to culture and politics, and a merely formal notion of plural democracy do not appear to be compatible with those minimal commitments.

However, the negative force of both of the strong resolutions considered disallow any comfortable assertion to the effect that marxism and pluralism must be smoothly converging. The high profile of philosophical argumentation at this level of the debate has worked to establish that aspects of the explanatory strategies of marxism and pluralism must pull in different directions. Even weak historical materialism entails an objectivist and developmental conception of the social totality; while class analysis, no matter how hypothetical its propositions are claimed to be, registers definite analytic priorities, priorities that the most critical pluralist might want to back away from. If the debate has undoubtedly moved from one of antagonism to dialogue and overlap, there is little prospect of outright convergence. In terms taken from another ongoing debate, we might say that our two traditions 'are condemned for the foreseeable future to coexist in tension' (Hirst and Woolley 1982: 160).

In this second part of the book I explore more generally how elements of tension condition the possibility of an eclectic or synthetic programme for social theory, that is, one which freely draws on both the marxist and pluralist perspectives. Several important strands of thought in contemporary politics and sociology claim, in fact, to have gone 'beyond' the allegedly stale confrontation between these two warhorses of social science. In my view, that kind of claim usually represents a statement of intent rather than of achievement. If, to illustrate, post-marxism leads, however tortuously, to a reformulated pluralist outlook, then the debate arguably has been rejoined rather than surpassed. Moreover, when more closely examined, sharp distinctions between the 'merely eclectic' and the 'genuinely synthetic', or between the radically novel resolution and the intelligent restatement of important traditional themes, prove hard to sustain. In chapters 7 and 8 I review important contributions to general sociology and state theory from that critical angle.

Meanwhile, it seems clear that novel substantive resolutions – especially in the shape of programmatic essays towards a more appropriate framework – inevitably raise questions about the adequacy of criteria for, and the object, of, social theory. The radical pluralist resolution, for example, which I dealt with mainly in terms of 'internal' critique, is actually a species of a wider challenge to perceived orthodoxy in the epistemology of the human sciences. This kind of referral of social theory to 'higher level' epistemological considerations has sometimes been regarded as a vital step in the proper 'grounding' of social scientific claims. But what is interesting about philosophical discourse today is the climate of uncertainty which surrounds the matter of the necessary foundations of enquiry (whether in natural or social science). Significantly from our point of view, general issues which have often been couched in a quasi-technical notation within specialist philosophy, are increasingly dealt with in the vaguer and denser vocabulary of, precisely, analytical and cultural *pluralism*. In other words, while the philosophical dimension of cultural theory continues to be relatively distinct, there can be no prior assumption that it operates on any 'higher' or more apodeictic plane. If anything, philosophy's inherent dependence on substantive insight has never been more apparent, and its immersion in the widespread 'crisis' of cultural understanding is plain. Since the decline of logical positivism, and in spite of several attempts (notably by scientific realists) to reimpose order, it is a widely shared view that 'the epistemology of causation, and of the scientific method more generally, is at present in a state of near chaos' (Cook and Campbell 1979: 10). The nature of the tendency towards philosophical pluralism is therefore of considerable significance for the changing shape of social theory.

2. Rescuing reason

There are two types, or perhaps two stages, of philosophical pluralism, and the extent to which the more radical type is entailed or encouraged by the more pedestrian sort is not easy to determine. The first pluralist move represents scepticism towards philosophical absolutes. In this mood, any tough proposal that there is a single model for science, or a sound foundation for knowledge, or a general theory of history will be met by pluralist caution, based on the possibility that there are always *many* useful paradigms for science, knowledge or history. The chief attitudes in play here are tolerance of alternatives and hesitancy about ascribing to the world some of the certitudes and totalities projected by our current theories.

The second, radical pluralist, move in philosophy involves the categorical assertion that no single theory or set of theories could *ever* approximately fit the diverse realm of experience. Indeed, restricted cognitive models of the nature of reality and experience simply fail to comprehend the multiple and compound modes of being that we inhabit. It follows that not only absolutist sentiments, but the privileged place given to apprehending life in terms of knowledge, is intrinsically illusory. It would seem here that the first pluralist move involves a pragmatic approach to epistemology, whilst the second involves the latter's militant rejection. Both types of pluralism have contributed in the past to the periodic liberation of philosophy from entrenched orthodoxies. But it is the radical sort of pluralism that is especially exciting when first encountered, since it appears to say that the whole project of philosophy itself and its hallowed components – reason and reality, truth and science – are misguided. Philosophy, that is, always seeks to stabilize, distinguish and reintegrate the elements of experience, whereas radical pluralism accepts the permanent *lack* of stable bearings, the inherent inadequacy of purely cognitive and representational schemas for human understanding.

The most powerful modern statement of the radical perspective was articulated by Friedrich Nietzsche. Nietzsche memorably described the vain (both senses) aspirations of philosophers to capture Truth and Reality as merely the mobilization of a vast army of *metaphors*. Metaphors, indeed, which have forgotten that they *are* metaphors; that is, concepts which (impossibly) seek to go beyond their basis in human will, language and imagination. For Nietzsche, there is no beyond (cf. Norris 1982: ch. 4).

The arguments of post-modernist theorists, for all their nuances and range of specialisms, basically follow this Nietzschean pattern. However, whilst the post-modernists mimic Nietzsche's iconoclasm when they embark on the project of radical critique, it has become apparent that few of them finally decide to bid 'farewell to reason' in the literal sense of that slogan (Feyerabend 1987). This process is worth exemplifying, for it draws attention to some interestingly ambiguous features of the more pragmatic pluralist option. Both the withdrawal from the radical option, and the ambivalence of the pragmatic one, I will suggest, reinforces the conclusion that current philosophical directions *cannot*, as is sometimes thought, be drawn upon unequivocally to support the more substantive radical pluralist perspective in social theory. Ironically, the post-marxist writers discussed in the last chapter can be seen in this light as having taken as virtually read the *success* of the post-modernist critique of epistemology just at the point where many other radical philosophical pluralists appear to be once again hedging their bets. I want briefly to illustrate this claim by reference to some of the most influential post-modernist accounts.

The critical method of deconstruction has formed a major part of the post-modernist critique. It arises as a reaction to the structuralist conceptions of language which dominated the human sciences in the period to the 1970s. In structuralism, language is seen as a stable set of interrelations between its elements, forming clear rules for syntactic and semantic construction. The structuralist outlook involved the generalization of this systemic approach to language into a number of domains of human interrelations, with (variously) the social system, the unconscious, and cultural mythologies being conceptualized analogously. Indeed, 'analogy' may not be a direct enough linkage, since most versions of structuralism assume with post-Saussurian linguistics that language itself is the definitive feature of social interaction and human competence.

The post-structuralist or deconstructive critique of structuralist motifs does not necessarily reject the linguistic emphasis. Rather, it takes language as *oversimplified* in structuralism, and questions the abstract unity attributed to the linguistically-inspired totalities which characterize the various applied paradigms of structuralism. Above all, deconstruction denies the *stability* of language, and rejects the ascription of a *correspondence* between the use of language and definite human intentions. Deconstruction, unlike structuralism, does not see language as an abstract storehouse from which we draw in order to supply messages about reality or to communicate personal states of mind. Instead, language is conceived as forever running away from its user in the very moment or context of its materialization as text. The distinction between text and context is thus broken and the previously taken-for-granted relationship between the terms text/meaning/intention is disrupted. As Christopher Norris summarizes: 'Deconstruction . . . starts out by rigorously *suspending* this assumed correspondence between mind, meaning and the concept of method which claims to unite them' (Norris 1982: 3). For any given text, it is claimed, the connotations and metaphors which are generated form a surplus of significance which goes beyond any specific implication imposed by an author's usage. Language runs free, and is essentially 'contaminated', thus constantly frustrating any pure referential or intentional function it may be thought to satisfy.

This apparently specialist linguistic claim is in fact a wider

assault on assumptions about philosophy and thought in
western culture. According to deconstruction, it is characteristic
of western philosophy to assume that thoughts mirror intentions, and then either succeed or fail in hooking on to the
world. But this assumption, it is argued, at once privileges
intentionality over writing, and treats language generally as a
transparent medium of representation, in which the world
declares itself to us. This conception becomes quite unsustainable once the 'polymorphic' nature of language is demonstrated.
Deconstruction, it is held, shows that signification is a process
in which meanings are always *deferred*, and that the widespread
linguistic practices of citation and repetition paradoxically
always point up connotative *differences* amongst meanings,
rather than similarities between the human subjects who
display them. Language, it follows, must be seen as intrinsically
ambiguous and opaque. It is true that philosophers habitually
imagine that the production of clear ideas can overcome such
intrinsic opacity, but this fond hope is merely a prejudice and
a fallacy, one which has dazzled and confounded the entire
Western rationalist tradition. There simply is no thought
outside linguistic usage, nor any usage which ultimately fixes
meaning. In order to try to secure certainty, philosophers
generally evince a 'metaphysics of presence', in which both the
objective and subjective intentions are held to be uniquely
spoken for in the very *person* of the philosopher, thus dispelling
the complications dealt out by language and textuality,
returning these once again to their transparent function. For
deconstruction, however, this is a metaphysics in the worst
sense, i.e. one which accords an unwarranted priority to
philosophical speech and ratiocination over the endlessly
slippery and affective surfaces of writing. When examined
closely, language can be witnessed as enabling an infinite
series of contortions and paradoxes which can be thrown back
in the face of any systematic attempt to derive ultimate
meaning from it.

As a specialist method, deconstruction is thus a practice of
close reading: an attempt to turn the tables on authors by
revealing the hidden motifs, tensions and intentions in *any*
textual construction whatsoever. As a wider cultural theme
and philosophical perspective, deconstruction culls from the

subversive manipulation of texts a number of rejections of classical epistemology. Above all, the evocation of 'reality' (whether subjective or intersubjective) as something outside textuality which possesses independent status in relation to 'ideas' is held, as in Nietzsche, to be nothing more than a figure of speech, negated in the fact and content of discourse. One consequence of this critique is that literary criticism is capable, in a way philosophy is not, of recognizing the essentially rhetorical, shifting character of all meanings, including those of philosophy itself. Thus, there is probably a vital conflict between literature and philosophy, and victory lies with the former (at least in its deconstructionist mode) due to its greater self-awareness (Norris 1982: 21).

The seductive flow of the deconstructionist move can, however, be interrupted at a number of points. For one thing, its characterization of orthodox philosophy is skewed. Far from being marked by attempts to group ultimate meaning in 'presence' and 'authenticity', it could be equally plausibly asserted that academic philosophy has woven a tortuous route *out* of speech towards an arcane lexicon of demonstration, logical elaboration and analytic, second-order discourse. In many ways, modern western philosophy has painstakingly sought to *abstain* from deciding 'ultimate' issues. The power of the sceptic to disrupt epistemic representational schemas is just as pervasive an influence as any supposedly unified concern to 'fix' a transparent word–world connection. It is also obvious that epistemology (investigation of the logic of word–world connections), while playing an important general role in modern philosophy, contains within it a diverse range of approaches (rationalism, empiricism, idealism, pragmatism, marxism etc.) which cannot without distortion be steamrollered over by deconstructionists as part of the same flat-earth illusions of western 'metaphysics'. Moreover, within western philosophy epistemology is only one branch. Logical and ontological ideas, ethical questions, and issues arising within substantive specialist areas are by no means always reducible to their epistemological implications.

Protesting against the 'misrepresentation' of philosophy and epistemology is perhaps a relatively minor point. More important is the problem that the very mode of critique adopted in deconstruction lends itself to counter-charges of reductionism. This is damaging because reductionism is frequently cited in the post-modernist literature as the very symptom of a dogmatic philosophy of *closure*, not one of textual openness. The standard deconstructionist gambit, however, is precisely to select a plurality of texts in a given field only to condense them into a format in which none other than 'the metaphysics of presence' is discovered. In *The Deconstructive Turn* (1984), for example, Norris examines a number of important modern philosophers – important above all because they are thought to show a quasi-deconstructive awareness of the power of language to subvert authorial intention and to broaden interpretive scope. However, these figures are forever trying to force their own linguistic strategies into producing 'external' and objective significance, thus committing the philosophers' fallacy of ignoring the auto-generative power of language. For all his appreciation of linguistic nuances, Ryle, for instance, restores in the end a 'phonocentric theme' (Norris 1984: 27). Wittgenstein, it is said, with great originality first of all poses, but then evades, the textuality of his own arguments (1984: 40). Frege's pathbreaking non-realist semantic logic is not enough, it is remarked, to halt the necessary slide into 'slippage or undecideability' (1984: 151). Kripke, in the very moment of erecting a hard-line referential function for language, fails to spot that it is the very *rhetoric* of his own text which makes his solution appear plausible (1984: 172). And so on.

What is significant about this process of criticism is, paradoxically, its rationalism and reductionism. The contradictions identified are presented as the *necessary* consequences of a given textual mode; and the key to their unlocking – the end point of the whole enterprise – is the awareness and practice of deconstruction. The message is always and everywhere the same: a text will run away with its author. There is precious little concession to a plurality of significance here. The method itself is a rationalist, self-justificatory one in that, sequentially, a problem is identified (the old authorial intentions are at work); a contradiction is explored (discrepancy between text and authorial presence); and a higher synthesis emerges (*recognition* of text–intention discrepancy). And this process of reading/reasoning is effectively instated as the Method for ascertaining the significance of the text in question.

According to this deconstructionist attitude, there is nothing but textual slippage, undecideability of meanings, and the free play of plural significance. If this is so, we seem to be faced not so much, as in Norris's initial characterization, with a 'bracketing out' of epistemological strategies, but rather with a full-blown counter-metaphysics of flux and text. The implication is not merely that the epistemological question of the relationship between words and things is problematical given the instability of language and reference, but that all sorts of apparent entities and relations are essentially textual, constellations of signification-potentials. It has been suggested that such a conclusion is not an abandonment of philosophy at all but a version of epistemological *idealism* (Rorty 1982: 154). However, even idealism posits a series of necessary *identities*, whereas the typical deconstructionist arguments lead to non-identity and arbitrary connection as the favoured ontic modes. This form of 'vulgar' deconstruction has been particularly prevalent amongst literary circles in the USA in the 1970s, and Norris tries hard to absolve the foremost deconstructionist, Jacques Derrida, from its excesses. 'What is in question, for Nietzsche and Derrida, is not some "alternative" logic of figurative language, but an open plurality of discourse where all such priorities dissolve into the disconcerting "free play" of signs' (Norris 1982: 59). But if signs *are* indeed wholly 'free' from intention, reference and cognitive ordering, then texts do indeed reveal a necessary indeterminacy, being entirely open to proliferation and figuration at will. Nothing more is needed to constitute 'an alternative logic'.

Perhaps in recognition of this problem, Norris and other subtle deconstructors have come to play down, and even reverse, the notion that deconstruction decisively disallows philosophical claims to rationality and meaning. In *The Contest of Faculties* (1985), Norris argues that deconstruction was really about ensuring a critical *awareness* of the affective presuppositions and rhetorical tropes at work in the presentation of systematic philosophies. It is thus the analytic *rigour* of deconstruction in the hands of its best practitioners, rather than any 'message' about textuality *per se*, that is held to be of value (Norris 1985: 14). The overlap between deconstruction in this sense and the tradition of analytical philosophy suggests itself at this point. Indeed, deconstruction can even be seen as *preserving* what is distinctive and critical in philosophy in a climate where the 'vulgar' conclusion might be that philosophy is merely one more form of writing.

This adjustment in Norris's position, though, is somewhat disingenuous, for a marked enthusiasm for slippage, paradox and the free play of signs was certainly present in his earlier work, as we have witnessed. Moreover, not only the US literary critics, but philosophical critics of western rationalism – figures such as Richard Rorty, from whose work Norris and others take a great deal – now appear to be cruelly double-crossed for their efforts, since Rorty (1982: 90ff.) is cited as supporting the vulgar conclusion. Certainly, a sober case has been made out that Derrida, in probing the 'unspeakable' condition of philosophical judgement, was in effect taking the classical Kantian investigation of foundations just one necessary step further (Gasche 1986). Yet here too, there is an appeal to the privileged status of philosophic reflection over other forms of exploration which, in rejoining the mainstream of meta-physics, must surely work *against* rather than extend, those parts of Derrida and deconstruction which mock, twist and subvert that tradition. The post hoc division of the de-constructionist movement into vulgar and philosophical variants is probably better seen as an admission that the project of pure critique has run into the sands.

Another post-modernist variant which converges on de-constructionism at many points is Jean-François Lyotard's critique of the 'grand narratives' of modern intellectual culture. Where deconstruction focuses on the mirage of stability in language usage, Lyotard accepts that all social thought and interaction takes place within language games, and it is these local contexts which are responsible for whatever stable meaning we derive. Lyotard locates the oppressive fixity of social and philosophical reference in its dependence upon totalizing categories. Typical of the modernist case of philo-sophical reflection, he argues, is the drive to legitimize our local values and concepts by constructing overarching edifying myths about the progressive march of science, or reason, or freedom, or the proletariat. In each case a particular type of practical, discursive strategy is projected on to the structure and dynamic of reality itself and buttressed by an objectivist epistemology to secure its conformity to reason and truth. The result is that each discourse erects a unique story-line for history, fitted out with privileged analytic concepts and self-confirming practical instructions. For all their differences, liberalism and marxism are argued to share this kind of rationalist and teleological structure. They both draw on typical Enlightenment modes of philosophizing to confirm that they alone carry the banner of progress and necessity.

As with deconstruction, the radical version of this critique appears to go all the way down. Notions of knowledge as representation are flatly rejected, and appeals to science are recognized to be a principal form of self-projection. Lyotard insists that no single grand narrative could be 'right', even in principle. Any number of competing narratives are available, and the appropriate analysis for them is not at all a logicist dissection and testing of their claims, but rather an examination of the 'agonistics' by means of which significance emerges within each discourse and amongst a plurality of discourses (Lyotard 1984: 10, 20).

The post-modern condition, for Lyotard, has witnessed the deepening crisis of these modernist narratives. A self-consciousness about the narrative mode itself has increasingly penetrated the structure of representational reasoning, he maintains. Lyotard may well have in mind here the turn away from general methodology and towards history in the philosophy of science, or the rebirth of narrative styles within historiography (Stone 1981), or the recent proliferation of micro-sociologies. In all three domains, the relation of exteriority between the concepts of a discourse and its object begins to disintegrate. Such transient, local language games are held to possess their own discursive rules, and their evaluative logic is essentially social rather than epistemic in some transdiscursive sense.

The element of pluralism in Lyotard's post-modern scenario is not only the admission of many possible narratives; it is also the claim that human subjects belong to, and are constituted, in *many* such games. There simply is nothing outside of these to seek to totalize. Our imaginary strategies and narrative splinters constantly shift: they are governed not by a unique narrative logic inscribed in the world itself, but rather by 'paralogy' – the permanent displacement of stable essential relations (Lyotard 1984: 22).

As in deconstruction, the problem with this view is that a pluralist concern for diversity has rapidly turned into an Anti-Philosophy. The possibility, for example, that the post-modern picture itself may just be one more narrative among other only has to be posed to appear inadequate to the real challenge which is delivered. For what is on offer is not really a plea for the coexistence of alternative perceptions; it is the destruction of the Enlightenment heritage altogether. In fully acknowledging the radical nature of the post-modernist picture, the conclusion emerges that it is itself a powerful *picture* of the development and crisis of cultural understanding. That is, post-modernism presents an alternative grand narrative. To be sure, as befits its emphasis on paralogy, this picture abounds with paradoxes. It is a totalized conception of local logics, an overall narrative of the progressive decline of the grand narratives. These are nevertheless general claims which ask to be addressed as such.

In fact, an important aspect of Lyotard's argument could be said to be a contribution to the sociology of knowledge taken in a fairly traditional sense. Lyotard is impressed not only by the complexity of social life in general, but by the profound changes going on in the modes and means of communication in the later twentieth century. The philosophic motif he resorts to most centrally, that of the language game, arises (as perhaps it did not for Wittgenstein, its originator) directly from the 'working hypothesis' that society in general has become computerized. Information is now pervasively and intrinsically packaged as a commercial phenomenon, with publicly agreed norms rapidly receding from view. It is the social compartmentalization of advanced industrial society which spurs ever more local and specialist access to specific systems technologies, and this bespoke character of strategic calculation intensifies the privatization of knowledge, further diminishing its (illusory) universal properties. Given this situation of literally innumerable language games, Lyotard argues that we are now much better placed to *choose* how society responds to us (1984: 10–13).

In this historically novel social context, several orthodox notions beg to be dismantled. The idea of society as a unified totality of functions, for example, fails to recognize both the *optional* character of micro-strategies and the absence of a single coherent focus for the distribution of language games. The idea that social individuals or subjects receive their identity from the traditional poles of social attraction (states, parties, classes, professions, intellectual traditions) severely underestimates the dispersion of individual selfhood across a number of language games, and indeed refuses to acknowledge the unprecedented *mobility* of social subjects.

Here it is not fanciful to suggest that Lyotard's argument is in effect a presentation of some well worn themes in mainstream sociology. Indeed, its similarity to conventional pluralism may already have registered. There is an emphasis on functional complexity, mobility, differentiation, and the absence of permanent allegiances; but no appeal is made to atomized individualism as such. Group and individual subjecthood, no less than 'society', is an *imaginary* unity, one which in practice is usually undermined by participation in a number of overlapping strategies and identities. The single major difference between the post-modernists and the pluralists of a previous generation is that the former pay closer attention to the serious effects of a changing modernity on our very conception of knowledge and its legitimating role in political choice. Without entering into that debate here, we can see that the structure of the post-modern argument, and perhaps its most plausible element, is that definite shifts in the character of society have led to a crisis in our understanding of the nature of subjective apprehension and political motivation, which must accordingly change. This pattern of argument is perfectly at home in a traditional conception of the sociology of politics. In his high Nietzschean phase Lyotard would have resisted any such domestication of his rejection of rationality (Dews 1987: 140). The central thrust of his more recent work, by contrast, requires empirical and theoretical evaluation of a fairly straight epistemological sort.

The upshot of these compromises within post-modernist thought is that some aspect of universality and cognitive rationality is rescued from the prospect of apparent intellectual chaos. We would, of course, expect realist-inclined philosophers both to fear and to attack the drift to irrationalism, subjectivism, nihilism and disintegration which post-modernist pluralism seems to embody (cf. Jarvie 1983, Trigg 1980, Rose 1984, Dews 1987). More surprising perhaps is the internal dynamic of post-modernism, the current phase of which has witnessed a marked step back from the radical pluralist option and an implicit settling for something more pragmatic, perhaps couched in the form of contingent facts about how humans make sense of the amplitude and infinitude which surrounds them.

Along these lines, Cornelius Castoriadis has weightily criticized the tendency to project 'ensemblist-identitary' categories as expressing the intimate logic of society and history. Taken radically, this seems to result in the conclusion that the very attempt to assess what the central social identities and significant practical ensembles might be is a mistake. In this mood, Castoriadis views the world which our categories posit as 'confronting' us as a *magma*, and even a 'magma of magmas', i.e. a molten manifold that is simply beyond expression in identitarian terms (Castoriadis 1987: 182). Our constructions of relevant 'social imaginaries', in Castoriadis's terms, are creative ways of 'leaning on' the amorphous potentials of the magma; they do not reflect any inherent natural structures of being.

For all that, Castoriadis concedes that no relevant social imaginary can be grounded in the sheer arbitrariness that accompanies this view of life as fluid chaos. Paradoxically, that view itself is charged with attributing yet another 'essence' to being (Castoriadis 1987: 341–2). It follows, then, that as part of our 'psychic economy', we must after all deploy and commit ourselves to the kind of identitarian categories which cut the world up in various ways. The crucial thing to remember, it seems, is that there are many ways of doing this and that no one set of categories can claim ultimate sanction outside of the creative process of signification.

My final example of the kind of strident and influential contribution which exemplifies the move from radical to pragmatic critique is Roberto M. Unger's assault on 'necessitarian' social thought as the basis for political theory. As with other post-modernists, Unger completely rejects the idea that social theory should aspire to the goals of natural science. It is in his view the very propagation of this mimicry – the 'naturalistic premise' – that has so seriously blighted social theory and political creativity. Even today, when there is a considerable degree of reflexivity and even anti-naturalism around, social theorists have failed to go far enough, and a thoroughly anti-necessitarian alternative has been only intermittently and incompletely formulated (Unger 1987: 25).

However, Unger's vehement call for emancipation from 'false necessity' is itself only incompletely and intermittently asserted. Against the powerful sway of 'deep-structure naturalism' in social science (exemplified above all by marxism), Unger urges us to 'pursue the initial, anti-naturalistic route of modern social thought to its outermost limits, and see what happens' (Unger 1987: 87). What happens, though, is not to Unger's liking any more than it is to that of Castoriadis, Lyotard, Foucault, et al. For the outer limit of anti-necessity is pure contingency, and the outer limit of anti-naturalism is unconstrained creationism. In fact, Unger is quite worried by each of these breaches of rational boundaries. He wants to repudiate the search for a single 'script' for our social routines, but not to the point where the very distinction between the constraining context of action and those routines is obliterated (Unger 1987: 151–2). Indeed, Unger's overall aspiration to supply an appropriate overall framework for social and political understanding (and political practice too) is a typically modernist ambition. Accordingly, he differentiates his own theoretical stance ('super-theory') from an unrelentingly sceptical anti-necessitarianism ('ultra-theory'). This latter view is considered to involve complete causal agnosticism with respect to social forces, and an unwitting positivism in accepting the fluid equivalence of whatever is given (1987: 9, 168). Morally speaking too, ultra-theory can be criticized for expressing mindless existential panic in the face of any settled contexts whatsoever.

The immodest ambition of Unger's prolegomena for a social theory of politics makes it vital to note, even at the programmatic level (for Unger is sketching a project, not a finished product), the compromise he makes with philosophical foundationalism. All his criticisms of 'ultra-theory' (the radical pluralist option, in my terms) are based on the defensibility of some kind of valid generalization about social constraints and conduct. If this is so, Unger is entirely wrong to proclaim that there are no a priori reasons for preferring his own super-theoretical perspective to the ultra-theoretical alternative (Unger 1987: 169). On the contrary, the main reason he gives in favour of his own view is *nothing* if not a priori, since it concerns the necessary conditions of stable, usable concepts for social understanding and application, concepts which ultra-theory systematically eschews and criticises. As a matter of cultural *temperament*, it may well be that Unger feels closer to the ultra-theorists than to necessitarians, and perhaps it is this affinity which makes him (generously) reluctant to force his reader to a choice as to which of the two pluralist options is the more promising. Nevertheless, the main thrust of his position is that if we remove the notion of an all-encompassing quasi-naturalistic social script for political action, then 'we can turn what looked like intellectual disintegration into a more powerful vindication of the original, inspiring ideas of modern social thought' (Unger 1987: 203). Unger, like the other theorists we have touched upon, is thus only a half-hearted post-modernist. The fear of nihilism, which he claims is an immature and unfounded reaction to the radical implications of ultra-theory, continues to mark the thinking of those like Unger himself who launch an apparently unflinching pluralist critique of grand narratives and the false necessity they are reckoned to display.

3. Objectivism and relativism

In spite of the weaknesses of the radical pluralist option, the post-modernist critique has nevertheless achieved remarkable currency by way of undermining naive objectivist and holistic assumptions. The recent compromises undertaken by prominent 'anti-necessitarian' thinkers has, in other words, made it no easier to revert to naturalism as providing the model for social theory. The less extreme pluralist option in philosophy, one in which various theories are assessed pragmatically for usefulness and insight, but not for their ultimate truth value or verisimilitude, remains, therefore, a credible fall-back position for pluralists. Indeed, a number of erstwhile philosophical *realists* have come to embrace openly aspects of the weaker pluralist option. This enhanced philosophical mobility has in large part come about as a result of intensive debate around the question of *relativism*. Indeed in a sense, relativism just *is* the problem of pluralism-versus-monism. For the relativist 'there is a non-reducible plurality of [conceptual] schemes, paradigms and practices; there is no substantive overarching framework in which radically different and alternative schemes are commensurable – no universal standards that somehow stand outside of and above those competing alternatives' (Bernstein 1983: 11–12). In a sense, the most challenging part of post-modernism is its avowal of cultural relativism as described here. This relativist picture is customarily pitted against the conventional view of science as a developing body of universal knowledge which enables increasingly systematic predictions and control over the environment. Science in this view is a cumulative enterprise which tells us about a reality (natural and social) which exists independently of our ideas concerning it. When serious scientific claims are made, or come to be accepted, there is a reasonable presumption that they describe or at least seek to describe a state of affairs in the world. Accordingly, an epistemic distinction between science and *ideology* or mere belief is necessary, because the latter do not generally possess either the methodological systematicity or the demonstrable empirical grip of the former. Theories are judged by theoretical and empirical criteria, and these conjointly provide the basis for establishing science's *adequacy to reality*. If we did not assume that successful science constitutes evidence that our knowledge is capable of increasing approximation to how things really are, then science would have to be considered utterly mysterious and arbitrary. Social science, in this respect, is not noticeably different in principle from natural science.

This strong objectivist or realist picture has come in for many criticisms and qualifications at the hands of relativists. The ideal it posits is claimed to be curiously ahistorical and purely normative. Real science, it can be protested, reveals all sorts of social and ideological influences which contaminate and endlessly defer the aspiration to a God's eye view of the world. Marxists can point to the conditioning of the scientific method by the forces of production of industrial capitalism. Feminists have pointed to the pervasive masculinist tendencies of specific scientific fields and the boys' adventure stories of scientific endeavour which feature 'man's progress' and his heroic struggle to adapt to, then master, intractable natural forces. Post-modernists emphasize the intrinsic presence of many different sorts of legitimating narratives which guide and structure our substantive beliefs. Foucault has argued that the enterprise of classifying phenomena according to definite types, types which become logically connected to a technology of control, is a pervasive feature of cultural institutions specific to the modern era. In his view, claims about science always come as part of a wider 'regime of truth', a moral system of closure and control (cf. Foucault 1980).

This wealth of diverse critique is in itself enough to throw doubt on the abstraction called 'pure' science which strives to secure an eternal relation of 'representation' with the external world. Moreover, since T. S. Kuhn's famous (1962) account of the humdrum occupational and psychological components of *actual* paradigm-shifts in science, the notion of scientific communities operating according to purely rational criteria of objective theory-choice has been largely discredited. By and large, Kuhn implied, scientists do not 'adhere' to a theory for any loftier reasons than the workaday ones of habit formation, occupational funding and peer-group beliefs. The actual *history* of science, in sum, does not reveal the rational conversion of whole bodies of scientists to a new view of the world by virtue of either new truths discovered or a superior Method. This idealized view ignores the pervasive *pragmatic* and idiosyncratic features of scientific 'progress' (Laudan 1977). Above all, across these varied and powerful critiques, there is a general philosophical consensus that nothing can be said or known about 'the real world' which is not intimately bound up with dense sets of *current* theoretical and cultural assumptions, expectations and technologies of experimentation. In taking these belief sets seriously, it is urged, we must openly debunk revered ideas of Science and Truth, since these hoary abstractions always tend to indicate an essential structure of knowledge over and above particular modes of scientific or cultural practice.

Against this relativist chain of thought, a classic objectivist response is to retort that since relativism involves the claim that everything is relative; and that this is itself a universal or decontextualised claim; then relativism itself, if true, must be false. Therefore relativism is false, or at least self-contradictory. However, critics of objectivism find this a very crude summary. Rorty, for example, has sharply condemned the classic refutation of relativism. If the latter is 'the view that every belief on a certain topic, or perhaps about *any* topic, is as good as every other', Rorty maintains, then 'No one holds this view' (Rorty 1982: 166). By the same token, of course, it can as easily be shown that if objectivism is taken to mean the context-free striving for omniscience, in effect the God's eye view, then few living objectivists are likely to be found. The debate thus becomes one of qualified relativism versus qualified objectivism/ realism, and from many quarters the call has gone out that we need to go 'beyond' the eternal oscillation between these two apparently unacceptable extremes (Hollis and Lukes 1982, Bernstein 1983). Relativists can modify the crude caricature of their views, for example, by pointing out that *moral* relativism is not entailed by *meaning*-relativism. That is to say, serious argument about the common plight of human beings does not founder just because our beliefs about the nature of the cosmos are culture-specific. A stronger view, *cognitive* relativism, conceives not just meaning but also *truth* as being context-determined. Yet even this does not necessarily involve an end to serious dispute about what exists and how. Cognitive relativists deny only that our knowledge can ever be held up against the world in itself and declared to be identical to it. Rorty sums up this line of thought (i.e. a negative one) by saying that 'several hundred years of effort have failed to make interesting sense of the notion of "correspondence" (either of thoughts to things or of words to things)' (Rorty 1982: xvii). In view of this modified relativism, the classic refutation looks to be inappropriate. For relativism is *not* claiming for itself a universal objectivity. On the contrary, it is saying that we do not need mystifying talk of Objective Reality in order to engage in significant conversation. In practice, for this purpose, relativists use the very same criteria as realists, namely a range of evidence, logical coherence, and fruitfulness for research. The difference is that relativists are happy to leave it there, making no attempt to sanctify working knowledge (as do the realists) by regarding it as the embodiment of Truth or Reason.

The realist, once satisfied that irrationality has been staved off, can then also relax into a modified position. *Of course*, it can be admitted, we make objective claims only within definite perspectives. Obviously, the 'adequacy' of our theories emerges opaquely, not as if science was the very mirror of nature itself. But our theories, when we consider them to be adequate, do demand some conviction that the world is more or less as they portray it. And from natural and social science we have a substantial basis for belief in a totality of existence composed of particular, and related, sorts of objects, processes and powers. However, we can probably never know this evolving amalgam in its totality, nor pretend that our own understanding of it can be anything other than linguistic and conceptual in character, i.e. *social and human*. Since the impulse to realism may in the end be a contingent fact about human beliefs, the idea of a real totality, knowable by us through science, must be accepted as a regulative ideal rather than as a given fact.

A compromise between objectivism and relativism seems to emerge with these modified epistemological outlooks. Indeed, Hilary Putnam has proposed that a modern pluralist standpoint in philosophy strives not so much to take sides between such arguably sterile dichotomies, but to break their stranglehold on sensible discussion (Putnam 1981: xi, 73–4). Pluralism in philosophy is therefore not a matter of defending relativism, whether in its subtle or 'irrationalist' form. But neither can foundationalism be sustained: there may be a plurality of coherent conceptual schemes, and no assertion about the right one corresponding to the structure of reality can help us in deciding which to prefer. In following this train of thought, Putnam chooses to characterize his pluralism as being expressive of the new type of philosophical outlook in the post-modern cultural era (Putnam 1983: 183). It consists in finding and following the 'narrow path' which lies between the 'swamps of metaphysics and the quicksands of cultural relativism/historicism' (1983: 226).

However, as in the marxism-pluralism debate in social theory, of which, I insist, this philosophical issue is very much a part, the new-found sense of synthesis seems at times as much an expression of acute puzzlement as it is a convincing solution. In Putnam's case, there has been a well-advertised climb-down from the adherence to 'external' realism to 'internal' realism, according to which we only ever know reality through *versions* of it, of which there are many. And yet, when the 'constructivist' aspect of relativism inevitably presents itself, namely that if we only ever have *versions* of reality there is simply nothing to be said about 'it', Putnam fudges. He refuses to accept even the possibility that competing versions might be incommensurable, and this is a gesture of resistance which a more committed relativist could only regard as a substantial hangover from Putnam's erstwhile metaphysical realism (Feyerabend 1987: 265f.). The lesser, 'compromise' claim is this: 'We don't have an Archimedean point; we always speak the language of a time and place; but the rightness and wrongness of what we say is not *just* for a time and place' (Putnam 1983: 247). Yet in an important way, this is as realist as you like. No doubt objectivity is always objectivity 'for us', but when strict relativism (my radical pluralist option) drops out of the running, the 'for us' is *not* a concession to subjectivism. Through science and practice we actually know quite a lot about what is 'for us' and what is not. It is only a radical relativist hangover that prompts the addition of 'for us' to any well-attested knowledge claim. Human knowledge has necessary *boundaries*, to be sure, but within those, the relations and objects it posits aim to capture, and succeed in capturing, at least some part of how things really are. That at least is a persuasive reading of what is going on here, though certainly, it has tb be conceded to sophisticated relativists like Rorty that the realism is in large part of the 'intuitive' rather than 'technical' variety (Rorty 1982: xxiii).

The half-way house between objectivism and relativism, realism and idealism once more appears to have no occupants. Or to put it another way, the pragmatic pluralist option does not represent a satisfactory third way between the classic (if now subtler) epistemic choices. Thus Putnam generalizes: 'we seem to be caught between our desire for integration and our recognition of the difficulty' (Putnam 1983: 303). What needs to be done, this implies, is to register a plea for philosophic tolerance, rather than outright reconciliation, as we learn to live with the tensions in play.

4. Realism, pluralism and social theory

To the committed scientific realist or objectivist, Putnam's vacillation will be regarded as the necessary consequence of his virtual abandonment of realism, and the same realist would probably insist that Putnam's conundrum can be resolved satisfactorily by taking an altogether firmer line. Indeed, to the scientific realist, the rift between the 'internal' or 'empirical' realist on the one hand and the 'conceptual super-idealist' or 'constructive empiricist', on the other is actually something of a sham. This is because the former, whilst insisting on the independence of reality from science/ thought, freely accepts that nothing can be assumed *about* that independent world outside of it. The real world thus plays a very gestural and shadowy role in understanding the nature of scientific knowledge. The latter array of theorists for their part insist that if we only ever have our current limited theories and experiments to work with, then logically speaking, the 'world' is constructed anew, and quite differently, with each change in vision of science. Nevertheless it is accepted by constructivists that outside this strict logic, that is, back in the practical world, we can comfortably settle into the kind of 'natural ontological attitude' which assumes the persistence and intractability of real forces and things (van Fraasen 1985: 246).

For the scientific realist, by contrast, there must be an altogether closer relationship posited between the deep structures of reality and the practice of science if this sceptical and anthropomorphic consensus is to be effectively countered. Thus:

> In the realist view, things are not simply real in the weak, epistemological sense of existing independently of the

knower. They are real in a strong, *ontological* sense . . . On this view science is precisely the use of reason to figure out what real mechanisms are causally responsible for the phenomena of experience. (Isaac 1987: 45–6)

So the inclination of scientific realists is to conceive the world not only as standing independent of current scientific knowledge, but as a rich, structured and active domain of causal powers. The internal realist's flat ontology cannot allow for this idea, and yet, the scientific realist argues, science itself is possible *only* on the assumption that it is dealing with such a world. The emphasis here is to break with a pervasive 'epistemic fallacy', one which involves reducing all questions about the nature of *being* to questions about our knowledge of it. Such a reduction invariably opens the door to scepticism and paradox (Bhaskar 1987: 23). For the realist, the concepts of natural necessity, structural identities and generative mechanisms are quite essential for comprehending any particular scientific construal of them.

One of the surprising consequences of realism as presented here is that relativism, epistemologically speaking, must be openly embraced. This is because to believe that real structures themselves exist in the form that current science dictates is to commit the epistemic fallacy, to risk once again reducing reality to our knowledge of it. The history of science, being replete with radical changes in what scientists have regarded as physically necessary, is caution enough to resist this temptation. But further, even the most materialist interpretations of natural necessity must be ultimately *idealist*, in that a particular conceptual construal of reality is isomorphically mapped onto it and declared to be the latter's 'own' internal essence.

For that reason, whilst natural kinds and essential structures can be established as necessary phenomena for science, there can be no definitive attempt to fix once and for all the essential nature of real powers. 'Scientific' realism is therefore not (as it might appear) a view which appeals to a particular state of science in order to justify a particular philosophical standpoint. Rather, its arguments are transcendental in character, being to do with what reality must be like for any science to be possible in the first place. So while realism involves a structural conception of real powers and natures, it cannot sanction, in advance of substantive debate, how those causal mechanisms are to be further described.

As elaborated, the scientific realist approach appears to stand as a major blockage to both radical and pragmatic types of philosophical pluralism. Its full and flowing depiction of things, processes and powers stands in sharp contrast to, for example, Putnam's ontological frailty, which can readily be exploited by more sceptical post-modernists to the point where reality and its rational apprehension are 'bracketed out' entirely. Yet it would be a mistake to see realism as resurrecting objectivism in any absolute sense. Realists accept both the relativity of all knowledge, and the *differentiated* nature of real processes. According to the latter proposition, 'reality' comprises a great many sub-domains of entities and properties. Structured interaction between these domains is a defensible working assumption, but it is not a foregone conclusion. A strategy of reductionism for theorizing relationships between domains is therefore bound to fail, since it violates the principle that a stratified conception of reality demands a range of different, equally valid, levels of abstraction in scientific enquiry.

In other words, scientific realism is not, after all, a defence of 'pure' objectivism against 'mindless' relativism. Nor, with respect to particular domains, can realists support theoretical monism. On the contrary, from a stratified ontology, and from the acceptance of epistemic relativism, only (methodologically) *pluralist* consequences follow. Realism certainly posits a 'depth' unity or system of articulations across the range of causal processes, and this aspect distinguishes it from radical pluralism. In sum, though, realism amounts to an 'integrative pluralist' orientation with respect to the analysis of substantive relationships (Bhaskar 1987: 156).

In spite of its many attractive features, especially with respect to radical pluralism, it can be asked whether realism is distinctively different from pragmatic variants of philosophical pluralism. For example, if relativity is accepted for epistemic categories, it must surely be endorsed for ontological ones too? Realists, we saw, accept that knowledge of real processes is achieved and generated within transient and limited sets of theories. Yet the claim that reality comprises causal powers, generative mechanisms, and so on, is itself a quasi-substantive and contestable proposition. Its plausibility arises in part because of the nature of our current scientific and everyday beliefs, that is, as the generalized outcome of specific sets of values and concepts. Realism, arguably, is as 'trapped' as any other interesting generalization about ultimates. A familiar component of realism, namely the correspondence theory of truth, might be called upon at this juncture to stave off such an objection. It could be proposed that just as our scientific theories can be considered as having truth-value, that is, as corresponding to how things really are, so too can ontological claims which derive from science and experience. However, any appeal to the correspondence theory is ruled out when relativism is incorporated into realism, on the basis that we can never step outside our changing contexts to verify truth-claims in any decisive way. So the saving move – which would regenerate metaphysical or external realism – is, in fact, unavailable.

Another way of endorsing realism has been to say that the successful practice of science is only explicable in terms of the progressive encapsulation of real processes by science. Here too a familiar and impressive relativist 'scissors' effect comes into operation. *Either* the realists' reference to the success of science is framed from the outset in terms of science's increasing 'capturing' of reality, which seems to amount to a 'monumental case of begging the question' in favour of realism (Laudan 1981: 262); *or* the cumulative and fruitful aspects of scientific growth are cited as a basis for realism. The latter criterion, though, cannot amount to definitive support, since scientific development might equally well be explained in terms of, say, puzzle-solving rather than increasing verisimilitude.

Without a correspondence theory of truth, or (perhaps better) a verisimilitude theory of scientific development (Hesse 1974), realism must make appeal solely to the strength of transcendental philosophical argumentation. By their very nature, transcendental arguments are 'absolute' or precon-ditional: they uncover what the world must be like for scientific categories to emerge and to change. Realism, in that sense, like all philosophy, is 'normative' with respect to science (Bhaskar 1987: 15). Yet, clearly, this understanding undermines to an extent the implicit promise given in the label, namely that 'realism' is a modern scientific philosophy rather than a timeless metaphysical one. Moreover, the necessarily absolutist cast of transcendental reasoning again breaks the bounds of relativity, giving philosophical realism a privileged status above the vicissitudes of scientific and substantive debate. Bhaskar is aware that there is a problem here: 'How are the premises of our transcendental enquiries to be selected without already implying an unvalidated commitment to the epistemic (moral, aesthetic etc.) significance of the activities analysed?' (Bhaskar 1987: 14). His solution appears to be the assertion that transcendental categories can be deployed in a 'non-absolute' sense. But this may merely be a terminological escape clause: on the face of it, and without considerable further elaboration, a non-absolutist transcendentalism is a contradiction in terms.

Scientific realism, then, has not managed fully to impose a qualitatively different type of solution on the issues confronted by pragmatic pluralism. Indeed, realists tend to be much more persuasive against the vagaries of anti-realism than they are in elaborating realism as a developed independent standpoint (cf. the realist contributions to Churchland and Hooker 1985). In the end, it may be that realism is best seen precisely as 'immanent critique' rather than offering a complete foundationalism. Before deciding this, a number of outstanding issues will need further exploration by philosophers. Above all, the status of realism as a *representational* theory remains unclear. On the one hand, realists are often to be found making claims about the way in which theories can be said to reveal or refer to (real) generative mechanisms. In this mood, realists are, whatever they may say, committed to some version of the correspondence theory of truth/science. Yet we have also seen that this corollary is sometimes denied. On the other hand, realism can be supported *without* elaborate epistemic justification, for example in terms of its role as part of scientific and everyday *practice*. In this construal, the point is not that realism reflects the essence of science, which in turn reflects the nature of reality; rather, realism requires that all representational theories be treated as derivative from processes of practical *intervention* in the world (Hacking 1983). On the other hand, if *this* plausible option is taken, the much sought-after superiority of realism over pragmatism would have to be given up, since pragmatic pluralism is typically countered by realists by means of tough statements about what the world must be like for our theories to fit it. And these are quintessentially representational claims.

A final consequence of sophisticated scientific realism – and in a sense the most important for our overall purpose – is its relation to concrete social theories. Realists confirm that the objects of social science – people and social relations – differ from those of natural science, and that this difference is a significant one. In particular, there are no systematic experimentation procedures (as in natural science) which artificially recreate the kind of systemic empirical regularities which isolate particular causal mechanisms. Social mechanisms are, in the normal case, opaque and partial: they are tendencies at best. Secondly, realists are concerned to emphasize that social mechanisms and processes may operate at different levels of abstraction. This means that accounts of society which are sometimes seen as competing perspectives on an issue – for example, 'societal' explanations of vandalism as against 'individual' explanations – could well be considered complementary. These explanatory levels do not so much clash as 'nest' into one another (Bhaskar 1987: 157). Thus, realism does not deny, and in fact it positively supports, the idea that a plurality of levels operate in the social domain, and that *within* each level, a number of factors, processes or mechanisms are usually in play. Furthermore, real plurality of this sort entails conceptual pluralism, given the nature of the object and epistemic relativity: no one theory can or should be expected to 'reveal' the complex totality.

Given this 'applied' format for scientific realism, it is no wonder that its version of integrative pluralism has proved attractive to many of the humanistic disciplines (Sayer 1984, Lovell 1980, McLennan 1981). However, we can already speculate that its attractiveness lies precisely in the unusual combination it effects of a weighty ontological vocabulary and a wholly permissive substantive orientation. Of course, as against the idealist and empiricist construal of the purpose of social theories, realism proves to be a persuasive saviour of determinacy. But many very different accounts could be given a realistic rationale, and yet continue to go down the same empirical track as before. Notably, the critical thrust of realism has been deployed for marxist purposes, as might be expected in a tradition which highlights depth explanation and tendential 'laws' of social development. But lately, as the permissiveness of realism's formal constraints have become clearer, some marxists have expressed disappointment with realism's failure to make much difference to concrete ideological or theoretical debate (Harvey et al. 1987).

Within our own field of theories of politics, democracy and the state, realism has also been taken up as setting out some of the necessary conditions for 'adequate' theorizing. An adequate theory, in the general realist terms we have been discussing, involves a working assumption of a structured interrelationship of real causal processes, together with a non-reductionist approach to the concrete phenomena of each causal sequence. One writer, Jeffrey Isaac, suggests that insofar as marxism fulfills those aspirations it can be defended as 'a genuinely scientific theory of power' (Isaac 1987: 9). Empiricist democratic pluralism, it is argued, fails to meet this adequacy condition. The idea that political theory grapples with societal causal powers gives us the basis of depth explanation of human affairs, which cannot be attained by focusing on political decisions alone, or even the hidden immediate constraints on decisions. On the other hand, it is allowed that there may be nothing wrong with conventional pluralist claims, if reformulated in realist fashion; and indeed marxism, in so far as it seeks to establish a definitive monistic account, is certainly not to be regarded as superior to pluralism, either substantively or methodologically (Isaac 1987: 196, 220). Concretely, class relations and the state indicate real causal powers: but these can only be seen as *mutually* interactive chains of determination. The suspicion which arises inexorably in accounts like this is that the defence of the scientific nature of marxism requires that it be significantly pluralized to the point where its role is perceived as just one, albeit 'indispensable' and 'critical', part of the analysis of 'some' forms of domination (Isaac 1987: 230).

Similar conclusions emerge from Bob Jessop's reflections on the state of marxist state theory. Again in this text there is a double-sided emphasis on both integration and plurality. It is almost taken as read, for example, *both* that a satisfactory approach to 'relations among relations' can indeed be established, but that this cannot be founded by 'subsuming' one set of causal powers under any other, in monistic fashion. Rather, a 'method of articulation' needs to be fashioned which will reflect the 'complex synthesis of multiple determinations' (Jessop 1982: 252).

This eminently plausible proposal neatly encapsulates the aspirations of realism in a phrase derived from Marx himself. However, in practice, the fear of 'subsumptionism' has been honed to a very sharp edge by a generation of relativism and anti-reductionism in marxist theory. Accordingly, Jessop's main concern is to get away (1) from a general theory of the state and (2) from a general theory of the capitalist state. Overwhelmingly, the emphasis is on multiple concrete influences in determining state institutions and policies. Once that kind of move into plurality is firmly taken, the overarching sense of synthesis correspondingly fades. Interestingly, the central term here – 'articulation' – is one which seems ambiguously to indicate both linkages and disconnections. Moreover, no 'method' for substantive study, literally speaking, arises from this principle at all, other than an injunction to look out for both differences and connections. Thus, the analysis of the state in capitalist society is held not only, and perhaps not even mainly, to be about how political forms secure the conditions of capital accumulation. Rather, it is about establishing first the range of relevant processes (representation, internal organization, and intervention), then second, examining within each process the range of relevant considerations. For example, in the sub-field of representation, pluralist, corporatist and parliamentarist channels of political significance can be recognized as having some independent force (Jessop 1982: 228–30).

The point here is not to dispute the value of these distinctions, nor the importance of a sense of the articulation between factors. Rather it is to show that 'integrative pluralism' or 'the method of articulation' or a 'complex synthesis of multiple determinations' are heuristic catchwords; they are not in any precise sense the grounds of theoretical adequacy. If they *are* regarded in that way, then a holistic theory such as classical marxism is bound to look 'inadequate' in the face of empirical plurality. Thus, predictably, Jessop reasons that although he has been trying to develop an adequate *marxist* perspective on the state, marxism turns out to be but one 'point of reference' for an adequate account of particular articulations (1982: 228). More generally, the initial search for adequacy in political theory is 'paradoxically' concluded on a 'note of indeterminacy' (1982: 258).

The thrust of this chapter has been to indicate that such a conclusion is far from surprising, given that a considerable part of the philosophical context of substantive theory construction is built around the tension between monistic aspirations for conceptual integration and the pluralist insistence on real diversity. Realism is of considerable value in abstractly indicating the way beyond the aporia of philosophical pragmatism. But its appearance as a systematic theoretical underpinning for social theory is somewhat deceptive, since in practice the persuasiveness of any particular articulation of theoretical generality and concrete complexity has to be taken on its own merits.

In conclusion, we might consider whether that summation is not something of a betrayal of the promise of realism. Surely the connections between realism, as a depth ontology, and marxism, as a systemic account of the shape of modern society, must be stronger and more compelling than the cited pluralistic scenarios for social theory? The implication of this prompt is that marxism, and realism, must be treated in a fully *essentialist* fashion rather than merely formalistically. After all, if realism posits causal powers, attached to natural kinds, as constituting the fundamental structure of reality, then specific investigators of both natural and social domains are committed to establishing just what these fundamental structures amount to. Here, there is no mere 'analogy' between natural forms and social processes: the latter every bit as much as the former exhibit deep (though frustratable) evolutionary tendencies (Meikle

1985: 10). And arguably, marxism is the only social theory which in form and content gives a persuasive rendering of these real processes.

That kind of forceful argument turns the 'scientific realist' position into an essentialist or Aristotelian one, and with that shift the attraction of methodological pluralism rapidly wanes. Similarly, the holistic character of marxism returns to the fore, not now as a reductionist obstacle, but as marxism's central advantage over multi-factorial rivals (Meikle 1985: 150). At this point, of course, an interminable debate about the nature of 'genuine' realism and 'genuine' marxism seems to be on the cards. The formalistic realist positively promotes the conception of real essences and tendential powers, but warns against any premature conclusions as to what 'essentially' these consist of. The markedly idealist consequences of the epistemic fallacy attend any attempt – even an apparently materialistic one – to settle causal essences. The Aristotelian realist can claim in response that scientific analysis demonstrably and ever more closely approximates to the real order of natural (and social) history and that formal 'realists' are really only reverting to Kantianism when they declare *both* their belief in a back-ground world of causal powers, *and* their inability ever to definitively specify it.

In parallel, the formal marxists will emphasize the potentially equivalent impact of counter-tendencies and contingent action upon supposedly fundamental evolutionary patterns in history. Essentialist marxists, by contrast, say that marxism is distinctive only on condition that it boldly affirms the analytic priority of such tendencies. Thus Scott Meikle, for example, singles out as the essential evolutionary process of modern history the growth and passing away of 'the value form', as identified in Marxian economics (Meikle 1985: 65–6). In a sense, the vast array of institutions and contradictions which concern empiricists and pluralists are the effects of this one underlying process. To the pluralistic realist, that kind of monistic claim spells reductionism for any detailed investigation. Given the depth of the philosophical pluralism discussed earlier, the idea that the 'meanderings' of history are explicable only as the 'vehicles' of the realization of the value form (Meikle 1985: 151) can only amount to a resurrection of the God's-eye view, marxist style. It would have to be asked: Why is *that* the necessary 'essence' of history, above all other contenders? Does not *any* categorical assertion of the known essence immediately draw attention away from the real, autonomous impact of those many apparently non-essential phenomena in human history? In other words, marxism, to be, precisely, 'realistic', must theorize rather than obliterate the complexity of causal processes, and the blockages to such processes. Such questions can, of course, be multiplied indefinitely, and the cycle of pluralism and monism re-enacted. Generally speaking, the cycle is unlikely to be broken apodeictically, and it is a notable feature of even scientific realism that it too gives rise to serious internal altercation.

7

ECLECTICISM AND SYNTHESIS IN SOCIAL THEORY

1. A pervasive conundrum

The considerations of the last chapter revealed that there have been significant moves towards a reconciliation between two commonly opposed philosophical stances. However, the persistence of tensions between them was evident too. These tensions rendered problematic the formulation of a satisfactory 'third way' between the poles of the various dichotomies. Usually, one or other of the general orientations (objectivism/relativism) is being argued for, albeit subtly; *or* a more pragmatic, pluralistic attitude is in play. This latter possibility in turn might represent either straightforward ambivalence, *or* a combination of elements of integration and plurality. In all cases, however, the claim that the contrary pull of these familiar epistemological motifs can be regarded as an outmoded metaphysical anxiety cannot be upheld.

A similar predicament, I maintain, confronts much social theory. This is partly because the philosophical issues are encountered within the more substantive debates; it is also due to the fact that specialist philosophy itself (however technical it gets) serves only to iron out the logical shape of general outlooks already in play within the wider culture. The conundrum shared by philosophy of science and social theory is that a pragmatically pluralist attitude to theoretical exchange and competition tends either to be a forerunner of further integrative commitment, or it is a prelude to methodological and metaphysical pluralism in the radical sense. The question of synthesis is therefore both urgent and difficult. The promise of synthesis, we should note, cannot be a matter of hope and assertion. For example, in an attempt to reconcile marxism and post-modernism, Mark Poster has proposed that a dialogue between historical materialism and the concepts of Foucault can advance the task of critical theorists to construct an appropriate analytic response to the 'age of information' (Poster 1984: 164). However, Poster appears to accept at face value the post-modernist characterization of marxism as producing a 'Leviathan of Reason' with 'the labouring subject' as its mythical emblem (1984: 57, 73). Foucault, by contrast, is acknowledged (in his middle phase, anyway) to have almost disavowed the project of social explanation. More specifically, the marxist concepts of the state and mode of production are rejected by Foucault for a vocabulary which highlights instead modes of information. This term refers to the coded practices of knowledge/power which construct relations of domination and resistance around sexuality, bio-politics and mechanisms of surveillance. It involves a decisive shift of substantive focus in Foucault which has its counterpart in a social ontology comprising 'a multiplicity of forces . . . dispersed, discontinuous and unsynchronised' (Poster 1984: 88). But this is Foucault (as Poulantzas (1980: 44) recognized) at his most radically pluralistic, in both political and methodological terms. Historical materialism simply drops out of the picture when this account is taken seriously, and even the proposed object of enquiry (mode of information) mimics marxist categories only in order to disclose them as obsolete. With the best will in the world, to propose a merger between marxism and (Foucauldian) pluralism conceived in this way is clutching at straws. Interestingly, Poster rests content in the end with the unexceptionable expectation that marxists will at least 'heed' the new critical developments (Poster 1984: 164).

A similar problem arises in sympathetic treatments of the exchange between marxism and deconstruction. The latter, Michael Ryan for example argues, is an intrinsically critical discourse, always working for the 'margins' against 'the centre', and so rubbing against the grain of the power relations which become enshrined in the discourses of fixed reason. As such, deconstruction is thought to be egalitarian; it leads to the 'plural diffusion of all forms of macro- and microdomination' (Ryan 1982: 8). Ryan feels that this is the basis for a 'critical articulation' between marxism and deconstruction. However, what is proposed here is once again not much more than the idea that theories which are critical of the status quo, and which share a broadly emancipatory goal, can learn from one another. In order to be hopeful in this regard, the questionable assumption has to be made that 'plural diffusion' can be equated with substantive egalitarianism, and that marxism's historical critique of capitalism is one which can be plausibly translated as a general project with 'marginality' at its heart. As is clear from much of our preceding discussion, though, these assumptions are extremely dubious. Deconstruction provides no internal guarantee against liberal pluralism, and marxism has usually involved more than taking the side of the underdog in any relation of power. Indeed, marxists have often been politically unsympathetic to 'marginal' resistance precisely because of its peripheral position in the long-term mainstream of class struggle. The idea of establishing a low common denominator between competing critical perspectives is reasonable and necessary, it can be agreed. But that project cannot be taken far as an analytical synthesis where marxism is consistently overdrawn as the embodiment of a tyrannical metaphysics, and where deconstruction is perceived as sharply breaking from the holistic logic of social theory.

Perhaps what is required here is a less holistic attitude to the rivalry between competing perspectives. In particular, the notion of alternative sealed and finished conceptual schemes which organize and dictate 'applied' reasoning can itself be challenged as a typical rationalist oversight (Davidson 1973–4). Of course, part of the effect of this point is to indicate that strong relativist positions, ironically, lean upon such fictions, as for example in the assertions of the incommensurability of paradigms, or the sheer otherness of 'other cultures'. An eclectic synthesis, on the other hand, requires to review the various paradigms as stores of concepts and tools which can be drawn from with impunity. That kind of sentiment is common when teachers of social and political theory appraise student needs. Thus Andrew Cox et al. maintain that 'a process of academic interchange' has to go on such that theories of politics must be judged for their *utility* rather than their truth (Cox et al. 1986: 207, 216). We need to move, that is, from an impulse to choose decisively between theories to an approach which emphasizes that each paradigm will be useful, will provide insights, depending on the aspect of the political process we are interested in. The respective strengths and weaknesses of theoretical perspectives can then best be judged by the criteria of, for example, parsimony of explanation, aspiration to comprehensiveness, selection of interesting material and so on. The validity or adequacy of the perspectives, in any ultimate sense, does not arise.

This pedagogic-eclectic standpoint looks very attractive. Yet the (apparently) value-free or commonsensical stance which recommends a blend of perspectives overlooks some important features of theory-construction. Some of the criteria that are declared useful for theoretical assessment, for instance, run against one another. The criterion of parsimony in social science has often been used precisely to *undercut* the aspiration to comprehensiveness. This is indeed the nub of the whole debate around how many *dimensions* the analysis of power should aspire to. Arguably, one-dimensional pluralism wins hands down on parsimony, and four-dimensional marxism takes the prize for comprehensiveness. In other words, there is a potential clash between the classical variants of the two traditions over the very *ranking* of judgemental criteria.

Moreover, the standpoint of 'utility' as a criterion for theory-choice in some ways prefigures the outcome of comparison such that pluralism is bound to look rather stronger than marxism. This is indicated by Cox et al. when they suggest that, at the empirical level of a problem, the most sensitive marxists are really rather like pluralists, maybe with a more turgid theoretical vocabulary (1986: 190). Pluralists are not, however, in turn said to be rather like marxists, but with a *thin* vocabulary, at the level of large-scale processes. This is partly because pluralists, we have seen, seldom go in for statements at that level. Now if we take a utilitarian approach to theory choice, and hold, as these authors do, that the most interesting things about society are its *particular* sectors, problems and issues, then it follows that the attempt to raise questions about the system *as a whole* could well be deemed so much unnecessary functionalist clutter.

It comes as little surprise then, that in this variety of eclectic synthesis, 'pluralism' is recovered rather more sympathetically than marxism. The latter's enduring problem is thought to be its 'monocausal' and 'non-falsifiable' logic (Cox et al. 1986: 190, 223), whilst its best representatives are said to see the state not as functionally connected to capitalism, but as a quite open-ended 'field of political struggle' (1986: 65). In marxism, it seems, the insights which most provide pragmatic utility are precisely those which are closest to substantive pluralism and furthest from the classical 'law-like' statements about the social system.

Beginning from a softening of the paradigms, this assessment has therefore moved rapidly on to the 'hard' depiction of just one of them, namely marxism. And because of the emphasis on synthesis, it now must appear as if marxism is the main obstacle to it. So, if 'monocausality' is a problem, *multi-causality* becomes the natural alternative. If the state is really nothing more definite than a 'field of political struggle', then it is open to the efforts of a range of interest groups struggling to get their voices heard. If theorizing at the level of the system as a whole is not useful, then *connections* between a variety of arenas of political interaction are both contingent and secondary. In short, a 'neutral' methodological eclecticism whereby theory choice is governed by insights, utility and particularity leads precipitously to *substantive* pluralism. Arguably, the seeds of the resolution are planted at the outset in the way the comparison is framed.

More ambitious calls for an eclectic theoretical project share the problems of the pedagogic strategy, and interestingly the onus always seems to fall on marxism rather than pluralism to rid itself of the absolutist features which block a more productive approach to the sociology of politics. The main charge is usually that there are deep logical problems with marxist explanation, problems which lead inevitably to re-ductionism or 'derivationism', whereby politics is granted no real autonomy. Marxism's inadequacy in this respect is held to stem from its relentlessly systemic character, something which intrinsically prohibits a full appreciation of the necessary plurality of particular 'aspirations, ideologies and ways of life' (Pierson 1986: 150). Developing this approach, as a prelude to some rigorous critical argumentation, Jean L. Cohen writes:

> [Marxism] is unable to provide the exclusive referent for an alternative vision of society or even for the dynamics of contestation and transformation in the present. More significant, the Marxian concepts of class, totality, system and history cannot serve as the standpoint from which to unify, theoretically and practically, the plurality of social struggles and movements in contemporary society. (Cohen 1983: xii)

Such firm tones of rejection seem to point inexorably to pluralism in the positive sense, and not the half-way house of eclecticism, though the latter is in fact the aim of the critique.

What is striking about this kind of protest is its exact repetition of arguments produced by the Popperian generation of critics of marxism (Popper 1962, Acton 1955, Mayo 1955), who are to be respected for at least consistently seeking the *victory* of pluralism over marxism. Modern commentators such as Cohen and Pierson, by contrast, are reluctant to take this path. They do seem to want to hang on to that in marxism which remains positive and worthwhile. It appears, for example, that, after all, Marx provided a 'peerless' critique of liberal ideology, and that he laid out an 'unsurpassed model for critical thinking' (Cohen 1983: xiii). Similarly, it is acknowledged that 'classical Marxism is not, in fact, premised upon the suppression of a genuine plurality of interests' (Pierson 1986: 189). But if these assertions are made in good faith, the uncompromising character of the eclectic-pluralist critique of the classical model is considerably overstated. The aim of the model recognized as 'unsurpassed' is precisely to facilitate depth analysis across empirical variety in order to establish the broad shaping forces of modern society. The concrete specificity of particular objects and forces is not at all obliterated, but their significance is firmly embedded in wider structural processes. 'Derivationism' might well be an ever-present *danger* in this kind of search for explanatory comprehensiveness, but as long as large-scale theory is thought to be valuable at all, reductionism cannot be its necessary outcome. And the critics do often concede in the by-lines that marxism can, with care, appreciate plurality.

There is thus a marked ambivalence in the texts of sympathetic eclectic critics of marxism. Certainly the rhetorical oscillation between total critique and partial recovery is sufficient to diminish the coherence of their own positive standpoint. Cohen, for example, posits the urgent need politically to 'articulate' an institutional domain in which the plural forces of party, union, movement, reform, and self-expression can be reconciled, whilst retaining their many differences (Cohen 1983: 227). Pierson, for his part, rightly acknowledges that such 'advances' in theory as this are essentially programmatic, and in a sense they are *bound* to remain that way, since eclectic insights inevitably entail 'a general loss of the explanatory comprehensiveness which has ever been one of Marxism's most theoretically appealing features' (Pierson 1986: 150). At such moments eclectic theorists might be better advised to declare their perplexity. Instead, hopes and expectations are generated about the desirability and availability of a synthetic resolution to the debate which tend to go unfulfilled.

2. A structurationist synthesis

It should not be thought that in criticizing eclecticism I am recommending that no effort be put into developing new synthetic *attitudes*, even where genuinely novel synthetic *concepts* appear unforthcoming. Rather, the point is to encourage a sense of the depth of the traditional theories and a sense of the difficulty of providing an eclectic perspective which is not also an expression of sheer ambivalence. One of the most impressive attempts to achieve a theoretical synthesis of the relevant type, one which operates right across all the levels of analysis in social theory, is the 'structurationist' perspective developed by Anthony Giddens. Part of the rationale for developing this perspective has been Giddens's belief that 'there are no easy dividing-lines to be drawn between

Marxism and "bourgeois social theory"' (Giddens 1979: 1). Giddens thinks it important to recognize the strengths of these existing traditions (with the probable exception of their functionalist components), but there is a great need, he suggests, to begin to mine a new vein in critical theory (Giddens 1982a: 64). The process of critique is central here, and Giddens has been preoccupied with developing a contemporary critique of historical materialism (Giddens 1981, 1985) as a preface to, or perhaps as a negative form of, the positive framing of structurationism.

This kind of perspective seeks deliberately to blur any clear distinction between ad hoc eclecticism and a considered middle ground or advanced synthetic resolution. This is a good thing, in that it reveals (if such a reminder were needed) that new ideas seldom arrive by way of sudden revelation. By the same token, however, *œuvres* which try to secure a fluid transition between critique and a novel set of categories often continue to bear the trace of the pervasive dilemmas or dichotomies which they seek to overcome. Overall, this is the conclusion I will develop in describing Giddens's valuable exploration of the middle ground.

Beginning from a positive evaluation of Marx's legacy, Giddens regards as crucial and correct Marx's conception of capitalism as structured and riven by class relations. Capitalism is intrinsically a class society, for Giddens, because only in capitalism does the appropriation of material surplus, through the sale of labour power as a commodity, form the central source of social division. The peculiar dynamic of the capitalist forces of production is crucial in understanding how class relations and class conflict take on a particularly vital role in the social life of modern times. More generally, Giddens has a certain temperamental or methodological sympathy for the way in which Marx uses social theory to inform his conception of political struggle. At his best, Marx develops an indispensable sense of human and class agency – of *praxis* (Giddens 1981: 2, 1984: 242) – which preserves the idea that people *can* become conscious of their situation, then act to change it, even when that situation involves weighty structural constraints which are apparently beyond their immediate control.

The qualification 'at his best' is significant, however.

Giddens shares with other critics the belief that Marx's theory of history is essentially an evolutionary model, in which the productive forces are primary, and that this dramatically undercuts a proper focus on human and social agency. For Giddens, *all* evolutionary schemas are dubiously functionalist and teleological in this way. That is, they involve propositions about what human outcomes are beneficial to the social system as a whole, and posit those effects as the very rationale for social change. This functionalist approach diminishes the sense in which human struggles, motives and actions determine how a 'system' muddles through in the first place. In fact, systems as such simply do not have needs or beneficial consequences.

In Giddens's terms, human agents are always *knowledgeable* about the social structures in which they operate: the latter do not operate 'behind the backs' of their creatures (Giddens 1979: 71). Evolutionary schemas are by contrast teleological, not merely because of their functional construal of outcomes, but because a logical series of particular outcomes is imagined, one composed of necessary stages towards an ultimate end-point for history as a whole. In spite of the emphasis on class struggle in Marx's life and work, historical materialism constitutes just such a 'stageist' theory of history in which the various component epochs are treated as progressive fore-runners for communism. For Marx, real history – the autonomous and co-operative self-direction of 'full' human individuals – *begins* with communism. For Giddens, this kind of view is demeaning towards the agents and struggles of present and past stages of 'pre-history', and it rigorously disregards the reflexive character of everyday practice. To correct this imbalance requires a perspective in which historical change is seen as considerably more open-ended.

On the other hand, when marxists do invoke agency in history, it is invariably class agency they refer to. For Giddens, this is plausible for capitalism, but not for societies prior to the modern era. The latter are class-divided, in that they frequently display pervasive material inequalities, but they are not intrinsically *class* societies, because the mechanisms of material production are not primary in establishing social distinctions and identities; *allocative* resources, to use Giddens's terms, do not have priority over *authoritative* resources (Giddens 1981: 4–5, 1984: 258).

Further, and crucially, Giddens regards marxism as nearly blind to major social forces and principles of causality other than class. Ethnic and gender divisions, for example. Also, marxism fails fully to appreciate the massive historical influence of war and violence in the character and development of modern civilization. Its reductionist approach to the *state* is especially important here, in that the forms of power storage and surveillance techniques available to nation states are only tangentially connected to questions of economic reproduction. The state has to be acknowledged simply as 'the purveyor of violence', a feature which in the contemporary world system has reached a 'terrifying peak' (Giddens 1982: 229). What more urgent reason is needed to critically review what marxism tends to *leave out* in its historical analysis?

Giddens squares up more than most contemporary critics of historical materialism to the implications of these charges, namely the onus on the critic to suggest a coherent alternative. Is it possible, in other words, to offer a more compelling perspective, one which does justice to Marx's insights, while more adequately theorizing the problems identified? The challenge is of course heightened by Giddens's appreciation that Marx's analytic vision operates at a number of levels of abstraction: from a general theory of human nature and social motivation, through a conception and outline of historical development, to a specific political diagnosis for the transcendence of capitalist structures. One of the relevant issues here (in the light of the post-modernist critique) is whether that extraordinary range of theorizing can any longer be expected to gell into a substantive theoretical 'system'. Giddens for his part does grasp this nettle, attempting to offer alternatives at each of these levels in the shape of the theory of structuration and a critical pluralist analytic framework for politics.

Giddens's intervention in the debates about how social interaction should be conceptualized does not stem solely from his worries about marxism. Rather he is concerned with the more general tendency for social philosophies to divide into two incompatible standpoints. These are, first, an objectivist or naturalist one which insists upon regarding human agents as the creatures of broader social forces. By and large, he thinks, most variants of marxism – functionalist, structuralist, positivist – come under this head. The major problem with structuralists is their tendency to see social systems as working 'behind the backs' of human actors, who are conceived as little more than 'dopes' for that reason (Giddens 1979: 52). On the contrary, Giddens insists, agents are knowledgeable and skilful actors whose practices *constitute* systems. Structures do operate, but only 'virtually': they have no existence outside of practice (1981: 26).

A second tradition in the human sciences regards human agency as entirely a matter of intentional plans and conscious reflection. This hermeneutic tendency has included some marxists for whom consciousness, struggle and vision are the major forces of hope and change. Against these appreciative or voluntarist currents, Giddens points out that subjective meanings and intentions become sedimented in institutions that become embedded in enduring spatio-temporal forms. Actions are always *situated* and involve supra-individual causes and effects as various as the unconscious processes of the individual psyche (1984: 49, 282) and the global institutional forces just alluded to. None of this is to deny agency, for Giddens, but voluntarist philosophies are one-dimensional in their conception of action. What is needed by way of correction is a stratified model, one which highlights the *unanticipated conditions* of action, and its *unintended consequences* (1979: 56).

Giddens therefore regards this logical opposition between structuralism and voluntarism as useless for proper social analysis. Instead, he proposes a concept of structuration in which the dualism of structure and agency is replaced by a duality: the double-sided process in which social practice constitutes the objective conditions which in turn constrain subjective action. This notion of 'duality of structure' is a central feature in Giddens's perspective, but it is also a slippery one, often presented in a rather loose and inconclusive way. For example, in one place, duality of structure appears as just one of ten elements in the theory of structuration (Giddens 1981: 27). Duality of structure is defined there as 'the essentially recursive nature of social practices. Structure is both the medium and outcome of the practices which constitute social systems'. In another place, duality of structure in the same sense is held to be one particularly 'essential' element of, or 'crucial move' in structuration (1981: 19, 1982: 10). In a third nuance, Giddens sees duality of structure not so much as an *element* in structuration, but as being 'logically implied' in the latter's various aims and rationale (1984: 25). One might even wonder whether there is any difference at all between structuration theory itself and the principle of the duality of structure. Indeed, Giddens never quite clarifies this basic query. He does gesture towards a solution by indicating that duality of structure forms an overall conception of social practice which the theory of structuration then converts into a heuristic for the substantive study of particular societies (Giddens 1984: 376). Yet that proposal looks weak again when structuration is defined in the most abstract and, it has to be said, fairly banal terms, as in this encapsulation: 'According to the theory of structuration, all social action consists of social practices, situated in time-space, and organized in a skilled and knowledgeable way by human agents' (1982: 9). More concretely, structuration is drawn up as referring to the *way* in which social practices become concretely established through the operation and interaction of *rules and resources* (1984: 25). 'Rules' refer to forms of signification/communication, and to normative principles. Resources are either allocative (material) or authoritative (social, organizational). These notions begin to look less abstract than the general conception of action.

Before considering them, it is worth remarking that the *meaning* of 'duality of structure', as well as its place in the substantive theory, is problematical. Giddens, of course, sees a dua*lism* as a schism between opposites, whereas his own conception of a 'duality' is intended to be more fluid and dialectical. But often in philosophical reasoning the very coinage of new terms, when set against the alleged polarities erected in discredited theories, is taken as sufficient to register an 'advance' in virtue of the very framing of the problem and solution. This philosophical tactic is, to be sure, one that every social theorist has occasion to adopt, but it may not be enough to vindicate the succeeding vocabulary. In that spirit, we need to ask what is it, exactly, that distinguishes a dualism from a duality, other than the assertion that they are indeed quite distinct? Perhaps the answer is that the understanding of the main problem in the new theory is notably different from that in the old. Yet in the case of the agency-structure issue, this appears not to be the case. Giddens in fact expresses some fairly orthodox 'subjectivist' sentiments, as for example in his many existential-sounding references to the fragility and finitude of being, or to the idea that the self-consciousness and knowledgeability of agents *always* makes a crucial difference to a social situation. Indeed, his insistence on the structural character of 'unintended consequences' and 'unanticipated conditions' looks to be compromised in such affirmations. This is especially so when the nature of *practice* is depicted not so much as collective struggle as the individual monitoring of interaction (cf. Urry 1982).

By comparison, Giddens hesitates over traditional 'objectivist' accounts. For instance, he acknowledges, but certainly does not accord parity to, the structural considerations generated by psychoanalytic and semiotic theory in the conception of the social individual. The main impression is rather that in the face of a barrage of literature aimed to 'decentre' the human subject, Giddens (rightly or wrongly) holds on to a fairly orthodox humanist notion of the conscious, rational self. In these interpretations, the aptness of the term duality of *structure* is doubtful. There is something strange in any case about a 'duality' which only has one term: in practice Giddens is usually dealing with structure-and-agency. But arguably the effective emphasis in his work is primarily and increasingly *agency*, or at least it is concerned to stress how partial specific sorts of structural constraints actually are. In earlier versions of his perspective, Giddens seemed content to regard structuration as those 'processes whereby "economic classes" become "social classes", and whereby the latter are related to other social forms' (Giddens 1973: 105). Later, however – and especially in the wake of his critique of historical materialism – this point of departure looks once again too structural, and Giddens is now reluctant to specify any substantive constraints at the general level of the theory of action. Understandably, this move is partly designed to prohibit the development of an a priori philosophy of social determination. However, that withdrawal does work to reinforce the feeling that 'duality of structure' is little more than a negative injunction (No structure without agency!) with the weight – if anything – on the voluntarist side.

In the more applied reaches of structuration theory, the problem of conceptual clarity reappears. The notion of the social 'rules' which agents follow is particularly slippery and in some ways unsatisfactory, as Giddens in fact allows (1979: 64, 69). The term suggests several contrasting meanings, one of which is Wittgensteinian: all social meaning is a matter of rule-governed behaviour. Another is the idea of prevalent social sanctions and moral norms. Yet another is the specific expectations that particular regimes of social interaction demand. None of these possibilities quite captures what Giddens has in mind, for again he does not seek to define rules as existing outside the practices which they regulate and from which they are generated. Giddens sees the citation of rules as that analytic strand of structuration which emphasizes the importance of meanings, significance and sanctions of agents as embodied in definite *procedures* (Giddens 1984: 18–20).

Procedural rules are bound up with the resources they govern/reflect. Giddens treats resources as of two kinds, authoritative and allocative. One of his main criticisms of Marx is that in historical materialism, allocative resources are given unconditional primacy. For Giddens, it is only in class societies (capitalism) that the 'dominion of human beings over the natural world' takes precedence over 'dominion over the social worlds itself' (1981: 4). Arguably, a misleading characterization of Marx's theory at this juncture has led Giddens into a dilemma of his own. For it seems as though Giddens has *reproduced* a division akin to Marx's own distinction between productive forces and social relations. We saw in chapter 4 that the question of how far such a rigid division reflects Marx's considered analytical practice has been hotly disputed. There is at least a strong case for thinking that Marx did not hold productive forces to be a purely technical or material set, outside of, and determining social relations. In straightforwardly reversing Marx's supposed priorities for pre-capitalist society, however, Giddens effectively reproduces the same formal structure, since it still looks as though allocative resources are 'purely' material and technical, leaving all the human aspect of domination in the category of authoritative relations. This seems especially problematic, given that Giddens places techniques of surveillance, spatial organization, and the physical means of information storage amongst authoritative resources *rather than* allocative resources. Perhaps influenced by the force of this kind of point, Giddens has lately refined the question of social domination as pertaining to the necessary *interweaving* of authoritative and allocative resources (1985: 8). The catch with this more flexible understanding, of course, is that it looks like a recipe for a wholly open-ended analysis of history, not an alternative social *theory* to marxism. If there are no prime movers in history, Giddens writes, 'the problem for social analysis becomes that of examining a variety of relations between allocative and authoritative resources in the constitution of social systems and in the dynamics of social change' (Giddens 1985: 8).

This formulation requires further reflection. With regard to the constitution of the capitalist social system, Giddens's initially generous concession to Marx on the transformative centrality of class forces and productive power causes an element of analytic uncertainty in his own developed project. It is true, Giddens continues to defend the 'centrality' of class to the analysis of capitalism. Yet when the theory of structuration is built up in conjunction with the critique of historical materialism, it is plain that Giddens thinks Marx's focus on class is far too restrictive, even in the case of capitalism. The rules and resources (and therefore structures) which agents draw upon and which constitute societies are after all extremely various. Aspects of surveillance, normative belief, ethnic and gender domination are 'authoritative' questions just as important as, and not reducible to, those of class. Ecological and military patterns especially involve resources in a logic of allocation which to a considerable extent cuts against that of capitalist productivity. The interaction of both types of resource generates a matrix of power which, even in capitalism – perhaps *above all* in the modern era – cannot adequately be treated in the marxist rubric of the primacy of production. It turns out, then, that Giddens must withdraw his one initial and unreserved plank of support for marxism. Neither in terms of the constitution of society, nor in the dynamic of modern capitalism is marxism defensible.

In *The Nation State and Violence*, Giddens expounds an analysis based on four relatively autonomous 'institutional axes of modernity' (1985: 338) and this comes as close as anything to date to a substantive alternative. These are, briefly, the dimensions of capitalism, industrialism, surveillance, and the centralization of the means of violence. Each strand has a specific social logic or domain, and generates a specific set of political claims and campaigns. Thus, industrialization concerns the transformation of nature, leads to a series of ecological movements, and involves a discursive context of moral rights and humanist priorities. Surveillance procedures are to do with the control of social space and information, giving rise to democratic movements which operate in the discursive arena of the political rights of the citizen/subject. The domain of private property and profits gives rise to class and labour movements with economic identities and outcomes at stake. Military violence dominates our modern sense of social order and peace, requiring intensive rethinking and campaigning around issues of general civil rights. Giddens is reluctant to give up the claim that class is central to capitalist society (1984: 162) but it seems plain that class relationships, while significant, cannot be 'central' in the sense of primary *over* other fundamental domains (1985: 318). Indeed, Giddens again notes that quite a list of social movements now needs to be incorporated: for example, nationalist, women's, ethnic, religious, student and consumer movements (1985: 318, 1982a: 67). That scale of inclusion will probably require the conceptualization of many parallel domains, movements, and discursive foci, to the four axes already highlighted. In general, the view of society now explored by Giddens is not so much a phase of *capitalism*, but rather of a much looser social totality, namely, civilization or 'modernity', only one major axis of which is the economic and class structure.

This series of elaborations of the relevant rules and resources of modern society is manifestly of a *pluralist* nature. It is pluralist in the analytic sense of accepting the equal causal weight of separate social spheres which require an autonomous theorization. This makes any 'global' analysis essentially one of juxtaposing and summating the different axes, not of theorizing an integrated or stratified hierarchy of social conditions and dynamics. It is pluralist in the political sense too, in that the various movements arising from the several dimensions of conflict have equally valid concerns which may be directed towards quite different parts of the dominant social order. Indeed, this latter phrase could well be regarded as illegitimate and metaphorical, since the theorization of the 'order' in question will depend very much upon which 'axis' of structures and demands it is being rotated around.

Giddens continues to be interested in analysing system transformation on a broad canvas, but this cannot be done via the kind of historical teleology he claims marxism resorts to. He is keen to record and reconstruct the ways in which societies develop, so the 'shape' of society over time is crucial to the broad sense of the process of structuration. But Giddens is interested as much in discontinuity as in progression, and he initiates a series of dramatic neologisms to capture the dynamic potency of those spatio-temporal locations which best convey the openness of change. Thus the transformation process in particular times and places constitutes an 'episode' rather than a grand scale 'transition' between pre-set stages of civilization. Similarly, the clash between different configurations of authoritative/allocative resources takes place along 'time-space' edges.

3. Functions and foundations

Overall, then, it is clear that whilst Giddens's synthetic enterprise has a bold architecture and ambition, it is oriented distinctly towards contingency and plurality. To criticize it effectively requires pointing up its many loose ends and conceptual ambiguities, as already indicated. It also requires stating that even in Giddens's hands, the sympathetic critique of historical materialism shades off into caricature, especially with regard to the accusations of reductionism and functionalism. Reductionism, to repeat, is an ever present danger in determinate social explanation, and marxists surely commit their share of the tendency to diminish complexity for the sake of a pre-established analytic priority. This does not mean, though, that the structure of marxist explanation *rules out* complexity, unless 'complexity' is simply equated with indeterminacy. Such an equation is as dogmatic as determinism itself.

Another form of the charge of reductionism or essentialism takes the shape of a critique of functionalist argument in general and in marxism. We saw in chapter 3 that the relationship between functional explanation and causal elaboration was central to the plausibility of historical materialism, but also that it was complicated. In fact, for all its familiarity, the question of functionalism must rank as one of the most important 'live' issues in the philosophy of social understanding. Giddens and other critics of functionalism and 'evolutionism' (which tends to rely on functional claims) foreclose on some difficult and unresolved problems in this area by focusing on three notorious weaknesses in functionalist theory.

These three drawbacks are that functionalism encourages sloppy thinking; that it is 'teleological'; and that it has conservative implications in playing down human agency for the sake of emphasizing the stabilizing forces at work on behalf of the entire social system. Generally, the illusion of functionalism is to treat society as if it were a natural organism. Now it is certainly the case that functional reasoning can be deployed in a manner which is dubiously self-fulfilling. In looking at social phenomena from the point of view of their role in facilitating a wider network of relations, we are easily led to treat the posited 'goal' of the system as necessary rather than possible, and to regard the phenomenon in focus as always successfully *meeting* the needs of the system. Moreover, the function which the phenomenon is alleged to serve can be mistakenly read as the chief reason for its coming into being in the first place.

This can be witnessed in some prominent marxist accounts of the state, as for example when Ralph Miliband asserts that 'the state's purpose has always been unambiguous, namely to help capitalist enterprise to prosper' (Miliband 1982: 95). This kind of statement implies (1) that there is an inherent and operative tendency for capitalism to reproduce itself, (2) that the state's overriding rationale lies in achieving this, (3) that it succeeds in its task, (4) that social systems (and, derivatively, institutions) have needs and goals, and (5) that individuals and groups whose decisions affect how the state operates have the same 'purposes' as it does. Each one of these implications is fallacious, stated as such, as is the logic which links them. As a means of guarding against this seductive but fallacious process of explanation, it is sometimes suggested by empiricists that proper social scientific accounts can take only two forms. The first is intentional explanations in terms of agents' motives (which can and must be 'teleological'); the second is the causal analysis of institutional effects, perceived and testable as delimited empirical particularities.

But something important is lost in the elimination of holistic functional propositions, not least that which motivates much of Giddens's own large-scale ideas: the sense that a properly *structural* account of social forces must look at the unintended consequences of action, and the enduring but not always empirically manifest tendencies which differentiate the possible types of society. It is worthwhile, therefore, to try to distinguish between valid or illuminating functional propositions and the dubiously self-fulfilling ones. In this light, the blanket condemnation of functionalism ultimately obscures more than it reveals. Unfortunately, Giddens's proclamation of a new 'post-evolutionary' perspective in social theory encourages just such an all-purpose condemnation.

We should note in this context that even from a neo-empiricist standpoint, the main accusations against functionalism (that it is necessarily a 'static' mode of thinking, or that it involves an inappropriate biologistic analogy) cannot be made to stick (cf. Nagel 1961: 531–3). As long as certain conditions for well-formed hypotheses are met, then functional explanations can take their rightful place alongside straightforward causal ones. For example, the identification of the function of a social item should refer to the properties of a 'system' which is smaller in scale than human society as a whole. In other words, the *context* of functional claims has to be clearly delimited. Secondly, respectable functional explanation cannot be teleological in the sense referred to, i.e. assuming a natural, necessary end point (but then natural evolutionary theory is not teleological in that sense either).

Thirdly, the specific functions posited cannot be regarded in advance as the *only* ways in which a goal or effect might be achieved. Fourthly, the very *sense* of the term 'function' needs to be carefully specified: it can amongst other things refer to relationships of mutual dependency between variables, or to the use to which a social item is put, or to particular contributions towards the operation and maintenance of a wider set of social relations, etc. Moreover, the functional qualities of a state of affairs can be either intended or unintended by the people affected. It follows from this array of criteria that 'functionalism is not a unitary and clearly articulated perspective in social enquiry' (Nagel 1961: 526). It also follows that particular functional explanations can be valid and valuable, especially when, in accordance with those guidelines, the very existence or explanatory primacy of some feature within a set of social relations is shown (or suggested) to be due to its functional facilitation of that set, or a crucial sub-set within it.

Returning to the marxist example in this light, the apparently small changes in formulation which mark Miliband's perspective from that of, say, Fred Block (1977), turn out to be all-important. Whilst Miliband's assertions appear to be dubiously sweeping, Block's rendering of the thesis that the state in capitalist society serves to reproduce the latter's characteristic tendencies is suitably tempered. The intentions of both capitalist owners and state officials are allowed to be various, and the service provided by the state for capital is thought to be neither inevitable nor exhaustive of the state's tasks. All the same, both the rash and the credible versions are organized around a functional generalization.

Whether functional explanations of this kind turn out to be persuasive or not will depend greatly on the extent to which they fulfil 'normal' criteria of empirical evidence and theoretical rigour. Indeed, it is interesting that empiricist and realist philosophers alike are keen to say that functional explanations are basically no different from causal ones. The principal objection to functional explanation is that the current existence of something seems to get explained by its later (contingent) consequences, and this is agreed by all to be impossible. However, this objection by no means dispenses with functions since functional explanation is a kind of gloss on hypotheses about the dispositional properties or powers of the phenomena in question (Bhaskar 1987: 142–3). As in the case of historical materialism, functional statements will be valid to the extent that the mechanisms in virtue of which the consequential functions are held to operate can be demonstrated to exist. If such mechanisms in functional contexts can be shown to be 'persistent features' of social relations (van Parijs 1981: 48–9), no mysterious 'backward causation' arises after all.

G. A. Cohen, it will be recalled, tentatively held to the view that functional explanations could be regarded as legitimate even in the absence of full causal elaborations. The exact import of Cohen's stance here is not clear, but this point could be taken as a note of caution in the face of this 'causalist' re-interpretation. *Is* it the case, we might ask, that a functional proposition can be construed entirely without loss as a causal account? After all, when we seek to diagnose the function of the state in capitalist society, we are not asking directly about how it came into being or how we can be sure that the posited function is secured, even though at some point along the line those (causal) questions will undoubtedly arise. In other words, the *defence* of functional explanation may well require *reference* to causal properties and sequences, but the type of explanation in play under each head remains to some degree qualitatively different. To ask about the *significance* (role, beneficial consequences) of an item in its wider context has an independent interpretive value, which is related to the fact that explanation is itself a pragmatic and human process, one which lends itself to a number of different (though related) 'aspects' (Achinstein 1983). The functional is arguably one *sui generis* explanatory aspect in this sense.

Finally, on this issue, we need to remember that although explanation in terms of causal powers seems to strive for objective 'adequacy', it is an epistemic fact that the ascription of cognitive adequacy to theories is revisable, not only according to further information but to changing criteria about what constitutes adequacy. So in practice, the dividing lines between 'adequate', 'legitimate-provisional', and merely 'speculative' causal explanations are sometimes hard to see, and are usually constructed retrospectively. The feeling that functional explanations without full causal elaboration close at hand are somehow less 'solid' than causal explanations themselves may thus be deceptive.

Clearly, much philosophical work remains to be done on these questions. For our purposes, the main upshot is that writers who brush off the idea of functionalism at an early stage in the proceedings run the risk of oversimplifying the issues, and of downplaying the important functional element in accounts of social significance. To the extent that Giddens falls into this category, he works against many of his own insights. For example, although he points out the dangers of scientism in the theory of ideology, Giddens ascertains the impact of the 'ideological aspects of symbolic orders' according to the extent to which they 'legitimate the sectional interests of hegemonic groups' (Giddens 1979: 188). From here it is but a short step to the perfectly reasonable functional proposition that the existence/persistence of certain types of belief system will tend to depend upon their suitability for the expression of dominant interests. One can of course further 'particularize' the contents of this proposition, and it will need careful research to establish, but its identity as a species of functional rather than causal-historical explanation seems obvious.

More generally, Giddens has much to say about the unintended consequences of action and about the institutional configurations they sustain. Similarly, some of Giddens's novel thinking about the *longue durée* of modern society is of an evolutionary nature. As Erik Olin Wright has pointed out, Giddens's idea that there has been a progressive 'space-time distanciation' in social relationships can be considered as a (non-teleological, retrospective) evolutionary proposition about the enhanced 'ability of people in a society to control allocative and authoritative resources in time and space for use in power relations' (Wright 1983: 30). Once a given level of distanciation is achieved, the account implies, a host of routines, ambitions and constraints are set in motion which make a reversion to the previous level extremely unlikely, other things being equal. This logistical and political nexus produces systemic tendencies, the functioning of which necessarily constrains a host of more ephemeral practices. The latter, in that case, can validly be explained by their part in

sustaining those structural tendencies of time-space distanciation.

The issue of functionalism is thus left unresolved by
Giddens, in spite of his efforts to suppress it. We saw that in
the course of the argument, the epistemological status of causal
and functional theories becomes a central focus. The last major
source of difficulty in deciding the value of the structurationist
synthesis that I wish to deal with is Giddens's general
oscillation over the nature of its epistemological bearings. This
question is conveniently encapsulated in the intriguing 1982
symposium involving Giddens and some commentators on his
work. In that exchange, Giddens expresses considerable
uncertainty about how, philosophically, to characterize the
kind of theorizing he engages in. On the one hand, parts of his
work show an inclination to realist epistemological tenets. He
believes for example that there are objective structures and
occurrences which are ascertainable through social science.
Indeed, in a nod to the virtues of positivism, Giddens has
stated that the 'facts' of the matter can be decisive in resolving
theoretical disputes. This is perhaps best taken as an anti-
relativist point about the commensurability of paradigms
(1982a: 74, 1979: 63). His invitation to see a greater sense of
'dialogue' between the ontological realm and that of theoretical
apprehension similarly belongs to a broad realist tradition, as
does his long-standing belief in the need to carve out a track
between empiricism and interpretive methods. More generally,
Giddens remarks on the 'futility' of trying to ignore or
obliterate the pertinence of epistemological foundations, as
evidenced in some positivist as well as deconstructionist
circles.

At the same time, though, Giddens is wary of the dangers of
an *overly* epistemological framework. This caution expresses
itself as a doubt about whether 'foundations' ever *can* be
established, even at the broadest level. He therefore rejects any
'firm' grounding for theory, favouring the idea of a 'multiplicity
of readings', and the overall tenor of his symposium reprise is
distinctly deconstructionist (1982b: 107). The tendency to want
to have it both ways enters Giddens's philosophical thinking
here just as it pervades his more substantive concepts. He is
not willing to support attempts to provide a 'grounding' for

theory, but nor will he support the claim that critical theory is ungroundable (1982a: 72). Yet this kind of vacillation, while entirely understandable, is probably not tenable in such an intuitive form. One is tempted to say: either theory is groundable or it is not. Either there are multiple readings with equally valid things to say (because 'reality' itself is a construction), *or* theory must aspire to the kind of substantive coherence which will be adequate to how things are in the world.

As a way of approaching the middle ground on which he stands, Giddens describes his work as 'firing critical salvoes into reality' (1982a: 72). This slogan is more cryptic than suggestive, and rather evasive too. What is the reality in question, and from what basis are the shots despatched? We have seen how structuration theory offers the promise of a substantive set of propositions, yet remains curiously formal: arguably, it is an approach to, or set of guidelines for, thinking about society, not a theory of society. Giddens gives relatively few recipes as to how to conceptualize under the banner of structuration, but one of them is that we should always seek 'a counterfactual conception of what people would know if they were in the circumstances that you're in' (1982a: 72). This idea too falls apart when probed closely. In the first place, the dictum seems unduly focused on the self-consciousness of subjects. Secondly, there is an uneasy circularity in play: if people really were to be conceived as in a position to know what I, in my position, know (and we may not even know how to characterize *that* adequately), then they would not, *ex hypothesi*, be in the specific relations and circumstances we want to analyse.

The methodological and substantive vagueness of structuration is exemplified when Giddens, in *The Constitution of Society*, examines some concrete research projects that he thinks conform to the 'main empirical implications of structuration theory' (1984: 289). High on the list is Paul Willis's *Learning to Labour* (1977). After some considerable time spent summarizing this text and others, however, what emerges as crucial is once more the duality of structure, translated into an injunction: in social science we cannot afford to treat structures without subjective understanding, nor analyse consciousness outside of social constraints. To that extent, granted, Willis's book certainly 'conforms' to structurationist principles. But it might also be thought to conform (and in the intention of its author it conforms more directly) to the investigative principles of a sensitive historical materialism. Interestingly, Willis none the less acknowledges finding it hard to escape methodological dualism in his search for a satisfactory blend of subjective and objective factors. This is embodied in the sharp difference in level and tone between the first (ethnographic) section of his key work and the later (theoretical) reflections. The point is, then, that whether cast as structurationist or (pluralistic) marxist, an appeal to important research of this sort does not in itself resolve the general tensions we have been concerned with.

From such reflections the question arises, how far is Giddens's work an apparatus of critique and suggestion, and how far is it a positive synthetic enterprise in its own right based on distinctive and productive concepts? From my discussion it will be clear that I prefer the former interpretation, and this hunch is confirmed first by Giddens's indecisive statements concerning the scope and role of social theory, and secondly by his expressed wish to produce useful concepts for substantive analyses rather than large-scale generalizations of a propositional kind (1984: xviii). Where his explanatory concepts *do* result in substantive propositions, they tend to be of the sort I have characterized as methodologically and sociologically pluralist. It is the supposedly monological traits of evolutionary schemas which disturb Giddens as much as their tendency to underplay agency. And it is the *range* of important general social mechanisms and divisions which strike him as important, and which renders classical marxism unsustainable as a general theory.

Nevertheless, it is equally important not to treat Giddens's work as conventionally pluralist. Philosophically, his temptation to endorse multiple readings on the one hand, is countered by the affirmation of realism on the other. Substantively, he is reluctant even in the later texts to say, sociologically, that class is just one autonomous 'factor' amongst others in the analysis of modernity. Indeed, there is no reason to think that his early trenchant critique of the Weberian brand of pluralism, in which Giddens pours scorn on the tendency endlessly to proliferate significant social divisions and differences, is any less valid for him now (1973: 103). The main feature of *The Nation State and Violence* is the effort to establish four or five central causal clusters in the modern world. The feeling continues to hover, indeed, that there ought to be a way of reintegrating these dimensions. After all, it is plausible to regard our current destinies as shaped by the *combination* of capitalism, industrialism, and the nation state system (1985: 5), and this cannot be adequately theorized in a merely additive, factorial way. In sum, we do not find in Giddens's work an advanced resolution to the debate between marxism and pluralism, either at a metatheoretical level or substantively. But his sensitivity to the difficulties of overcoming stubborn polarities ensures a productive exploration of the eclectic options, and that in itself is a contribution towards synthesis.

8

STATISM: TWO VARIANTS OF A THIRD WAY

In key respects, Anthony Giddens's project forms part of a more general climate amongst social theorists, many of whom might otherwise be reluctant to endorse the detail, or the label, of 'structurationism'. For example, the contention that it is above all in reflections about the formation and powers of *nation-states* that advances on marxism and pluralism must be registered is widely shared. There is also a growing consensus that methodological progress in social science requires the steadfast development of appropriate 'middle range' concepts and theories.

These common goals explain the typical form of dual critique which characterizes much contemporary theory. On the one hand, the rejection of reductionism and evolutionism (especially in marxist analysis) leads to the attitude that the long-term, impersonal forces which have shaped modern society are – and have always been – much more contingent and politically manipulable than has often been supposed. On the other hand, the institutional forms in which political action and ideologies have operated must be regarded as a good deal more *structural* than allowed for in voluntaristic schools of thought such as pluralism. In the attempt to bridge the perceived chasm between deep-structural and agency-oriented accounts, a growing number of challenging and well-researched works on the development of modern society have emerged (*cf.* Mann 1986, J. A. Hall 1985, 1986, Eisenstadt 1987). A major emphasis running through such texts is that the theoretical orthodoxies of social science, and especially marxism and pluralism, have been too 'society-centred' and that it is high time the autonomous powers and structures of *the state* were more explicitly built into overarching theoretical frameworks.

In this chapter, as a contribution to an evaluation of the now-extensive 'statist' current, I examine two variants of the concern to handle state 'inputs' in a non-reductionist fashion. One is Theda Skocpol's comparative sociology of social revolutions and state-building. Skocpol has been in the forefront of those calling for a state-centred approach, and her work in many ways has set the pace for subsequent historically-oriented investigations of relations between states and societies. Surprisingly, whilst the value of Skocpol's contribution has been justly proclaimed, critical evaluations of its explanatory texture are harder to come by. In offering an appreciation of that type, I will be arguing that although the proposal to 'bring the state back in' to social theory and research (Skocpol 1985) is a very positive one, the idea of a distinctive statist model is much more problematical. The inexact import of 'state-centred' accounts, moreover, is shadowed at the methodological level by Skocpol's interesting but indecisive considerations on the role of theoretical categories in concrete research.

My other exemplar of statism is the corporatist or 'neo-corporatist' perspective on interest-intermediation in the advanced industrial democracies. This important *œuvre* conveniently takes us from the threshold of the modern era (as depicted in Skocpol's principal work) to some of the latest patterns in state-society relations. Corporatist theory, like other variants of statism, has also made explicit its points of departure from conventional marxism and pluralism, and it similarly carries the promise of a productive synthesis. However, once again my assessment indicates that claims by enthusiasts of this current of thought to have established some kind of epistemological break with the resident orthodoxies are at best premature. Within the umbrella of debate represented by corporatism, we find a notable diversity of unresolved issues and standpoints, amongst which the influence of classical marxism and pluralism continues to be felt.

In appraising the two variants of statism in this way, the

complexity of the idea of *explanatory adequacy* in social science
needs to be brought out. This is particularly the case for
debates and discourses where different levels of abstraction
mingle together. Overall, my intention is not to deny that the
avenues opened up by statism are very valuable, or to refute its
claims in some definitive way. The point is rather to try to curb
the fashionable tendency to go in for sweeping dismissals of
society-centred traditions on the grounds that they are manifestly 'inadequate'. As sheer alternatives, I conclude, state-
centred theories are not obviously *more* adequate, and much
logical and substantive work remains to be done on the
proposition that each 'aspect' of the explanatory situation
'supplements' or 'complements' the other.

1. State-centredness

The main dimensions of the critical diagnosis of society-
centredness will be familiar from material discussed in
previous chapters. Pluralism is held by statists to ignore more
or less totally the structural role of the state, in that the latter is
perceived purely as an allocative mechanism, distributing
benefits according to the relative preferences of social interest
groups. Rather than look at the state as a matter of institutional
regulation and control, conventional pluralism, for instance, is
obsessed with the issue of which private groups get 'what,
when and how' (Krasner 1984: 225). The very emergence of
interest groups, moreover, together with the relative effectiveness of the way in which their demands are cashed by the
political process, tends to be assumed as given by the process
of modernization and social differentiation. Putting these two
features of pluralist thought together, it might be said that 'to
explain transformations . . . a pluralist would either have to
refer to broad, amorphous evolutionary trends at one extreme
or to the immediate manoeuvrings of interest groups at the
other' (Skocpol 1980: 157).

It is accepted by statists that this characterization of
pluralism is *almost* something of a caricature. After all, Dahl
was very much concerned with the role of public officials, and
in fact if the caricature fitted pluralism exactly there would be

no need for a state (governmental process) at all, since interest groups would spontaneously and harmoniously negotiate their way to democratic equilibrium. Nevertheless, it is clear that the state's profound *shaping* of the realm of competing interests and its constitutive, contested place in dynamic modernization has been underplayed by pluralists. Also, the conception of state officials as having distinct private interests stemming from their privileged location – something which has certainly been noted as significant by both pluralists and more state-centred writers (Nordlinger 1981) – does not go far enough. In a fully state-centred picture, state interests must be conceived as the organizational imperatives which stem from the state's centrality as an institutional *form*, not from personal benefits alone.

We may suggest in passing that this delineation still fails to do justice to pluralist protests against overly metaphysical or reverential presentations of the centrality of the state as a social form. Indeed, Skocpol badly misconstrues and devalues this original pluralist impulse, as outlined in chapter 2, when she describes pluralist inattention to the state as merely a matter of boredom in the face of dry, legalistic constitutionalism (Skocpol 1985: 4). That said, the point is well taken that in conventional pluralism at any rate the emphasis on institutional imperatives was largely missing.

As for marxism, statist writers are generally happy to acknowledge that in modern marxist variants the problem of the 'relative autonomy' of the state has been vigorously wrestled with. Once again it could be reasoned that if the thesis of 'class rule' were literally true, such that one class automatically and directly controlled another, there would be little rationale for a separate state structure. Lenin himself clearly saw that it is precisely because the state embodies the authoritative deployment of 'special bodies of armed men' (Lenin 1970: 9) that it becomes such a key target for the contending classes. Taking this kind of insight further, western marxists, as we saw in chapter 4, regard it as axiomatic that on many occasions the state has to act against immediate capitalist interests in order to secure the collective interests of the capitalist class as a whole, and the stability of the social orders in which capital accumulation flourishes.

The reaction of statists to this kind of qualified marxist insight is twofold. On the one hand, they see the 'relative autonomy' theorists as departing considerably from typical marxist analysis, which is (contentiously) regarded as a quasi-*behaviourist* problematic. That is to say, marxism is regarded as plausible insofar as particular groups of class actors can be found directly initiating or gaining from particular state policies (Krasner 1978: 5, King 1988). Since a great many state actions cannot be explained in this way, it is maintained, marxism is generally implausible. However, once the fairly crude dichotomy between state-centred and society-centred approaches is up and running, statists are in fact appreciative of the variety of subtle 'relative autonomy' stances. In her examination of explanations of the New Deal, for example, Skocpol discusses three marxist possibilities. The 'instrumentalist' variant is judged to be quite unfounded, but more 'structuralist' definitions, especially that of Block, seem to her to produce an 'impeccable explanation sketch'. The importance of this marxist variant is that plenty of space is allowed for state managers to act as such within the general imperatives of capitalist accumulation (Skocpol 1980: 185).

For all that, Skocpol would press the point that even the best marxist analyses allot to the state an analytically *derivative* role in explaining social and policy transformations, and this will no longer do. Indeed, nothing less than an 'intellectual sea change' is required to redress the imbalance (Skocpol 1985: 4). Theoretically and substantively, 'a distinctive type of explanatory approach' is needed, one 'highlighting the structural features of states and the pre-existing legacies of public policies' (Weir and Skocpol 1985: 100). In that light, even subtle marxism must be seen as 'false because reductionist' (Mann 1984: 185). The only route forward, it appears, is to recognize the state as a fully autonomous determinant of historical patterns and events (Skocpol 1980: 156–7). The state as an analytic variable, in sum, possesses 'a structure with a logic of its own' (Skocpol 1979: 27).

This peppering of quotations from various statist texts is necessary to indicate that at least in principle – as a major hypothesis – a strong programme of state-centredness is envisaged. Negatively, this involves a detailed critique of alternative (marxist) accounts. Positively, it means explaining key events or policies in a qualitatively new way. In both dimensions, Skocpol's contributions have been seminal in taking the debate forward. She has fully recognized the importance of the marxist concern with 'structural dynamics', but thinks that where this dimension is divorced from the finer detail of 'causal explanation', problems arise, notably in the shape of the familiar trio of evolutionism, teleology and reductionism (Skocpol 1980: 186). For example, in an early and searching review, Skocpol showed how Barrington Moore's (1969) work took the *dual* process of modernization (capitalist markets plus state-formation) to involve essentially a one-way evolutionary adaptation of political structures to (presumed) independent commercial 'impulses' (Skocpol 1973). Not only does this series of claims look suspiciously reductionist to Skocpol, it systematically omits to show how the international context of rival states itself *constructed* opportunities for 'internal' modernization. Marxists tend to take this enveloping inter-state system for granted as merely the contingent context of primarily internal, economically-powered growth. This treatment of specific and *multi-dimensional* causal variables as being a function of a unified, all-encompassing logic of capitalist growth Skocpol regards as highly questionable. Yet such assumptions, she concludes, are built into the very pattern of explanation offered even by such eminent marxist scholars as Immanuel Wallerstein and Perry Anderson (Skocpol 1977, Fullbrook and Skocpol 1984).

Theoretically, the state-centred alternative requires the endorsement of several propositions. One is that state institutions are staffed by career officials who will often act in a self-interested way. More importantly, and at times counteracting this emphasis, states are 'first and foremost sets of coercive, fiscal, judicial and administrative organizations claiming sovereignty over territory and people' (Orloff and Skocpol 1984: 730). The state's main tasks are thus to maintain public order and to secure a sufficient revenue base for its own reproduction, which, we might add, increasingly must include sufficient provision for a certain level of collective goods (Gurr and King 1987: 37). The third crucial rationale for state-centred analysis is, as mentioned, the peculiar dynamic, at any given time, of military, cultural and economic competition in the international network. Taken together, these three features of state identity make likely some serious conflicts of interest between state policy on the one hand, and all manner of social groups and classes on the other, even dominant classes. Far from being 'exceptional', or short-run, as marxists argue, the state's tendency to act *against* the (short- or long-term) economic interests of particular dominant classes is something we may expect to witness as a matter of course (Skocpol 1973: 18, 1979: 27).

The key standpoint of the state-centred perspective is that the three analytic elements cannot be subordinated to any set of propositions about the wider social functions of the state. Applying these theoretical insights to the great social revolutions in France, Russia and China, Skocpol (1979) rejects the traditional marxist proposition that prevailing class interests and economic structures determine the fact and the course of revolutionary transformation. Accordingly, she is not prepared to see these phenomena classified as contrasting instances of general types ('bourgeois revolution', 'proletarian revolution' etc.). Instead, she regards them as cases of modernizing upheavals in which autonomous state-centred variables played a central part. Specifically, in each case, the initial revolutionary momentum was generated by the weakening of military and administrative structures in states that were confronted with severe external competition. And the main outcome of all three revolutions was a dramatic *strengthening* of state powers within society. The makers of the modernizing revolutions, for their part, were not class warriors (whether bourgeois, peasant or proletarian). Rather, they were intellectual cadres whose professional and political identities were forged in the shadow of intermittent, weak, but persistent attempts by the state to restructure the economy and polity. From niches carved out from within the volatile matrix of officialdom in this phase, the new *enragés* could reflect on, and organize to overturn, the shabby compromises struck between feeble political leaders, rival state interests, and recalcitrant upper-class elements. Further turmoil born of peasant rebellion and military/fiscal incapacitation led to the successful replacement of the corrupt *anciens régimes* by the revolutionary order of the new state-building elites.

The statist perspective developed in this account of the classic revolutions can be generalized to apply to smaller-scale epochal conjunctures. For example, Skocpol has deployed a counterfactual style of reasoning in order to improve upon marxist and liberal-pluralist analytic narratives of the emergence of welfare legislation in the early twentieth century (Orloff and Skocpol 1984). If social spending on welfare were the necessary reflex of the needs of the capitalist economy at a given stage, it is asked, then why did state welfare emerge in Britain but not in Massachusetts? The same sort of comparative query can be put with respect to levels of working-class struggle (where the latter is isolated as the main explanatory variable), for on both counts Massachusetts appears to have had a socio-economic profile very similar to that of Britain. Indeed, there existed parallel legislation of a *regulative* sort in the two areas. Yet this was not the case with social spending provision.

Against the competing idealist hypothesis which would forefront the stronger sway that liberalism held in the USA, Orloff and Skocpol point out the considerable lasting influence of Victorian laissez-faire in many spheres of British intellectual and official circles. Moreover, the 'New Liberalism' often cited as representing Britain's more interventionist ideology from the late nineteenth century, has a direct counterpart in the American Progressive movement. The solution, it is suggested, must lie somewhere other than in class interests or prevailing ideas. More plausibly, the positive development of state welfare in Britain is due to the way in which institutional precedents (e.g. the various Poor Laws) and administrative capacities (the Civil Service) rendered a politics of social provision more *realistic* in that country. Conversely, US federalism, the lack of a civil bureaucracy and established political parties, together with a widespread suspicion of official corruptibility, made the establishment of public welfare programmes altogether less feasible in the United States, and certainly more revolutionary in the circumstances.

A third instance of statist revisionism is the explanation of political responses to the 1930s' depression. Skocpol has shown that little evidence exists for the view of the New Deal in the USA as a clear-sighted handling of crisis by the capitalist class. Even if the New Deal measures led in some way or other to capitalist restabilization (which itself is questionable), 'U.S. capitalists did not plan or promote these measures' (Skocpol 1980: 168). A more subtle marxist claim would be that the reforms can be explained by a combination of labour movement pressure and state officials' relatively autonomous action (which tends to be greater when the capitalist 'veto' is weak, as in times of recession). This orientation, Skocpol allows, has much to commend it. All the same, labour 'pressure' should not be taken to be equivalent to 'class struggle' in any strong sense of the term. The complexities of the Democrats' need to weld together a wide variety of political constituencies must be taken into account in explaining both the relative advantages for labour and their ultimate failure to materialize. Indeed, state officials, for their own reasons, prompted and facilitated labour-related initiatives 'from below'. Overall, the idea that the New Deal was an internal strategy geared to capitalist restabilization steadfastly ignores the fact that the effectiveness of the Recovery programme only surfaced in the 1940s, that is in the profoundly shaping inter-state military context. And *comparatively* speaking, we need to note that ideas on state economic management and social-democratic strategies made more rapid and more decisive progress in those countries (such as Sweden) where existing policy and procedures already reflected the state's commitment to social coalitions (Weir and Skocpol 1985: 148–9).

The message across these several pivotal cases is that specific institutional configurations, and the state interests they involve, are the decisive factors in socio-economic developments. The question which has to be tabled at this juncture is whether state-centredness, taken in the strong sense, is actually convincing. But we can best approach that issue by as it were retracing our steps through Skocpol's presentations to see whether the strong statist view does in fact shine through as the main thrust of this body of scholarship. Certainly, we have seen, there are places where statism looks to be put forward as an uncompromising new paradigm in social theory – 'the *state-for-itself*' model, as one of Skocpol's marxist commentators describes it (Miliband 1983: 66). Yet both in programmatic statements and in the texture of the case studies another possibility emerges: that statism is designed to complement rather than replace society-centredness. The upshot of this construal is, paradoxically perhaps, that there is *no* necessary 'centre' of analysis at all.

2. Bringing society back in

Admiring readers of Skocpol may have noticed that my earlier summary of the main drift of *States and Social Revolutions* was very schematic. This is partly, of course, because a rich investigation of that type cannot be briefly encapsulated in any form without the risk of mutilation. More importantly, however, I was careful to tailor my summation to the requirements of strong state-centredness, and it is this truncation in my view that does the breadth of the text little justice. What is lost, however, is precisely the *society-centred* dimension of analysis which Skocpol brings to bear on the explanatory task. When the full force of this point is registered, it is clear that neither the 'primacy' nor the 'autonomy' of state-centred phenomena can, in any logically accurate sense, be sustained. Indeed, there is considerable doubt as to what the object and analytical ordering of Skocpol's explanatory procedure actually are. Something of this can be illustrated by reference to a review by Randall Collins (Collins 1980: 647–9), himself an eminent 'new wave' comparative scholar. Having noted the several blows that *States and Social Revolutions* rains on 'long-standing Marxian ideas', Collins characterizes Skocpol's positive train of thought as follows. The 'main causes and consequences' of revolutions are said to be essentially political, though the process does have an ideological 'dynamic', whose 'most basic condition' is military breakdown, which itself is 'caused' by international pressure. Weakness in the face of such pressure is in turn located in the general failure to 'expand' the key 'internal structures of surplus extraction and domination'. This kind of summary succeeds not only in suggesting a number of diversely 'crucial' causes, conditions and contributory processes, but ultimately runs together internal and external factors, politico-administrative and socio-economic tendencies.

In Skocpol's own accounts this kind of complex causal nexus is confirmed. State incapacitation is held to have 'prompted', 'occasioned', or 'inaugurated' social revolution, but incapacitation is in turn 'explained' by internal and external modernizing 'pressures' (Skocpol 1976: 181, 192). If this is so, then Skocpol's immediately subsequent remark that military administrative incapacitation was both the 'fundamental cause' and the 'crucial trigger' looks odd. It is logically odd because Skocpol seems to be annulling the distinction between levels of causal ordering that she invoked a moment before. It is substantively odd because, in spite of her evident dislike of overt evolutionism, it is plain that in the broad sweep, Skocpol sees the various forms of state 'adaptation' to such *intensifying* modernizing pressures as the significant content of the revolutionary process. The distinction between fundamental causes and crucial triggers is thus important, but state incapacitation as such is not well suited to serve as the fundamental cause.

Indeed, although the strong statist standpoint appears to rule out economic and class factors as central explanatory factors, they enter Skocpol's analysis at a number of points, sometimes as (parts of) fundamental causes and sometimes as crucial triggers. The description of the process of modernization itself, for example, is described as being to a large extent the development of capitalist commodity production, first in agriculture, then in industry. While emerging as a major 'external' or inter-state pressure, commodification also of course has a vital 'internal' moment both for the initially disadvantaged states when they come themselves to 'develop', and crucially for modernizing pioneer states. The advantages accruing above all to Britain 'transformed means and stakes in the traditional rivalries of European states' (Skocpol 1976: 180). That we are moving away here from anything resembling one-dimensional statism can be emphasized by way of a formulation issued by Skocpol in the heat of her generally non-marxist engagement with Wallerstein. 'The dynamics of the European states system ensured that capitalist relations would spread both across Europe and over the entire globe through state initiatives by competing powers and through military concepts, as well as through market expansion' (Skocpol 1977: 1087). In this proposition, state actions are undoubtedly vital, but the core of modernization resides in the global expansion of capitalist markets, a process which is thought to be 'ensured' by inter-state competition.

High on the list of lower-level factors cited by Skocpol as structural 'contradictions' which help explain *ancien régime* vulnerability is the stranglehold exercised by the landed upper classes over tax reform and democratic-bureaucratic expansion. Now it is perfectly true, as Skocpol demonstrates, that the state itself over a long period *created* a vast range of new occupations and economic locations, and these partially transformed the income of the 'nobility'. The reactionary defence of 'privilege' in the 1770s–80s in France was therefore not at all simply a matter of shoring up seigneurial dues and feudal title in the classic medieval sense. Agrarian monarchical bureaucracies, Skocpol insists, were post-feudal formations in which the state itself constituted the offices and rights which generated a considerable amount of 'proprietary wealth' (Skocpol 1979: 58–9).

Be that as it may, it remains the case that around 85 per cent of the population in France were peasants in a traditional sense, and the major revolutionary potential lay in the endemic economic exploitation that this fact represents. The growing pressure to expand the tax base of the regime and to introduce greater commercial productivity ran head-on into the 'backwardness' of the mode of production. While it is obviously the case that an endemic situation cannot be the trigger for a revolutionary upheaval (for then we would have to ask: why not permanent revolution?), there is no denying the fundamental conditioning status of this type of class oppression, nor can the immediate causal significance of its conjunctural *intensification* be disputed. On the contrary, Skocpol firmly asserts that peasant rebellion was the very factor which made the various revolutions *irreversible*, i.e. made them revolutions in the strict sense (Skocpol 1979: 117, 1976: 192).

In all this, the role of the new state-building elites becomes considerably less outstanding than many commentators on Skocpol have understood. Certainly, if modernizing pressures and state incapacitation set the revolution off, and peasant

rebellion rendered it irreversible, its ultimate *success* was due
to the state-building cadres. The new professional-bureaucratic
state was indeed the principal visible result of the social
revolutions which affected the agrarian bureaucracies. However,
as with the 'fundamental causes' and contributory forces of the
revolutionary process, its outcome too is conceived as 'sym-
biotically co-existent' with the full emergence of 'national
markets and capitalist private property' (Skocpol 1979: 162).
This dual outcome cannot be perceived as 'bourgeois revolution',
because the state facilitates and even 'guarantees' capitalist
preconditions without itself being determined by capitalist
class agencies. But nor is it reasonable to see capitalism simply
as a state *strategy*. Rather, the theorist is compelled to posit
some general functional adaptations to intensifying class and
economic 'pressures', which are then concretized *and qualified*
by reference to particular political forces, opportunities and
conflicts which converge above all on the state.

This more rounded perspective seems to me to capture what
is going on in Skocpol's work far better than any unilateral
statist thesis. Essentially, her investigations demonstrate the
limited character of the traditional marxist account of social
revolutions, and its falsity when particular class agencies are
depicted as ever-resident at the helm of the ship of state.
Nevertheless, the broad lines of the historical materialist
notion of the transition from feudalism to capitalism are still
visible. Indeed, Skocpol's best treatments occur when she
conveys the phenomena of fiscal crisis and revolution as
totalizing conjunctures which display several types of 'indispensable' conditions and triggers. Without recalcitrant
agrarian class structures, no fiscal crisis. That is one (society-
centred) emphasis, as is the related deduction that upheaval
from below is required to turn administrative chaos into social
revolution. On the other hand, without state incapacitation in
the face of inter-state competition, no *intensification* of modernizing pressures. And without state-building revolutionary
organization, no modern, state-sponsored facilitation of capitalist relations. Those state-centred emphases continue to
stand out.

3. Causal analysis and general social theory

As *critique*, then, state-centredness has proved impressive, but the kinds of considerations in the last section can be bolstered by citing further 'statist' announcements at the general level to show that something more complex is going on. Thus, Skocpol declares that it is only 'the most encompassing social determinist assumptions' of the old traditions that she is concerned to exorcize. The point is *not* that 'state-determined arguments are to be fashioned in the place of society-centred explanations' (Skocpol 1985: 20). The problem is therefore not that marxists and others have failed to notice state variables; rather, the latter have not been taken seriously *enough* (Skocpol 1980: 200). These modulations serve to refute the claim that states are to be taken as *primary* analytical foci in the kind of intellectual framework represented by Skocpol.

If state phenomena are not necessarily primary, then this must in part be because they are not *autonomous* either. Paradoxically, in view of the many cautions directed against even subtle forms of marxism, Skocpol often refers only to the 'partial independence' of state-related variables (1973: 34), their 'potential' autonomy (1979: 29). The question of *how far* this potential is realized in particular conjunctures, moreover, is a question of 'structural' analysis, typically involving a mix of societal and organizational criteria. State autonomy here thus becomes a limit point for analysis, a never-realized ideal type which is no more empirically plausible than the possibility of the complete subordination of state to society. Pragmatically speaking, it is always *degrees* of autonomy we are dealing with: a state autonomy which 'can come and go' according to the wider context (Skocpol 1985: 14).

This manifest settling for a vantage point which foregrounds the *relative* autonomy of the state is as open to charges of theoretical vacillation as any marxist version of the same thesis. But there is no call for consternation here, since the idea of complete freedom from significant external social constraints is close to absurd. Even if features such as the maintenance of public order and the ability to secure a revenue base are isolated as prime criteria for state autonomy (cf. Gurr and King

1987), the 'play' that is available to states in the handling of these matters is arguably always tightly bounded by the nature of the wealth-producing structure and the degree to which subordinate classes are able or willing to endorse the social order in the broadest sense. That point is of course by no means *sufficient* as a basis for the analysis of the role of the state, but it is a perfectly *necessary* part of it.

Interestingly, reluctant though they are to sponsor functionalist forms of explanation, theorists of state autonomy themselves tend to resort to general functional propositions which reinstate a concern for societal relativity in accounting for the limits of state action. Overall, I have argued, Skocpol sees the state-building process as a series of more or less successful adaptations to the development of modernization, which is itself conceived as a dualistic evolutionary pattern. Michael Mann, a still more definite advocate of state autonomy, also considers his approach to be 'dualist' in that it combines internalist and externalist components. Mann however fails to see the irreparable damage done to statements of pure state autonomy when he characterizes the latter as the special 'usefulness of enhanced territorial-centralization to social life in general' (Mann 1984: 211). Whatever this may mean exactly, it plainly represents a functional claim indicating the orientation of state power around central social tasks and structures. The 'play' enjoyed by the state in the diversity of its function, together with the flexibility it exemplifies in its dealings with social forces, is unquestionably substantial. But it is also necessarily bounded and variable – not unconstrained or open to quite arbitrary manipulation. At this point the debate runs the risk of descending into pedantry, but the point is worth making that the onus is firmly on those who are bothered about the theoretical 'fudging' implied by the phrase relative autonomy, or concerned that it harbours a reductionist option, to produce a coherent *literal* reading of the notion of state 'autonomy'. This they have failed to do – with good reason.

I have been highlighting two main features of Skocpol's writings. One is the oscillation between a strong statist refutation of traditional (especially marxist) perspectives, and a view of state-centredness which is designed to 'complement' society-centred insights (Orloff and Skocpol 1984: 746). Secondly,

I have indicated at various points that Skocpol's conception of historical causality and explanatory primacy is generally quite loose or unclear. In rounding off this discussion, it is valuable to note how Skocpol views her own methodological stance.

In the essay 'Emerging agendas and recurrent strategies in historical sociology' (1984), Skocpol designates her practice as 'analytic' historical sociology. This position seeks to use a number of theoretical hypotheses and available 'master agendas' to identify and characterize significant causal regularities across diverse social contexts. Skocpol contrasts this approach with two others. The first is one whereby a single master agenda is applied to particular cases, which are thus conceived as embodying instances of the 'laws' prescribed by the general theoretical models. The second is the study of particular socio-cultural formations, an interpretive project which is focused on the distinctive trajectory of the peculiar qualities of a single case. The interpretive resources which furnish this strategy are neither universal laws nor causal regularities, but rather cultural *meanings*, of two kinds: those which characterize the culture studied and those which motivate the historian's project itself. The first alternative strategy is said to typify structural-functionalist historiography, whilst the second is exemplified by the humanistic socialist outlook of E. P. Thompson.

The superiority of Skocpol's preferred approach, in her view, lies in taking a cautious approach to the validity of general theories. These are to be cashed in as hypotheses, and *alternative* hypotheses should be aired wherever possible. However, the stance advocated constitutes a historical *sociology*, because theories are indispensable in suggesting the causal orderings without which history dissolves into a chaotic narrative flux. Analytic strategies also make maximum use of the comparative method, an invaluable tool for research. Whereas the 'general law' and 'cultural interpretation' models are interested in establishing, respectively, the conformity of the particular case with a general law, or the uniqueness of the case, the analytic model is interested in a range of comparisons and contrasts. This procedure maximizes cross-contextual generalization without suppressing the fact that some differences do really make a difference.

Skocpol's sketch of the methodological options seems attractive, but a number of questions and reservations should be lodged. For example, it is not clear what *status* the classification itself claims. As a rough and ready guide to the field of historical sociology it is certainly useful, indicating a continuum of approaches within which a number of important writers can be distributed. That it is a guide of this pragmatic sort is further indicated by the fact that most writers cited by Skocpol either fail to fit the three boxes exactly, or else a case could be made to that effect. For example, the 'analytic' category itself receives as many unambiguous entries as the other two, and includes Barrington Moore and Robert Brenner, neo-marxist writers with whom Skocpol could be expected to have numerous disagreements over method and explanation as well as over substantive priorities. Indeed, in many places throughout her work, Skocpol tends to indicate that she considers marxism to be an overly universalist explanatory project, one which conforms, if anything, to the 'general model' methodological standpoint. By contrast, her own preference has been to disavow such totalizing macro-theoretical frameworks (Burawoy and Skocpol 1982: vii, Skocpol 1984a: 19).

In that light, possibly the only thing that distinguishes 'analysts' from others is their use of the comparative method. Against this construal, Skocpol's own hope that the latter will not be taken in a dry and narrowly technical sense should be borne in mind (Skocpol 1984: 382, 384). The problem is, that on the more generous understanding of the logic of comparison and distinctiveness that she seems to prefer, scholars of the calibre of Anderson, Thompson and even Smelser could hardly be disqualified from the favoured investigative type. Indeed, although the isolation of 'causal regularities' is said to be a hallmark of the analytic approach (1984: 374), and although this suggests that analysts will be interested in cross-context *similarities* between cases, Skocpol confirms that they are in fact just as interested in *differences* (1984: 377). Substantively, her account of responses to the Great Depression reinforces this concern for differentiation among cases. In that comparative case study, some familiar candidate terms for causal prime movers (class struggle, mode of production) are found to be inoperable outside considerations of state strategies and organizational attributes. The latter, though, are further deconstructed into yet lower-level variables. Responses to the 'capitalist crisis', it turns out, are ultimately the product of very particular institutional and intellectual histories. For instance, those nations whose political precedents allowed certain sets of ideas (e.g. Keynesianism) to be given an early hearing were more responsive to state-led social democratic measures (Weir and Skocpol 1985: 148–9). Whether or not this is a reasonable assessment, it seems to differ little in its theoretical logic from an old-fashioned, 'genetic' approach to institutional pecularities.

At best, then, Skocpol's typology of research strategies is suggestive. Its lack of logical depth indicates that, in parallel with important substantive ambivalences, Skocpol is groping somewhat for consistency at the meta-theoretical level of discussion. Interestingly, although she never uses these terms explicitly, her typology of strategies represents fairly directly what in the philosophy of history has long been known as the debate between the 'nomothetic' or positivist option, the 'ideographic' or interpretive option, and something else in between. The plausibility of Skocpol's stance is that given the well-known demerits of the first two options, the invention of a label ('analytic historical sociology') together with a method ('comparative logic') seems sufficient to take us some distance along the third path. My foregoing comments should counsel against that presumption. Skocpol herself allows that the analytic model is not after all a self-sufficient alternative. It cannot substitute for grand theory, she allows, since it is the latter alone that supplies the range of explanatory hypotheses which guides analysis. Nor, we have seen, does causal comparison diminish the task of understanding uniqueness: it rather enhances it. The 'pragmatic' conclusion which emerges is therefore that 'it should not be surprising that the most ambitious historical analysts end up borrowing emphases from our first two strategies of historical sociology' (1984: 385).

Skocpol's work vividly and intelligently explores the terrain of synthesis between marxist and pluralist substantive insight, and between realist and instrumentalist models of explanation. But it neither provides nor seeks a coherent solution to the tensions in either domain. In each sphere, the notion of explanatory *emphasis* emerges as something requiring further

exploration. Classical marxism cannot be considered 'inadequate' on the grounds that it produces grand theory, for
that is held by Skocpol to be an honourable and necessary task.
Nor is it inadequate because it settles on illusory or minor
causal relations, for they are not in fact considered to be minor.
Rather, all grand theories emphasize some aspects of complex
social totalities and underemphasize others. This, indeed, is
why statism cannot be elevated to the level of a new reigning
paradigm without being regarded as positive *and* negative in
just the same respects. The explanatory situation, therefore, is
one in which different causal emphases can alternately be
combined or played off against one another. In a sense, it can
be expected that one theory's 'fundamental cause' will be
another's 'contributory factor', each emphasizing a different
aspect of the whole. Under yet another aspect, both might be
entertained *together* as 'indispensable but inadequate', taken
as a total causal profile.

The overarching problem heré is this. Granted that there are
always many aspects of a social process to consider, and thus
many explanatory emphases to be registered and combined,
what justification is there for considering some factors or
configurations to be more fundamental than others? An
instrumentalist view of explanation would lead to a negative
answer: there are as many aspects as there are questions. It
follows that no big theory can exhaust or definitively order the
explanatory emphases (cf. Achinstein 1983: 195). The latter
indeed, while referring to real complexes, are always and only
partial hypothetical tools, which comparative research can
sharpen. On a more realist construal, the assumption of a
structured ontology is itself sufficient reason for supposing
that some integrative theoretical sets might be more comprehensive with respect to real causal orders than others.
Comparative empirical research then plays a decisive part in
the retroductive analysis which follows the theoretical redescription of the component elements of a conjuncture (cf.
Bhaskar 1978: 125).

Both of those methodological standpoints accept a plurality
of legitimate causal emphases and the openness of social
contexts, thus making definitive theoretical elaboration impossible. They also value comparative analysis. But their

respective attitudes to the task and status of both theory and reality are very different. In my view, Skocpol has to date either abstained from this level of theoretical assessment, or perhaps has fallen inadvertently between the two options. On the one hand, master agendas are certainly indispensable and comparative sociology can more adequately refine them. On the other hand, master agendas are very useful and probably necessary, but they inevitably register contrasting emphases, which are unlikely ever to be squared either with each other or with the complex empirical record. We should look forward to a future engagement between Skocpol and such matters, for some extended clarification seems to be in order.

4. The two phases of corporatism

My second illustration of a statist 'third way' which seeks to avoid the antinomies of marxism and pluralism is neo-corporatist theory and research. In assessing this *œuvre* I can be somewhat briefer. This is because corporatism shares many of the methodological aspirations of state-centred historical sociology. And when it is put forward as *displacing* the traditional perspectives, corporatism suffers from weaknesses of the same sort that afflict unilateral state-centred discourses. As part of the moral of the story this can be asserted prior to the customary procedure of exegesis and argumentation, partly because readers who have followed the drift of my presentation up till now will not be surprised by such a conclusion. More importantly, though, a pre-emptive indication of the very partial nature of the corporatist breakthrough is appropriate in view of the fact that the principal neo-corporatist commentators have themselves in the 1980s become notably and explicitly more reluctant to put this brand of statism forward as a qualitatively new departure for political theory. In contrast to the bolder statements of, and hopes for, corporatism in the early 1970s, the scholarly consensus tends now to revolve around a fairly modest common denominator: the attempt to understand and classify 'certain important tendencies in a number of Western societies' (Grant 1985: 26).

Chief among the empirical reasons for the scale-down of

corporatist ambitions is the resurgence of free market policies in the western democracies in the last decade. Prior to this development, theses about the strengthening of the state seemed naturally to suggest an equivalent weakening of private interests. New Right theory and practice, however, has significantly advanced both central state power *and* prominent types of private interest. And it has done so at the expense of the kind of state *structures* in the realm of economic planning and functional representation that corporatist theory had forefronted. It is not the case that corporatist ideas have been shown to be quite inapplicable or irrelevant to recent political configurations,' and we should expect to see their revival as revamped alternatives to the current dominant ideology of 'free markets plus strong state'. All the same, it is clear that the setback for corporatist initiatives in policy-making has created an opportunity critically to reflect on the consistency and status of corporatist theory.

In pursuing this task, proponents of corporatism have become aware – perhaps more so than the historical sociologists discussed earlier – that the temptation to reify the state as an autonomous, singular and purposive entity in political conjunctures carries distinct penalties as well as advantages. The 'autonomy' attribute has been undermined not only by the sort of argument I conducted in the last section, but by the active presence of neo-marxists working under the roomy corporatist umbrella. The attribution of singularity and purposiveness to the state has been questioned by two other theoretical contributions. One is old-fashioned pluralism – or, more accurately, the realization among corporatists that pluralists did after all have some idea about state-centred traditions of political thought and in that knowledge preferred to posit a wide variety of decision-making locations within and outside the official governmental realm.

Secondly, the post-modernist climate has made it a duty on the part of any self-respecting analyst to hesitate before registering any claims which assume either ontological unity or motivational coherence. It might be better instead to think of 'the state' as a convenient jumbo-term for a number of fragmented and multifaceted institutional identities. As part of the post-modernist revaluation, Michel Foucault in particular

(1980: 60f.) has proposed that power is exercised – and corresponding resistances are generated – within innumerable 'micro-situations'. It is a fallacy, on this account, to define notions such as power or sovereignty exclusively in terms of any one source, even the state. As noted by Poulantzas (1980: 44) Foucault's thinking here bears a striking resemblance to aspects of conventional pluralism. Yet coming as it does from the influential post-structuralist camp, this observation serves only to further open the debate about the value of statism in relation to its society-centred alternatives. Few of these recent moves in social theory have been lost on corporatist commentators, and the notion of corporatism as a 'third way' has been tempered as a result.

The initial attraction of the corporatist paradigm, and its central focus, can readily be set out. Corporatism refers to the process whereby negotiations between organized interest groups in industrial democracies become institutionalized within, and mediated by, the state itself. In macro-economic terms, corporatist trends in the post-war period have supplemented and even supplanted market mechanisms as the chief regulators of employment, wage levels and the 'social' objectives of the economy. In political terms, the formalization of *collective* interests and their embodiment in various channels of policy-formation work against, and possibly bypass altogether the traditional parliamentary forms of representation. It follows that corporatism, in the sense of strategic co-operation between the state, business and labour organizations, carries at least the potential for a new type of political economy.

The main theoretical thrust which inaugurated this sense of the novel potential of corporatism was an accentuated break with pluralist orthodoxy (cf. Schmitter 1979, Berger 1981, Grant 1985, Cawson 1986). Several of the relevant criticisms of pluralism are very much akin to those of the statist writers already considered, turning principally on the general neglect of the state in society-centred analysis. Corporatists are particularly keen, though, to emphasize that the pluralist conception of politics as based on an analogy with the marketplace of supply and demand is woefully outmoded. Far from being responsive and neutral, the state is proactive and interventionist in its treatment of interest group pressures. Moreover, the pluralists tended to be extremely vague about the nature both of group identities and the 'pressure' they are said to exert. Pluralism is also excessively sanguine about the responsiveness of the system to a vast array of consumer interests. In the corporatist view, by contrast, there is a qualitative difference between all manner of voluntary and consumer associations and the main *organized, centralized* interests in modern society. It is the latter that are crucial and they tend to be functionally grounded, that is to say, based around the roles and expectations of large collectivities of people as they are located in the social division of labour. There may, according to this criterion, be important divisions between rural and urban interests, or perhaps between age-related and religion-related cleavages. But typically, in modern society, the major functional interests are very few in number, often coming down to the relationship between business organizations and labour movements. Other cleavages tend to be significant in relation to these. Organized interests must also normally possess a monopoly of authoritative representation with respect to their nominal functional constituencies.

It follows that the political process itself must be to an extent reconceptualized, for organized interests are not really re-presented in the customary mechanisms of democratic govern-ment. Rather, when the interests are powerful enough to command the state's institutional reorientation around them, the logic of interest-intermediation operates outside or alongside parliamentary procedures. Functional representation, in short, begins to dominate territorial-individual representation. It could even be argued that to regard the political process as a form of 'representation' at all is to fail to perceive how indivisible the nexus of intervention and representation actually is. Far from being pre-given, social interests are from the start articulated, compromised and reconstituted within the evolving norms of corporatist bargaining. Often, though not exclusively, corporatist practice will take the shape of 'tripartite' structures of consultation and policy-formation.

Previous characterizations of pluralism given in this book can be invoked here in order to warn against its further caricature, this time at the hands of corporatists. In fact, a noted first-phase pluralist has reasonably spoken out against the frequent lapse of 'professional memory' which is witnessed whenever brave new corporatism is juxtaposed one-sidedly against burned-out pluralism (Almond 1983). In addition to the several 'complications' to the caricature already rehearsed, it can be validly pointed out that from within the pluralist mainstream there emerged works dealing with the history and mechanics of state-organized interest representations which must be considered early and substantial ventures in corporatist research (e.g. Beer 1969, Rokkan 1966).

More than this, there is a case for saying that corporatism has actually retained much of the basis of pluralist thought, and has consequently inherited some of the damaging lacunae which also mark it. For example, the state, while given a more interventionist focus, is not theorized in corporatism any more than in pluralism as a particular *type* of social agent or as having a distinctive function with respect to economic interests. If that protest is countered in turn by the suspicion that it carries precisely the kind of society-centred bias that is in question, it can still be argued that corporatists show no sign of agreement about what the interests or role of the 'state-for-itself' may be. It is true that one line of thought (e.g. Pahl and Winkler 1975) did suggest that a new form of centralized control and a correspondingly distinct type of political economy was captured by the concepts of corporatism. However, this view has relatively few adherents, other than as descriptive of fascist forms of corporate economy. In regard to more 'normal' cases, most commentators prefer to continue to place corporatist institutions in the context of an advanced capitalist economy, and resist the view that the state so overwhelmingly directs the process of interest bargaining that normal democratic channels have ceased to be relevant to the legitimacy of political decision-making.

It seems, then, that for a theory which forefronts the role of the state, corporatism does not automatically yield up a coherent or compelling discussion of that aspect. Philippe Schmitter, one of the chief proponents of the corporatist research programme, has responded to this absence at the heart of corporatism. But rather than responding by formulating a tougher corporatist account of the state, Schmitter backs off

the idea altogether, complaining that 'we are being asked to
bring the state back into our analyses precisely when it least
resembles what it was historically and theoretically' (Schmitter
1985: 33). Leaving aside the possibility that, *contra* Schmitter,
the state's identity may well have *increased* rather than
decreased in coherence over time, he is here falling back on a
pluralistic understanding of the diversity of state interests,
vested in multiple agencies and rules. For example, there are
governmental interests, in the restricted sense of actions
designed to reproduce particular political regimes. There are
also the self-preserving practices of civil servants, often
couched in the form of a defence of the public sphere and
national interest. And there are the interests of the central,
national state *vis-à-vis* both international forces and more
localized political challenges to its legitimacy. Yet corporatism
is not necessarily subsumed under any of these important
institutional heads, separately or together (Schmitter 1985: 41).

One consequence of the inability to theorize the state as a
self-standing interest is that the general social constraints on
corporatism come once again to the fore. In phase one corporatism, there were in fact some markedly pluralist overtones in
the idea of (competing and compromising) organized interests.
True, no automatic equilibrium between interests could be
assumed prior to the intervention of the state in interest-
intermediation. The corporatist state is more of an active
partner in the negotiation and direction of interest bargaining
than a neutral 'broker'. Even so, the dominant inclination is to
continue to treat relations between social groups as, precisely,
a matter of bargaining, jockeying and negotiation. The scenario
is thus one whereby state, business and labour are envisaged
as roughly equal power centres, balancing out their contrary
impulses. The suggestion that corporatism does not differ very
much in these respects from pluralism can be mitigated by
pointing out that corporatism is not committed to the view
that competing interests (including the state) are actually *equal*,
or that equilibrium is ever achieved. On the contrary, at best
we are dealing with the effective 'mutual deterrence' which
interests exercise over each other, and thus with a dynamic
precarious set of balance mechanisms (Schmitter 1985: 36).
However, this qualification seems rather cosmetic, and in any

case there is a corresponding move in conventional pluralism. The whole point of the idea of 'countervailing powers' was exactly that considerable inequalities among interest groups could at least be held in check by a fairly low level of threatened retaliation in the socio-political arena.

Substantively, moreover, some corporatists have indeed been susceptible to the idea of equality amongst the 'peak associations', and between the latter and the state. In his major study of 'corporate bias' in the British political system, for example, Keith Middlemas offers the view that the representative associations of labour and capital jointly rise to the status of 'governing institutions' and indeed become part of the 'extended state' itself (Middlemas 1979: 323–4). That kind of proposition is highly controversial. The significant leaps towards corporatism in Britain identified by Middlemas occurred first of all during periods of war as a result of necessarily enhanced state direction, and secondly in the aftermath of the crushing defeat of the labour movement by the government and capitalist alliances in the General Strike of 1926. Perhaps the nearest that working-class organizations have come to being 'estates of the realm' was in the Labour government's 'social contract' initiatives during the 1970s. Yet it seems appropriate to regard that (unsuccessful) policy – certainly its later history – as the direct consequence of the severe pressure exerted upon Labour by national and international finance, with a view to controlling inflation and 'managing' the capitalist economy. In this context, labour movement demands simply had to be disciplined.

At the more local level of dual or tripartite channels, there is also evidence that it is those interests which are *already* privileged in the social structure that are the net beneficiaries of corporatist arrangements (Grant 1985: 18). For example, the direction of concessions in major British cities appears to be predominantly one-way: from the local and national state to the Chambers of Commerce (King 1985). These counter-examples are of course limited, and they cannot offset the productive research questions which corporatism generates. But they do clinch two points. One is that corporatists cannot after all afford to skip pluralistic issues about 'who gets what, when and how'. The other is that corporatists can sometimes be seen to share with pluralists the highly *dubious* normative predisposition to treat interest associations as approximately equivalent forces accruing approximately equivalent benefits from the socio-political system.

What, then, of the relationship between corporatism and marxism? In view of the nub of the last paragraph, together with the reluctance of corporatists to propose that a new state-controlled order is under way, a marxist construal of corporatism looks promising. Certainly, authors who would not normally regard themselves as marxists accept that corporatism is often a class strategy for the regulation of labour rather than a middle ground between capitalism and socialism (e.g. Crouch 1979: 20, Schmitter 1979: 32). More emphatically, it can be argued that the advantage of corporatism to capitalists is that it appears to achieve in one fell swoop the integration and co-ordination necessary for advanced industrial growth *and* the political incorporation of the working class. The latter is encouraged through the very institutional neutrality that seems to be conferred by corporatism, elevating labour to quasi-governmental rank. Indeed, insofar as corporatist academic theory sustains this twin illusion of state neutrality and labour movement equality, it could be said to be part of the ideological rationalization of advanced capitalist society.

Along these marxist lines, it has been asserted that corporatism amounts to 'state structured class collaboration' (Panitch 1981: 42). In an increasingly global setting for monopoly capitalist enterprise, the role of national states in regulating the accumulation of capital has become vital. Corporatism, in this view, is a novel institutional form; but its very novelty and formality are rooted in the need to reproduce familiar long-term goals associated with the capitalist system. Thus:

> The mode of production is fundamentally unchanged, social relationships remain hierarchically stratified, imperatives of profit and accumulation exercise unvaried sway, class conflict is barely assuaged, critical contradictions persist and indeed, while more intricately cloaked under the mantle of harmonisation, repressive state power lurks as a more likely potential source. In other

words, corporatism may well emerge as Capitalism's most apposite shell. (Newman 1981: 56)

Theoretically, the 'fundamentalist' marxist assessment which is illustrated here is notably reductionist: the 'form' of politics has precious little impact on the underlying, and in a sense unchanging, logic of capital. From a different neo-marxist standpoint this juggernaut account of capitalism creates serious obstacles to realistic analytic and political assessment. Above all, the combative and constructive pressure of working-class politics seems to go by the board. Without negating the capital-enhancing properties of corporatism, a rather more positive appraisal can be made. For example, it can be maintained that corporatist structures are partly the *product* of working-class struggle and its effective organization. The impact of labour organizations on the capitalist state, as witnessed by the development of extensive social welfare provision, is thus testimony to the partial success of social democratic politics, not the result of its craven failure. True enough, capitalist forces will always be trying to wrest the initiative away from organized labour and its political representatives: but corporatism is an achievement which represents at least a 'historic compromise' in the 'democratic class struggle', which cannot be interpreted solely as the product of capitalist design (Korpi 1983).

Taking this constructive attitude even further – and with the Swedish case in mind – John Stephens (1979) has more or less advocated a 'corporatist road to socialism'. Aimed against theories which treat the capitalist state as a functional unity, Stephens prefers the rubric of 'the state in capitalist society'. On that interpretation, the unstable contradictions of the latter are shared by the state, making it possible for programmes and institutions to develop which might dramatically, if perhaps only gradually, transform that capitalist integument into a socialist one. Corporatism is not, therefore, either the harbinger of pessimism or the force which stalls the (mythical) glorious proletarian revolution. Instead, corporatism can be seen as a disparate balance of forces through which progressive changes can in the right circumstances be forged. By and large, capitalism *without* corporatism is likely to be more brutally individualistic, chaotic and possibly more oppressive too. Also, 'left corporatists' would argue, the expectation that working class consciousness will sharpen and 'mature' with the intensification of capitalist exploitation has ever been a fatal flaw in the fundamentalist marxist outlook. It is much more likely in their view that progressive developments will emerge in a capitalist society where the strength of the labour movement is officially recognized.

In fact, orthodox marxists do not often take stark 'fundamentalist' postures to the limit, nor do they always offer rigged functionalist claims. The argument is not: corporatism is functional for capital (it provides integration and stability), *therefore* that is what brought corporatism into being. The origins of corporatism and welfare can be accepted as in large part the result of 'the challenge of labour', just as social democratic gains can be regarded as valuable contingent additions to working-class resources and repertoires (cf. Panitch 1979). For all that, the fact remains (in the straight marxist line), that corporatism *has subsequently proved* itself to be 'functional' for capital in advanced democracies, and this should leave marxists in little doubt about the dangers of socialistic-sounding inflexions of corporatism. Better altogether to renounce this new type of class collaboration (Panitch 1981: 28).

This stance, though less functionalist than it first appears, remains problematic. It lacks the imagination to ask crucial questions about just *how* functional corporatism is for capital. Are all its variants equally capitalistic? Could it be transformed at least in *some* socialistic ways? Would not a non-corporatist state strategy for capital be *more* damaging to long-term labour interests? Given the political developments in the 1980s in the industrial democracies, it seems clear that given the choice, capitalists would rather not make the partial compromises that corporatism involves. Corporatism represents a promising avenue for capitalist growth most of all when market-based routes are blocked for one reason or another. Certainly, the price of capitalist entry into corporatist bargaining is low in these circumstances, but as it becomes institutionalized, corporatism represents a progressively higher cost to capital (Grant 1985: 24). It is likely that more political and structural opportunities for the Left will be found in this situation than in alternative capitalist contexts.

It does require a further leap of imagination and conviction, though, to treat corporatism *per se* as holding great potential for systemic transformation. To say that socialist progress *can* be made is one thing. To expect that capitalist strength can be effectively dissipated by that means alone is quite another. The idea that pervasive structures of economic power can be fundamentally altered through particular mechanisms of political representation involves an inadvisable degree of faith in the power of contingent, incremental change and in the charisma of democratic argument. Orthodox marxists can persuasively insist that contestation within official political processes is necessary but insufficient to effect such change. Without denying the leeway for contingent negotiation and struggle, corporatism does represent an opportunity for the capitalist class to turn contestation by subordinate groups into accommodation and quiescence. The extent to which they avail themselves of that opportunity is not an entirely contingent matter in the sense of being arbitrary or accidental. The 'needs' of capital accumulation, modernization and profitability can be met in more or less conducive political circumstances. *That* these mechanisms must persist is not, however, an option for the capitalist class or any social system which is geared in so many ways to its well-being.

Corporatism comes out of these theoretical engagements as something of an enigma. There is almost a greater likelihood of agreement on what corporatism is *not* than what, in any overall theoretical sense, it does represent (Grant 1985: 7–11). For example, to see corporatism as a statist doctrine now seems exaggerated. Corporatism, far from resolving the state/society oscillation, reproduces it, in two main ways. Firstly, the state/society contrast reappears as a continuum of empirical cases, running from 'state corporatist' variants at one end to 'liberal' or 'societal' corporatism at the other (Schmitter 1979). This provides a rough and ready guide to empirical classification rather than a substantive theory. However, even as a descriptive typology it leaves something to be desired. Mussolini's Italy is commonly cited as a key instance of corporatism which resides indisputably toward the statist end of the scale. Other cases tend to be more vaguely distributed across the rest of the spectrum. Thus social-democratic Austria and Sweden have been taken to be cases of 'strong' corporatism, and Britain prior to the 1980s can be seen as hovering somewhere between 'medium' and 'weak' corporatism (Lehmbruch 1982). This scale of assessment is no doubt useful, but its lack of rigour, whether in conceptual or empirical terms, is striking.

Another form of the state/society polarity occurs in the difference of emphasis implied when corporatism is considered as a pattern of policy-making rather than as a factor in interest-intermediation. Of course, corporatists might reasonably say that *both* aspects are important and that corporatism, perhaps alone amongst social theories, holds the promise of bringing the different emphases together. Nevertheless, I have suggested that corporatism does not in fact provide a distinctive account of the interventionist state. Nor does it escape the grip of pluralist influences when regarded as interest-intermediation (the very term is resonant with conventional pluralist implications).

Perhaps, then, it is better *not* to see corporatism as the sort of 'macro' social theory which competes with (and surpasses) the likes of marxism and pluralism. To understand it in these terms might trigger off a search for the definitive analytic essence of corporatism which would seem to lead only to disappointment. This can be fairly asserted even though the value of corporatism as a descriptive typology or as a means of calibrating 'an enormous variety of occurrences' (Cawson 1986: 71, Nedelman and Meier 1979) can openly be recognized. It is thus doubtful that, at this lower or 'meso' level of abstraction, corporatism represents a coherent 'synthesis' of marxism and pluralism (Cawson 1986: 6). But neither is it correct to say that the terminology and thrust of corporatism, however incomplete, can be decoded without loss into the rhetorics of class struggle or group competition. Whatever its weaknesses in positive conceptualization, corporatism does suggest – and exemplify – the symbiotic character of the political and economic aspects of state policy in the advanced industrial democracies. As a general phenomenon, this is not all *automatically* taken care of by the analytic repertoire of the two traditions.

When pitched at a lower level of abstraction than that of the social totality, corporatist insights can be used to generate fruitful synthetic propositions. For example, a 'dual politics' thesis has been developed to register the interesting way in which the logic of state-society relations in Britain depends on the social sector or sphere in question. Thus, in policy forums concerned with the planning of *production*, recognizably corporatist negotiating channels tend to emerge. On issues of collective consumption, especially at local or regional level, a more distinctive pluralist scenario holds, with competing pressure groups lobbying partially responsive state agencies (cf. Cawson 1985).

It could therefore be claimed, in the light of this sort of observation, that insofar as corporatism represents a focus on those specific sectoral logics which operate 'below' the level of the social system as a whole, it offers the possibility of a combination of marxist and pluralist insights. In saying this, it is important to be aware that there are as many arguments to be had about the empirical characteristics of corporatist arrangements as there are about the status of corporatist theory. There is considerable uncertainty, for example, as to whether corporatism at any level can cope with the idea of *informal* liaison between functional groups and state officials, or whether by contrast official tripartite structures sanctioned and directed by the state must constitute the essential feature of corporatism. There has also been a debate about whether corporatism is principally a mode of dealing with industrial relations between capital and labour, taken in the fairly narrow sense of wage-bargaining. Finally, there has been a relative shift of emphasis in Schmitter's work towards postulating the elements of an associationalist *culture* which might complement and indeed underpin corporatist institutions. Part of the idea here is that unless a social ethic of compromise, 'package-dealing' and tempered sectional demands is encouraged, corporatist institutions and leaderships are unlikely to be stable (Schmitter 1985).

Taken together, these emphases cover a considerable range of phenomena, and in all cases the relationship between corporatism and pluralism in particular is manifestly one of overlap rather than disjunction. Even when restricted to the sphere of industrial relations, corporatism deals with the reality rather than the ideal type of interest negotiation. This typically falls *between* 'statism' and purely pluralist bargaining (cf. Crouch 1983). Taking the much broader tack of examining the ideological prerequisites of corporatism also invokes key elements of the pluralist tradition, notably the normative emphasis on a civic culture of tolerance and compromise in the acceptance of imperfect pluralism. This parallel is striking enough to render somewhat bizarre Schmitter's belief that his adding the associationalist culture to corporatism further separates it from pluralism (1985: 55). Indeed, Schmitter's own conception of the 'modern social order' is far more classically pluralistic than anything in the first-phase corporatist texts, since it is pictured as 'composed of a mix of institutions with different actors, motives, media of exchange, resources, decision rules, cleavage patterns and normative foundations' (Schmitter 1985: 51).

One of the significant things to emerge from the relative chaos of the corporatism debate is that it could be profitable to explore the ways in which pluralism, marxism and corporatism can be politically, if not necessarily logically, reconciled. In a move which resembles Schmitter's but, with greater sensitivity to the richness of the various political traditions, Paul Hirst (1986) has pointed to the importance and attractiveness of associationalism as formulated by the guild socialists. Cole and others developed a vision of democratic socialism which managed systematically to avoid both statism and excessive pluralistic individualism. Decision-making was envisaged as taking place in a federal structure of semi-autonomous democratic associations, which in turn were defined by their corporate character as vital functional groups (chiefly *producer* groups). Hirst does not propose that this programme could be directly updated and profferred as the solution to the current crisis of legitimacy of both state-collectivist and liberal-individualist political formulae. The guild socialists can be criticized as having overstated the identities conferred by production as compared with *user* interests. Also, there may be a *number* of valuable ways of constructing a two- or multi-tiered representative system which manages to combine functional and territorial-individual forms. The guild socialists tended to minimize the importance of the latter and the need for general constitutional constraints. Still, the credibility of associationalism is precisely that in concrete political terms corporatist *and* pluralist elements can be recognized as necessary parts of any viable democratic socialist project.

That kind of analysis, I take it, is not intended as providing any radical solution to the corporatism debate. Indeed, the message is probably that when diverse insights are couched as big theories the ensuing confrontation may be counter-productive. Whilst not necessarily agreeing with that, the purpose of citing Hirst's argument – and the brunt of this whole section – has been to suggest in a similar vein, first, that corporatism, as big theory, does not break the mould of traditional concerns. However, secondly, what is certainly achieved in considering the impact of 'meso-level' and 'normative' corporatist ideas is the sense that there is much scope for further theoretical and political development within (and across) marxism and pluralism themselves. Corporatism, if not quite a 'synthesis', does succeed in indicating a set of concerns and processes which require to be addressed in a fresh, non-reductive spirit.

9

CONCLUSION: 'MODEST ECLECTICISM' AND THE RESTRUCTURING OF SOCIAL THEORY

In drawing the book to a close, I want to try to avoid a trap which many authors of works such as this fall into. That is the temptation to launch out, in the comforting certainty that only a few pages remain, into summative and promissory statements which manifestly over-extend the reach and character of the discussions which have preceded them. A number of the theoretical appraisals and positions developed earlier could, I believe, bear further elaboration and justification; yet on the whole the book is as much about encouraging the appropriate intellectual *attitude* to the debates encountered as it is about establishing some sort of superior niche within social theory.

One side of the preferred attitude is to accept at least the possibility that we stand on the brink of a new social epoch, the distinctiveness of which may require us to introduce categories and discourses which severely puncture the modernist ambience of conventional marxism and pluralism. In that spirit, I recast and added to the substantial inventory of problems and weaknesses that the classic variants can be presented with. On the other hand, I have maintained that it is not the decisive replacement of outworn criteria by fresh insight which will mark social theory in the coming period, but rather the relatively inconclusive jostling of theoretical traditions, the scrambling of ground rules for comparison and assessment, and the oscillation between post-modernist disruption and modernist retrenchment.

In that context, it is vital to acknowledge the continuing heuristic and substantive *strengths* of the respective mainstreams, and to appreciate the complexity of some of their modern representatives. As important, there is a real need to show how apparently pathbreaking models can be quite as problematical as the orthodoxies they seek to replace. Often, indeed, their most telling components are contemporary reworkings of traditional themes, or the astute blending of aspects of different traditions. Whether or not such eclectic outcomes are to be credited as major synthetic advances or (by contrast) bewailed as a string of borrowed ideas may ultimately be a pedantic or subjective matter. Yet the speculative scaling of theories into the dramatically new, the intelligently progressive, and the merely derivative is seldom an innocent game. Regrettably perhaps, this staging of contests of rank is partly what gives social theory its academic lustre. More importantly, shade changes in analytical formulation can both trigger and reflect significant shifts in political orientation. All the more reason, then, to try to achieve the right balance between old and young pretenders.

Let me then conclude the book by exemplifying again its two main angles. Positively, this involves a final encapsulation of the marxism-pluralism debate and the prospects for their fruitful – if ever-uneasy – co-existence. 'Negatively', a short assessment of another important transcendent project is tabled. In his luminous trilogy on the past ills and imminent liberation of political thinking, Roberto Unger (1987, 1987a, 1987b) presents an arresting scenario for our theoretical and practical predicament. Unger is particularly interesting for me because he identifies, only to decisively reject, the kind of stance I have been progressively promoting. If, however, in the manner of chapters 5 through 8, this directly threatening posture can be warded off, and itself destabilized, then the following adjudication of 'marxism versus pluralism' cannot be sold short.

Marxism should be seen even now as the major perspective in social science which strives to provide a coherent materialist analysis of the systemic dynamics of modern society. It is also, *par excellence*, the tradition in which the inescapable connections between epistemology and substantive research, and between

social theory and political practice, are made. These achieve-
ments and aspirations can be applauded, even where their
detailed articulations are found wanting; or where reservations
are felt concerning the excessive weight which is placed on
philosophical reasoning in some 'big' theories of social
structure and historical change. In pacification of this distrust
of meta-empirical commitment, it can be reiterated that there
are only two plausible escape routes. One is the fully fledged
post-modernist critique of rationalist narratives in social
theory. I argued that this kind of outlook either deprives us of
any coherent foundation for systemic thought and change; or,
in the by-ways of its headline critique, post-modernism has
issued forth new approaches which actually confirm the power
of integrative theoretical schemas, at least as a cultural fact
about our mode of cognitive apprehension.

The second escape from big theory and its meta-theoretical
grounding lies in the rigorously empirical analysis of the
political inputs and outputs of given institutional settings. As
a temporary rebuke to the hubris of Theory, and as the
necessary framework for the latter's instantiation, an empiricist
orientation has much to commend it. But no assault upon
holistic conceptualization – whether in the name of positivist
scientificity or post-modernist irony – has succeeded altogether
in eliminating from social theory its ambition to devise
conceptual maps which point political and social struggles in a
certain direction. Methodological narrowness aligned to political
complacency was found to be precisely the aspect of conventional pluralism most in need of repair. In that light, the
wrenching of pluralism out of the positivist legacy and into a
more critical engagement with historical generalization and
social philosophy has been important and welcome. Bearing in
mind the precedent of 'original pluralism', we can even say
that following a sojourn in the descriptive imagination, in
which grander assumptions are suppressed rather than eliminated, pluralism has in effect *returned* to some of the classic
goals of Enlightenment sociology.

The weakest part of marxist analysis, as with all systemic
theories, lies in the rigidity of its derivations from the macro-
level of societal dynamics to the micro-level of social identity
and political motivation. Even where – especially where –

epochal categorization (capitalism) and class analysis (bour-geoisie/proletariat) can be shown to possess a legitimate 'objective' quality, the expectation that people will experience and act on their situation in 'structural' terms carries enormous explanatory risks. I noted earlier that assertions of analytic primacy do not entail reductive monism, but it is easy to see how the clarity of the designated primary mechanisms comes to be overstated. Correspondingly, the multiple sources of constraint and identity get flattened out. Most notably, marxists have handled social movements and upheavals as essentially class phenomena, where often on the ground no such singularity of causality or purpose exists. Politically, the analysis of capitalist development has had welded into it the cultural condition and emancipatory mission attributed to a specific historical class force – the industrial proletariat. As capitalism and its subcultures move on from their classic expressions – changes which materialist sociology can readily explain – the directness of the connections between the abstract understanding of the 'places' within production relations and particular political/cultural projects has been lost.

A loosening of those connections does not however render marxism invalid or obsolete. The broad-scale categories of historical materialism, when applied by writers sensitive both to the problem of reductionism and to the challenge of pluralism, continue to produce an impressive array of theses and sugges-tions about the politico-cultural impact of developments in the modes of production. This can be witnessed in the quality of recent studies of marxist orientation, ranging from the investi-gation of the legal frameworks of primitive societies (Newman 1983), through class struggle in the ancient world (Sainte Croix 1979), to the effects of early European modernity on traditional communities (Wolf 1982), to the global theatre for the move from liberal to 'organized' capitalism (Hobsbawm 1988). In such works, marxism's facility for describing pervasive struc-tural forces, and the general cultural configurations within which the detailed fabric of political life is constructed by groups of historical actors, is re-established.

Marxism and pluralism emerge from this summary as compatible, but not merely in the bland sense of both being valuable. The relationship follows the logic of social theory as I have outlined (and defended) it. That is: without the necessary developmental and structural benchmarks supplied by macro-level theories such as marxism, the place and significance of meso- and micro-level pluralist investigations would be difficult to gauge. Of course, this does not mean that for particular purposes investigations at lower levels of abstraction have no logic of their own or that 'structural' factors must be invoked ad nauseam. But it does suggest that however equally essential marxist and pluralist insights are, it is the latter which 'supplements' the former and not vice versa. My firm theoretical orientation is thus a pluralistic marxism rather than critical pluralism.

In the book, I have been at pains to follow that kind of declaration with the caution that we need to be aware of the ways in which the 'supplementarity' of pluralism can be overturned, thus disrupting even the most reasonable and provisional marxist framework. For one thing, the idea that marxism deals with structure and necessity, while pluralism gets all the contingency and surface politics, is unsatisfactory. In the light of the impact of statism, it is clear that institutional forms, albeit bounded by considerations of material production and reproduction, constantly re-organize the latter and them-selves operate as causal constraints on what is politically possible. In response to this problem, it has been proposed that political-institutional forms might be conceived along the lines of an analogy with the determining influence of a mode of production on society generally. Thus we might speak of a prevailing *mode of domination* constituted by the combined elements of techniques and relations of power, which can be treated as 'producing' particular political outcomes (Mouzelis 1986: 220f.). This interesting suggestion manifestly requires further elaboration, above all because it is in the nature of analogies and metaphors to mislead as well as illuminate, by suppressing crucial differences between the processes being compared. For example, any human practice whatever (the making of jokes, the completion of doctoral theses) can be redescribed as a mode of production comprising technical and social elements and revealing a causal sequence. In the meantime, the conventional marxist's belief that, above all, it is the societal mode of production of economic material life which is decisive, and not any of those (important) 'productions' which supply a more delimited range of determinations, remains persuasive.

The second persistent source of tension which unsettles pluralism's supplementary status turns on the question of analytic plurality rather than the emphasis on the substantive role of social groups. The crux of explanatory pluralism is that there can be no objective 'primacy' of one factor over others within a structural constellation, or of one structural line over others. Primacy is rather a matter of the local, internal weightings of variables relative to a specific set of concerns. Analytically and politically, this literal reading of the pluralist temperament at some point or other must disrupt the inextinguishable traits of objectivism in the marxist world-view. This problem is sharply etched, for example, whenever the 'marriage' of marxism and feminism is under consideration. Are these perspectives in competition over *which* structural line (crudely, class or gender) is primary? Or can the different processes highlighted by each be rearticulated into a common concern without obliterating the distinctiveness of either theoretical approach? These questions have yet to be satisfactorily answered, partly because they raise profound problems of logic as well as politics.

Politically, too, pluralistic developments within marxism can only be taken so far without threatening to abolish what is distinctive about the latter. It is common and advisable for marxists to accept, for example, that there are a number of salient social contradictions and movements *other* than those of class – ethnic identities, the women's movement, ecological struggles, and so on. But marxists cannot easily accept, without loss of identity – as pluralists *can* accept – that these social movements have entirely different causes, autonomous status, and radically conflicting priorities. Marxists must in effect reserve the translation rights for such varied movements, striving to reinterpret them as converging on progressive issues which in turn bear important connections to the struggle to transform capitalism into some more socialistic nexus of wealth and power. Here lies one of the most urgent exemplifications of the 'eternal' oscillation I have tried to emphasize between the modalities of integration and diversity.

To be fair, this political problem is neither exclusive to marxism nor susceptible of final solution. The import of feminism itself, for example, is dependent upon the way in which the same sort of dilemma is handled. One of the key emphases in freeing the assessment of women's oppression from straight marxist or liberal categories has been to insist upon the necessary differences which obtain among social relations, and therefore upon the *autonomy* of the different movements of social liberation. This eminently pluralistic development within feminism, breaking any preconceived unity of 'mankind' or 'the working class', has proceeded to gather a deeply disintegrative momentum. For by the very same token it can be asked what ultimate validity the categories of women, sisterhood, 'herstory' etc. have when they must themselves inevitably foreclose on the multiple identities amongst real women. In attempting to cope with this deconstructive, post-feminist drift, those feminists who fear the political and intellectual consequences of the primacy of pluralist 'difference' (e.g. Barrett 1987) find themselves in a parallel situation to many marxists. The common feature is that a certain body of categories and traditions are defended as much for their integrative commitment and sense of genuine community of interest as for any particular item of doctrine. Indeed, some feminists have taken a sharp turn back *towards* orthodox marxism as a response to feminist pluralism, since the integrative credentials of class analysis are at least well established, throwing up a protective shield which may help to stem the apparently endless proliferation of causes and subjectivities (Weir and Wilson 1984).

The relation of supplementarity which exists between marxism and pluralism is thus defensible in many respects, though it comes under constant pressure of disruption. Some commentators would regard that double-edged situation of co-existence and contradiction as conclusive evidence of the explanatory *failure* of both traditions (cf. Holmwood and Stewart 1983). By contrast, I have defended a more 'conservative' view: the traditions provide a considerable armoury of analytic tools which can often combine at different levels of abstraction to provide satisfying and significant, if always incomplete, accounts. In this view, the tensions described actually serve a productive function, preventing any complacent lapse into dogma, whether of one kind or another. The leverage gained by this attitude can be illustrated with reference to two of the most important 'structural' social developments of our times.

Some prominent tendencies within the capitalist democracies, for example, have been pulled together under the suggestive heading 'disorganized capitalism'. Writers who favour this term (e.g. Lash and Urry 1987, Offe 1985) are eager to emphasize how disorganized capitalism differs from the phase of 'organized' capitalism, just as the latter dramatically changed key aspects of its own preceding context, liberal capitalism. In today's world we are witnessing momentous alterations in economic mechanisms, institutional forms and cultural consciousness. The nation state, for example, is becoming less central to the organization of economic and political resources, the relevant settings for which now have, simultaneously, a more international and sub-national character. The nature of production and work itself has become both more flexible and less salient as a determinant of people's life-chances and self-understanding. Finance capital has become substantially independent of industrial capital, while the scale of manufacture itself has continued to shrink. The staggering capacity of modern technology for creative task-adaptation has been exemplified once more in the new generation of sophisticated control systems and personal computers. Generally, the growth of service functions, and of the sprawling middle-class stratum who derive their status and income from services of many kinds, is evident. Consequently, although the traditional working class has not disappeared entirely, its size has declined rapidly, and probably irreversibly. The entire cultural fabric of organized capitalism – big factories, big cities, the dominance of wage-labour in social life – has been profoundly reconstituted. This process has had pronounced impact on political institutions and strategies, especially those based on class identity, whose familiar parameters are no longer in place. Political constituencies are more transient and more varied, and their substantive focus is as likely to be derived from normative questions pertaining to chosen life-styles as from the rigorous distribution of life-chances.

That kind of sketch does not have to be developed at much greater length to reveal the potential it holds for updated pluralistic analysis. Similarly, some of the phrases and implications seem directly introduced to weaken the marxist image of 'organized' capitalism. But it should be noted that writers who favour such a picture are careful not to precipitate the slide into pure post-modernism, or to advocate a sociology of 'post-industrial society'. Thus Scott Lash and John Urry remind us that capitalism still exists tangibly enough to give the new perspective the name it bears, and that its disorganization should not be mistaken for 'high entropy random disorder'. Rather this epochal sub-division embodies the 'fairly systematic disaggregation and restructuration' of capital itself (Lash and Urry 1987: 8).

In order to account for such restructuration, some classical marxist theses need to be brought once again into service, for of course Marx himself was continually impressed by the revolutionary dynamism of capitalism. When the disappearance of the manufacturing proletariat is touted, for example, we need to remember that in part it has been *transported* rather than eliminated, from the First to the Third world, and indeed has been dramatically enlarged in the process (Harris 1983: 265f.). When the decentralization of capital is noticed, we should not forget that its *concentration* in a smaller number of controlling hands has continued apace. Opportunities for further expansion of the process of capitalist competition and integration will surely emerge as the feasibility of commercial development improves in presently inhospitable terrain (e.g. Antarctica), or indeed of outer space (Kidron and Segal 1984). When the growth of service sector comes to be not only instanced but explained, a necessary reference point is Marx's thesis of the rising organic composition of capital: the progressive replacement of living labour by machinery and the capitalist imperative to derive proportionately greater surplus from fewer directly productive labourers. Accordingly, an ever greater proportion of people could be expected to become involved in the realization of surplus value and the extension of commodity production: thus the expansion of markets into every aspect of life-style choices and the shifting numerical balance of commercial and productive labour. Generally, here, we can accept the promptings of the 'capitalist regulation' theorists (e.g. Aglietta 1979) to the effect that the amazing mobility of international capital is tailored to forever seek out ways in which the cost of wage-labour can be diminished. Since this search is a response to complex cultural standards of expectation and consumption, and to the ways in which nation states are compelled to periodically 'decommodify' some parts of the circuits of production and exchange and 'recommodify' others, there can be no question of any purely economic laws working themselves out with iron necessity. Yet the chief characteristic of capitalism as a social force – its amoral exploitation of advantages to enhance profits – is strikingly apparent in the magpie-like raiding of national nests by transnational corporations for favourable inducements to settle and diversify.

Lastly, we need to mark that although theories of 'state monopoly capitalism' should be further demoted in the light of the move towards a local-global context for both politics and production, the intrinsic society-centredness of marxism (and pluralism, for that matter) could prove to be more resourceful than state-centred outlooks for the analysis of the coming epoch. The demise of neo-corporatism as a star attraction, for example, is due to its being rooted in the earlier phase of organized capitalism, centring on the state's role as an actor in the relations between the big battalions of capital and labour. These organizational forms, and the unity of the state itself, are now subject to processes of severe fragmentation. Marxism and pluralism, as theories jointly attuned to system-wide tendencies and local divisions of interest, thus look set to wreak some revenge on corporatism and similar 'meso-level' concepts which looked at one point poised to displace them. That some hallowed pieces of marxist wisdom are also shaken up by the evolution of disorganized capitalism is not to be doubted either, mostly those concerning the narrow interpretation of class politics and economic reductionism. But just as the features of organized capitalism can be immanently deciphered in the tendencies of liberal capitalism which were identified by first generation marxists, so too can disorganized capitalism be derived in part from the contradictions of its predecessor, with the aid of much the same conceptual apparatus.

Another major opportunity for interweaving marxism and pluralism is presented in the analysis of the restructuring currently under way in the Soviet Union. While statist commentators will perhaps regard the reform process as superficial, and though a liberal-individualist approach will probably highlight the historic personalities of particular leaders, a subtle blend of marxist background concepts and those of pluralist group dynamics begs to be developed. This is because the immediate sociological context of *perestroika* is the rapidly growing and densely layered civil society which now exists in the USSR. The inseparability of political and economic causes needs to be emphasized here (cf. Lewin 1988). The opportunities to democratize the Soviet polity and tackle the manifest functional inadequacies of its economy are explicable only in terms of the historic configuration whose contradictions are now dramatically unfolding. The systemic aspects of state-led post-capitalist societies are arguably unthinkable without marxist categories, especially those of the mode of production and of transitional social formations, while the phenomena which produce multiple social identities and subjective allegiances (urban growth, consumption sub-cultures, party status, functional expertise, educational creden-tials) are classic pluralist territory. The cases of disorganized capitalism and reformed state socialism thus give plenty of scope for the rejuvenation of marxist and pluralist insight, in tandem as well as separately.

What general implications, finally, does my treatment have for the direction of social and political theory? Roberto Unger has characterized its development as follows:

> By the 1980s social theory, imprisoned in discredited orthodoxy or dissolved into flaccid eclecticism and mock scientism, had failed to adjust its theoretical instruments to its original aim. It had simply forgotten about the aim. It continued to use, in more fragmentary fashion, all the conceptual strategies that betrayed thought to false neces-sity. Because these strategies no longer belonged to a cohesive and deliberate theoretical project, they stopped being mistakes, and became superstitions. (Unger 1987: 139)

For Unger 'false necessity' means the illusion that the causes which operate on human actions and relationships can be treated as if they are fully determined natural mechanisms. In this sense, his general account of the progress of social science is probably right: its history witnesses a growing awareness of the specificity, variability, and malleability of social constraint. (Whether or not this perception was the 'original aim' of social theory is another matter.) It is also true that social theorists have, paradoxically, tended to persist with concepts and methods which are geared more towards universality than specificity, to objective constraint rather than local strategy. It is this paradox and its intensification that I have been concerned to spell out for the case of marxism and pluralism.

Moreover, on the philosophical level, 'mock scientism' is an appropriate, if unduly dismissive, condensation of the effort both to recognize the particularity of the *object* of social science (human relations) and yet to approach its analysis from the rational scientific standpoint. In chapter 6 especially I touched on this problem, which is exemplified by two common but contrary responses to the influence of scientific realism. For those attuned to the uniqueness of the (historical) human condition, realism is simply the latest form of pseudo-naturalistic metaphysics; by contrast, for those to whom the project of objective social science is still in principle attractive, realism as elaborated pluralistically by the likes of Roy Bhaskar (1979) begins to look more like 'qualified *anti*-naturalism' than scientism (Benton 1981).

Unger's framework is thus provocative. Throughout the preceding discussions of this book, for example, I have been keen to say that while there are severe weaknesses in the explanatory fabric of 'strong' versions of marxism and pluralism, it is highly dangerous to assume that a convincing alternative can simply be strung together from an untheorized, pragmatic-pedagogic concern to move with the times. Even if a coherent, productive departure from prevailing norms is currently unavailable, there is still no compulsion to rest content with 'flaccid eclecticism'.

So far so good. But the terms of Unger's discussion involve in my view a dramatic exaggeration of the extent to which the available orthodoxies have been thoroughly discredited. They also set in motion a pincer movement which entraps not only the flaccid eclectic option but also the further intellectual profile that Unger dubs 'modest eclecticism'. The modest eclectic position is in fact acknowledged by Unger to be notably superior to the flaccidly eclectic one, principally because it reveals a 'heightened self-awareness' of the difficulties in reconciling hard theory with soft reality, and because of its refusal to resolve them by simply settling for a variety of pragmatic relativism. This syndrome I described earlier in terms of the conundrums of philosophical pluralism: the search for (theoretical) integration in the face of (real) diversity.

In short, 'modest eclecticism' seems to include the general standpoint I have been most concerned to explore. To see this conclusively, let us again listen to Unger:

> The modest eclectic dilutes and combines the traditional claims of positivist social science and deep-structure social analysis. He believes that the appeal to a script can be made plausible only if the constraints and tendencies are recognised to leave open a broad range of variation . . . But though he wants to limit the scope of his explanations he does not want to change their character. For the modest eclectic accepts the assumption that only by referring to a script can we explain social situations and historical transformations . . .
>
> If the modest eclectic comes out of a Marxist tradition he may insist that there is something to the story about forces and relations of production . . . If the modest eclectic comes out of the positivist tradition he will be attentive to the importance of the institutional arrangements that define the setting for the ordinary deals and disputes of social life. (Unger 1987: 139–40)

We can of course quibble with the implied assimilation of pluralist concerns to positivism here. The survey of pluralism I offer in chapter 2 should suffice to indicate that the negative connotations which positivism evokes today apply only to the (methodological) part of one strand of pluralist thought: empirical democratic theory. And in chapter 3 I argued that whatever the 'something' is that modest marxists retain from the story about forces and relations of production it cannot be the idea of a comprehensively determining 'script' which dictates the roles of historical actors. Evolutionary social theory cannot be open to infinite multilinearity, but its conjectures are for the most part retrospective and conditional, not predictive and unalterable by human agency.

More questionable still is the claim that Unger's own theoretical and practical proposals must be understood as the intransigent refusal to become similarly entrapped in the web of eclecticism. A number of methodological and substantive considerations at the heart of the vision of *Politics* do not bear this claim out. We should remember from an earlier summary that in spite of the attraction of deconstruction for him, Unger preserves the rationalist belief in a full-scale explanatory perspective, and the expectation that the latter will produce a sharper and truer political programme. His persistent reiteration of how 'relentlessly anti-necessitarian' his approach is (e.g. 1987a: 1), is further compromised by the admission that if the distinction he proposes between institutional contexts and everyday routines is to be productive, the former must be conceived as 'shaping and constraining'. Indeed such constraint can even be acknowledged to exhibit a kind of 'second order necessity' (1987a: 58, 259). The implied suggestion here would seem to be that Marx and other 'necessitarians' advocated a picture of human practice as governed by some sort of naturalistic *first order* necessity. But this (mistaken) extrapolation is also sensibly qualified at a number of points. We should observe too that Unger himself is not averse to resorting to naturalistic propositions as major premises of his theory of action. The distinction between inherited formative contexts and chosen routines, for instance, is reckoned to be in part a matter of our deep human need 'to settle down in a social world and make out of it a home' (1987: 151). The permanently agitated texture of radical pluralism, it follows, is not something that people could adapt to very easily.

Unger thus in his own distinctive way reproduces a fairly familiar conception of social relations and their appropriate conceptual representation. He also offers an evolutionary perspective, albeit one which is again designed to enable us further to break with unilineal and determinist models. This is the thesis that over time, modern society has displayed enhanced 'negative capability', that is, the relative independence of thought and politics from pre-given social hierarchies of one kind or another. The development of early modern states can be envisaged in this light as negotiating a cycle in which increments of the crucial evolutionary quality of 'plasticity' are achieved under pressure for societies to retrench into variants of the natural economy (Unger 1987b). Moreover, the cumulative and conflictual growth of societal plasticity is central to our understanding and transformation of *contemporary* cycles of reform and retrenchment. In spite of the extensive negative capability now available to us in a bid to transcend our dependence on formative contexts, Unger sees a regrettable tendency to revert to a necessitarian and naturalistic mentality with respect to the very possibilities of transformation. This mentality is evidenced in a hidebound, forked vision of free market sovereignty on the one hand and welfare state or state socialist reformism on the other. Urging that we pursue more radical democratic goals, Unger advocates a revamped 'petty bourgeois' ethic, in which autonomous individuals collaborate in a scheme of empowered democracy. Crucial to this new regime is the transformation of absolute property rights into collective, circulating capital funds which can be democratically drawn upon for particular chosen projects (1987a: 27). A thoroughly denaturalized theoretical outlook can actively help here to break with the common premiss of orthodox reform proposals: that institutional arrangements come in unalterable combinations of economic, political and cultural components. The state of negative capability is nowadays such that, in Unger's estimation, a great many different combinations of institutions, and contrasting theoretical genealogies, can be reimagined and embodied in a new political ordering. Petty commodity production could thus feasibly and commendably be associated with a democratic polity whose main characteristic would be organization on the basis of currents of opinion rather than that of hierarchical stations. An appropriate civic culture of radical democracy can also be evoked, one in which no unrealistic assumption about the sheer altruism of the citizenry need be made. Rather, the new co-operative culture can be regarded as a 'zone of heightened mutual vulnerability', requiring only a shared interest in the minimization of conflict

(Unger 1987a: 536). All in all, the new society would move firmly towards an unprecedented alignment of the external societal framework with our deepest projects as original, autonomous and imaginative individuals (1987a: 364).

That much in this unusual blend of spiritual and analytic interests is original and infectious is not to be doubted. What is objectionable is the suggestion that Unger's intervention dispenses altogether with 'modest eclecticism', and that the latter, as he describes it, is but a poor apology for strenuous theory. On the contrary, even from this sketch it can be seen that Unger no less than the other synthetic writers we have considered remains fully within the reach of that misdescribed category. In spite of his post-modernism, for example, Unger cannot disguise his own residual rationalism. In spite of the critique of marxist unilinealism, he indulges his own naturalistic and evolutionary inclinations. For all the references to the contingency of connections between economic, political and cultural ensembles, Unger also posits some tendential correspondences which require similar degrees of ('denaturalized') development across these spheres if decisive transformation is to be possible (1987a: 164). Indeed, Unger's retention and development of the established trio of spheres – economic organization, political forms and cultural consciousness – is surprisingly conventional, for that pattern of distinctions and connections is surely an obvious target for radical departures from orthodoxy.

In postulating his petty bourgeois alternative too, there are signs that Unger's novelty is in good part rhetorical only. He openly acknowledges, for example, that his proposals for theory and practice are best thought of as a 'proto-theory' having several optional clauses, rather than 'the complete job' (1987a: 33, 325–6). The content of the vision, moreover, is set up in terms of joining together the valuable elements in liberal anti-statism, communal corporatism and revolutionary leftism (1987a: 21–5). Clearly, if this is the task, the relentless critique of the various orthodoxies somewhere along the line must give way to a more appreciative understanding of their potential and achievement, and this is exactly what transpires (1987a: 391). These modulations in tone and substance are to Unger's credit, for he draws on a number of central propositions from the traditions he appears to treat with contempt. From pluralistic corporatism, he holds on to the importance of combining associational and neighbourhood-based political forums with representative democracy (1987a: 479–80). From critical pluralism is derived the essential condition that the central state in empowered democracy must not be 'hostage to faction', particularly business factions, but instead should be continually decentralized (1987a: 370). And from marxism comes the basic and – it cannot be emphasized too strongly – entirely *revolutionary* idea that progress towards the liberal ideals of self-fulfilment will remain the prerogative of a privileged minority class until the accumulation of capital in private hands is systematically reversed (1987a: 369f.).

It turns out, then, that if we understand by 'modest eclecticism' the productive liaison between the kind of structural constraints emphasized by marxism and the pluralistic analysis of multiple group identities, then Unger's own enterprise is, precisely, modestly eclectic, since the methodological and empirical tensions examined earlier in this book can readily be found in the volumes of *Politics* as well. As with Giddens, Skocpol, Mann and other leading writers, Unger is clearly engaged in an *unfinished* dialogue with the allegedly valueless orthodoxies, and it cannot be easily concluded that the newer contributions possess obviously preferable explanatory resources, for all the benefits of hindsight that they command.

In sizing up the state of contemporary debate in social theory, we therefore need to be aware of the dangers of either projecting or receiving new efforts as if their tools and formulations represent completely coherent and distinctive visions of life which somehow must wage war on, and defeat, existing ones. In that sense, the widely repeated idea of Kuhn's that paradigm-changes in science effect a kind of *gestalt*-switch on investigators has had a deleterious impact on social theory. In spite of my reservations about post-modernist forms of critique, the notion of theoretical engagement consisting in the contrasting appeals of different *vocabularies* (cf. Rorty 1986) seems a more useful register of intellectual struggle than the clash of rigid and always incompatible conceptual boxes. It has been the overall contention of this book that the vocabularies of marxism and pluralism continue to provide the terms – and the tensions – through which classical and contemporary issues can most productively be addressed. Within this increasingly intricate eclectic dialogue, pluralistic marxism is best placed to supply the necessary integrative framework for the important range of social subdivisions which characterize the modern world.

BIBLIOGRAPHY

Abercrombie, N., Hill, S., and Turner, B. (1980) *The Dominant Ideology Thesis*, London: Allen & Unwin.

Achinstein, P. (1983) *The Nature of Explanation*, Oxford: Oxford University Press.

Acton, H. B. (1955) *The Illusion of the Epoch*, London: Routledge & Kegan Paul.

Adamson, W. L. (1981) 'Marx's four histories', in *History and Theory*, Beiheft 20: *Studies in Marxist Historical Theory*, Boston: Wesleyan University Press.

Aglietta, M. (1979) *A Theory of Capitalist Regulation*, London: New Left Books.

Alford, R. R. and Friedland, R. (1985) *Powers of Theory*, Cambridge: Cambridge University Press.

Almond, G. (1983) 'Corporatism, pluralism and professional memory', *World Politics*, vol. 35, no. 2.

Almond, G. and Verba, S. (1965) *The Civic Culture: political attitudes and democracy in five nations*, Boston: Little, Brown & Co.

Almond, G. and Verba, S. (1980) *The Civic Culture Revisited*, Boston: Little, Brown & Co.

Althusser, L. (1971) 'Philosophy as a revolutionary weapon', in *Lenin and Philosophy and Other Essays*, London: New Left Books.

Amin, S. (1978) *The Law of Value and Historical Materialism*, New York: Monthly Review Press.

Austin, J. L. (1962) *How to Do Things with Words*, Oxford: Clarendon Press.

Bachrach, P. and Baratz, M. S. (1962) 'Two faces of power', *American Political Science Review*, vol. 56, no. 4.

Bahro, R. (1978) *The Alternative in Eastern Europe*, London: Verso.

Balibar, E. (1970) 'The basic concepts of historical materialism', Part III of L. Althusser and E. Balibar, *Reading Capital*, London: New Left Books.

Barker, E. (1915) 'The discredited state', *The Political Quarterly*, Feb.

Barker, E. (1928) *Political Thought in England 1848–1914* (2nd edn), London: Thornton Butterworth.

Barrett, M. (1987) 'The concept of difference', *Feminist Review* 26.

Baudrillard, J. (1975) *The Mirror of Production*, St Louis: Telos Press.

Beer, S. H. (1969) *Modern British Politics*, London: Faber & Faber.

Bentley, A. F. (1967) *The Process of Government* [1908], Cambridge, Mass: The Belknap Press.

Benton, T. (1981) 'Realism and social theory', *Radical Philosophy* 27.

Benton, T. (1984) *The Rise and Fall of Structuralist Marxism*, London: Macmillan.

Berelson, B. R. et al. (1954) *Voting*, Chicago: Chicago University Press.

Berelson, B. (1970) Extracts from *Voting* (1954) in Kariel, H. (ed.) 1970).

Berger, S. (1981) *Organizing Interests in Western Europe: pluralism, corporatism and the transformation of politics*, Cambridge: Cambridge University Press.

Bernstein, R. (1983) *Beyond Objectivism and Relativism*, Oxford: Blackwell.

Bets, D. de (1983) 'Liberal democratic theory in America', in Wintrop, N. (ed). *Liberal Democratic Theory and its Critics*, London: Croom Helm.

Bhaskar, R. (1978) *A Realist Theory of Science* (2nd edn), Brighton: Harvester Press.

Bhaskar, R. (1979) *The Possibility of Naturalism*, Brighton: Harvester Press.

Bhaskar, R. (1987) *Scientific Realism and Human Emancipation*, London: Verso.

Block, F. (1977) 'The ruling class does not rule: notes on the Marxist theory of the state', *Socialist Revolution* 33.

Bluhm, W. T. (1965) *Theories of the Political System*, Englewood Cliffs: Prentice Hall.

Bobbio, N. (1987) *The Future of Democracy*, Cambridge: Polity Press.

Bobbio, N. (1987a) *Which Socialism?*, Cambridge: Polity Press.

Bowles, S. and Gintis, H. (1986) *Democracy and Capitalism*, London: Routledge & Kegan Paul.

Breitling, R. (1980) 'The concept of pluralism', in Ehrlich, S. and Wooton, G. (eds) *Three Faces of Pluralism*, London: Gower.

Brenner, R. (1985) 'Agrarian class structure and economic development in pre-industrial Europe', in Aston, T. H. and Philpin, C. (eds), *The Brenner Debate*, Cambridge: Cambridge University Press.

Brown, A. (1974) *Soviet Politics and Political Science*, London: Macmillan.

Burawoy, M. and Skocpol T. (eds) (1982) *Marxist Inquiries: studies of labour, class, and states*, Chicago: University of Chicago Press.

Callinicos, A. (1987) *Making History: agency, structure and change in social theory*, Cambridge: Polity Press.

Campbell, A. et al. (1960) *The American Voter*, New York: John Wiley.

Carchedi, G. (1977) *On the Economic Identification of Social Classes*, London: Routledge & Kegan Paul.

Carillo, S. (1977) *Eurocommunism and the State*, London: Lawrence & Wishart.

Castoriadis, C. (1987) *The Imaginary Institution of Society*, Cambridge: Polity Press.

Cawson, A. (1985) 'Corporatism and local politics', in Grant (1985).

Cawson, A. (1986) *Corporatism and Political Theory*, Oxford: Blackwell.

Churchland, P. M. and Hooker, C. A. (eds) (1985) *Images of Science*, Chicago: University of Chicago Press.

Cohen, G. A. (1978) *Karl Marx's Theory of History: A defence*, Oxford: Oxford University Press.

Cohen, G. A. (1982) 'Reply to Elster', *Theory and Society*, vol. 11.

Cohen, G. A. (1983) 'Forces and relations of production', in Matthews, B. (ed.), *Marx: 100 years on*, London: Lawrence & Wishart.

Cohen, G. A. (1983a) 'Reconsidering historical materialism', in Chapman, J. and Pennock, J. R. (eds) *Nomos*, vol. XXIV: *Marx and Legal Theory*, New York: New York University Press.

Cohen, J. L. (1983) *Class and Civil Society: the limits of Marxian critical theory*, Oxford: Martin Robertson.

Cole, G. D. H. (1914–15) 'Conflicting political obligations', *Proceedings of the Aristotelian Society*, vol. XV.

Cole, G. D. H. (1920) *Social Theory*, London: Methuen.

Collins, R. (1980) Review of Skocpol's *States and Social Revolutions*, *Theory and Society*, vol. 9.

Cook, T. D. and Campbell, D. T. (1979) *Quasi-Experimentation*, Chicago: Rand McNally College Publishing Co.

Cox, A. et al. (1986) *Power in Capitalist Societies: theory, explanation and cases*, Brighton: Harvester Press.

Crouch, C. (1979) 'The state, capital and liberal democracy', in Crouch, C. (ed.) *State and Economy in Contemporary Capitalism*, London: Croom Helm.

Crouch, C. (1983) 'Pluralism and the new corporatism: a rejoinder', *Political Studies*, vol. 31.

Crozier, M. J., Huntingdon, S. P., and Watanki, J. (1975) *The Crisis of Democracy: report on the governability of democracies to the trilateral commission*, London and New York: The Trilateral Commission.

Dahl, R. A. (1956) *A Preface to Democratic Theory*, Chicago: University of Chicago Press.

Dahl, R. A. (1961) *Who Governs?*, New Haven: Yale University Press.

Dahl, R. A. (1971) *Polyarchy*, New Haven: Yale University Press.

Dahl, R. A. (1980) 'Pluralism revisited', in Ehrlich and Wooton (eds) (1980).

Dahl, R. A. (1982) *Dilemmas of Pluralist Democracy*, New Haven: Yale University Press.

Dahl, R. A. (1983) 'Comment on Manley', *American Political Science Review*, vol. 77, no. 2.

Dahl, R. A. (1985) *A Preface to Economic Democracy*, Cambridge: Polity Press.

Dahl, R. A. and Lindblom, C. E. (1953) *Politics, Economics and Welfare*, Chicago: Chicago University Press, 2nd edn with new Preface, 1976.

Davidson, D. (1973–4) 'On the very idea of a conceptual scheme', *Proceedings and Addresses of the American Philosophical Association*, vol. 47.

Dews, P. (1987) *Logics of Disintegration*, London: Verso.

Diamond, S. (1974) *In Search of the Primitive*, New Brunswick: Transaction.

Doyle, W. (1980) *Origins of the French Revolution*, Oxford: Oxford University Press.

Dunleavy, P. and O'Leary, B. (1987) *Theories of the State: the politics of liberal democracy*, London: Macmillan.

Duncan, G. (ed.) (1983) *Democratic Theory and Practice*, Cambridge: Cambridge University Press.

Duverger, M. (1974) *Modern Democracies: economic power versus political power*, Illinois: The Dryden Press.

Easton, D. (1953) *The Political System*, New York: Alfred A. Knopf.

Eckstein, H. (1979) 'On the "science" of the state', *Daedalus* 108, Fall.

Eisenstadt, S. N. (1987) 'Macrosociology and social theory: some new directions', *Contemporary Sociology*, vol. 16, no. 5.

Elliott, G. (1987) *Althusser: the detour of theory*, London: Verso.

Elster, J. (1982) 'Marxism, functionalism and game theory: the case for methodological individualism', *Theory and Society*, vol. 11.

Elster, J. (1985) *Making Sense of Marx*, Cambridge: Cambridge University Press.

Feyerabend, P. (1975) *Against Method*, London: New Left Books.

Feyerabend, P. (1987) *Farewell to Reason*, London: Verso.

Figgis, J. N. (1914) *The Divine Right of Kings*, Cambridge: Cambridge University Press.

Fine, B. et al. (1984) *Class Politics: an answer to its critics*, London: Leftover Pamphlets.

Fine, B. and Harris, L. (1979) *Rereading Capital*, London: Macmillan.

Follett, M. P. (1918) *The New State: group organization the solution of popular government*, London: Longman, Green & Co.

Foucault, M. (1980) *Power/Knowledge: selected interviews and other writings*, ed. C. Gordon, Brighton: Harvester Press.

van Fraasen, B. (1985) 'Empiricism in the philosophy of science', in Churchland and Hooker (1985).

Fullbrook, M. and Skocpol, T. (1984) 'Destined pathways: the historical sociology of Perry Anderson', in Skocpol, T. (ed.), *Vision and Method in Historical Sociology*, Cambridge: Cambridge University Press.

Furet, F. (1981) *Interpreting the French Revolution*, Cambridge: Cambridge University Press.

Galbraith, J. K. (1952) *American Capitalism*, London: Hamish Hamilton.

Gandy, D. R. (1979) *Marx and History*, Austin: University of Texas Press.

Garson, G. D. (1978) *Group Theories of Politics*, Beverley Hills: Sage.

Gasche, R. (1986) *The Tain of the Mirror: Derrida and the philosophy of reflection*, Cambridge, Mass: University Press.

Geras, N. (1981) 'Classical marxism and proletarian representation', *New Left Review* 125.

Geras, N. (1987) 'Post-marxism?', *New Left Review* 163.

Giddens, A. (1973) *The Class Structure of the Advanced Societies*, London: Hutchinson.

Giddens, A. (1979) *Central Problems in Social Theory*, London: Macmillan.

Giddens, A. (1981) *A Contemporary Critique of Historical Materialism*, vol. 1, London: Macmillan.

Giddens, A. (1982) *Profiles and Critiques in Social Theory*, London: Macmillan.

Giddens, A. (1982a) 'Historical materialism today: interview with Anthony Giddens' conducted by Bleicher, J. and Featherstone, M., *Theory, Culture and Society*, vol. 1, no. 2.

Giddens, A. (1982b) 'Reply to the critics', *Theory, Culture and Society*, vol. 1, no. 2.

Giddens, A. (1984) *The Constitution of Society*, Cambridge: Polity Press.

Giddens, A. (1985) *The Nation State and Violence* (vol. 2 of *A Contemporary Critique of Historical Materialism*), Cambridge: Polity Press.

Godelier, M. (1986) *The Mental and the Material*, London: Verso.

Gorbachev, M. (1987) *Perestroika*, London: Collins.

Gottlieb, R. S. (1984) 'Feudalism and historical materialism: A critique and a synthesis', *Science and Society*, vol. 48, no. 1.

Gottlieb, R. S. (1987) 'Historical materialism, historical laws and social primacy: further discussion of the transition debate', *Science and Society*, vol. 51, no. 2.

Graham, K. (1986) *The Battle of Democracy*, Brighton: Wheatsheaf Books.

Gramsci, A. (1971) *Selections from the Prison Notebooks*, London: Lawrence & Wishart.

Grant, W. (1985) 'Introduction', in Grant, W. (ed.), *The Political Economy of Corporatism*, London: Macmillan.

Gurr, T. R. and King, D. S. (1987) *The State and the City*, London: Macmillan.

Hacker, A. (1967) 'Power to do What?', in Connelly, W. (ed.), *The Bias of Pluralism*, Chicago: Atherton Press.

Hacking, I. (1983) *Representing and Intervening*, Cambridge: Cambridge University Press.

Hall, J. A. (1985) *Powers and Liberties*, Harmondsworth: Penguin.

Hall, J. A. (ed.) (1986) *States in History*, Oxford: Blackwell.

Hall, S. (1975) 'Marx's notes on method: a "reading" of the "1857 Introduction"', in *Cultural Studies 6: Cultural Studies and Theory*, Birmingham: Centre for Contemporary Cultural Studies.

Hall, S. (1977) 'The "political" and the "economic" in Marx's theory of classes', in Hunt, A. (ed.) *Class and Class Structure*, London: Lawrence & Wishart.

Hall, S. and Schwarz, B. (1986) 'State and Society, 1880–1930', in Langan, M. and Schwarz, B. (eds), *Crises in the British State*, London: Hutchinson.

Harding, N. (1981) *Lenin's Political Though*, vol. II, *Theory and Practice in the Socialist Revolution*, London: Macmillan.

Harre, R. (1979) *Social Being: a theory for social psychology*, Oxford: Blackwell.

Harris, N. (1983) *Of Bread and Guns: the world economy in crisis*, Harmondsworth: Pelican.

Hart, V. (1978) *Distrust and Democracy*, Cambridge: Cambridge University Press.

Harvey, D. et al. (1987) 'Reconsidering social theory: a debate', *Society and Space*, vol. 5.

Held, D. (1984) 'Power and legitimacy in contemporary Britain', in McLennan, G. et al. (eds), *State and Society in Contemporary Britain*, Cambridge: Polity Press.

Held, D. (1986) *Models of Democracy*, Cambridge: Polity Press.

Held, D. and Pollitt, C. (eds) (1986) *New Forms of Democracy*, London: Sage.

Hellman, G. (1979) 'Historical materialism', in Mepham, J. and Ruben, D. H. (eds), *Issues in Marxist Philosophy*, vol. II, *Materialism*, Brighton, Harvester Press.

Hesse, M. (1974) 'A realist interpretation of science', ch. 12 of *The Structure of Scientific Inference*, London: Macmillan.

Hindess, B. (1983) *Parliamentary Democracy and Socialist Politics*, London: Routledge & Kegan Paul.

Hindess, B. (1987) *Marxism and Class Analysis*, Oxford: Blackwell.

Hindess, B. and Hirst, P. Q. (1975) *Pre-capitalist Modes of Production*, London: Routledge & Kegan Paul.

Hirst, P. Q. (1985) *Marxism and Historical Writing*, London: Routledge & Kegan Paul.

Hirst, P. Q. (1986) *Law, Socialism and Democracy*, London: Allen & Unwin.

Hirst, P. Q. (1987) 'Retrieving pluralism', in Outhwaite, W. and Mulkay, M. (eds), *Social Theory and Social Criticism: essays for Tom Bottomore*, Oxford: Blackwell.

Hirst, P. and Woolley, P. (1982) *Social Relations and Human Attributes*, London: Tavistock.

Hirst, P. and Woolley, P. (1985) 'Psychoanalysis and social relations', in Beechey, V. and Donald, J. (eds), *Subjectivity and Social Relations*, Milton Keynes: Open University Press.

Holton, R. J. (1985) *The Transition from Feudalism to Capitalism*, London: Macmillan.

Hobhouse, L. T. (1918) *The Metaphysical Theory of the State*, London: Allen & Unwin.

Hobsbawm, E. J. (1969) *Industry and Empire*, Harmondsworth: Penguin.

Hobsbawm, E. J. (ed.) (1982) *The History of Marxism*, vol. 1, *Marxism in Marx's Day*, Brighton: Harvester Press.

Hobsbawm, E. J. (1988) *The Age of Empire*, London: Weidenfeld & Nicolson.

Hollis, M. and Lukes, S. (eds) (1982) *Rationality and Relativism*, Oxford: Blackwell.

Holmwood, J. M. and Stewart, A. (1983) 'The role of contradiction in modern theories of social stratification', *Sociology*, vol. 17, no. 2.

Hsiao, K. C. (1927) *Political Pluralism*, New York: Kegan Paul, Trench, Trubner.

Hunt, A. (1977) 'Theory and politics in the identification of the working class', in Hunt, A. (ed.), *Class and Class Structure*, London: Lawrence & Wishart.

Hunter, F. (1953) *Community Power Structure*, Chapel Hill: University of North Carolina Press.

Isaac, J. C. (1987) *Power and Marxist Theory: a realist view*, London: Cornell University Press.

Jarvie, I. C. (1983) 'Rationality and relativism', *British Journal of Sociology*, vol. 34, no. 1.

Jessop, B. (1982) *The Capitalist State*, Oxford: Martin Robertson.

Johnston, L. (1986) *Marxism, Class Analysis and Socialist Pluralism*, London: Allen & Unwin.

Kariel, H. (1961) *The Decline of American Pluralism*, Stanford: Stanford University Press.

Kariel, H. (ed.) (1970) *Frontiers of Democratic Theory*, New York: Random House.

Kaye, H. J. (1984) *The British Marxist Historians*, Cambridge: Polity Press.

Kelle, V. and Kovalson, M. (1973) *Historical Materialism*, Moscow: Progress.

Kelso, W. A. (1978) *American Democratic Theory: pluralism and its critics*, Westport: Greenwood Press.

Kemp, T. (1971) *Economic Forces in French History*, London: Dobson.

Key, V. O. (1964) *Politics, Parties and Pressure Groups*, (5th edn), New York: Crowell.

Kidron, M. and Segal, R. (1964) *The New State of the World Atlas*, London: Pan Books.

Kiernan, V. (1983) 'History', in McLellan, D. (ed.), *Marx: the first 100 years*, Oxford: Fontana.

Kiernan, V. (1987) 'Problems of marxist history', *New Left Review* 161.

King, D. S. (1988) 'Political centralization and state interests: the 1986 abolition of the GLC and MCC', *Comparative Political Studies*, vol. 21.

King, R. (1985) 'Corporatism and the local economy', in Grant (1985).

Kolakowski, L. (1978) *Main Currents of Marxism*, vol. I, *The Founders*, vol. II *The Golden Age*, vol. III, *The Breakdown*, Oxford: Oxford University Press.

Korpi, W. (1983) *The Democratic Class Struggle*, London: Routledge & Kegan Paul.

Krasner, S. (1978) *Defending the National Interest*, Princeton: Princeton University Press.

Krasner, S. (1984) 'Approaches to the state: alternative conceptions and historical dynamics', *Comparative Politics*, vol. 16, no. 2.

Kuhn, T. S. (1962) *The Structure of Scientific Revolutions*, Chicago: University of Chicago Press.

Laclau, E. and Mouffe, C. (1985) *Hegemony and Socialist Strategy*, London: Verso.

Laclau, E. and Mouffe, C. (1987) 'Post-marxism without apologies', *New Left Review* 166.

Laibman, D. (1984) 'Modes of production and theories of transition', *Science of Society*, vol. 48, no. 3.

Lane, D. (1985) *State and Politics in the USSR*, Oxford: Blackwell.

Larrain, J. (1986) *The Reconstruction of Historical Materialism*, London: Allen & Unwin.

Lash, S. and Urry, J. (1987) *The End of Organized Capitalism*, Cambridge: Polity Press.

Laski, H. J. (1917) 'The pluralistic state', *Philosophical Review*, vol. 28, reprinted in Nichols (1975).

Laski, H. J. (1919) *Authority in the Modern State*, London: Oxford University Press.

Latham, E. (1952) *The Group Basis of Politics*, Ithaca: Cornell University Press.

Latham, E. (1964) 'The group basis of politics: notes for a theory', in Munger, F. and Price, D. (eds), *Readings in Political Parties and Pressure Groups*, New York: Crowell.

Laudan, L. (1977) *Progress and its Problems: towards a theory of scientific growth*, London: Routledge & Kegan Paul.

Laudan, L. (1981) 'A refutation of convergent realism', in Jensen, U. J. and Harre, R. (eds), *The Philosophy of Evolution*, Brighton: Harvester Press.

Lecourt, D. (1977) *Proletarian Science: the case of Lysenko*, London: New Left Books.

Lehmbruch, G. (1982) 'Neo-corporatism in comparative perspective', in Lehmbruch, G. and Schmitter, P. (eds), *Patterns of Corporatist Policy-making*, New York: Sage.

Lenin, V. I. (1970) *State and Revolution*, Peking: Foreign Languages Press.

Levine, A. (1987) *The End of the State*, London: Verso.

Lewin, M. (1988) *The Gorbachev Phenomenon*, London: Radius.

Lindblom, C. E. (1977) *Politics and Markets*, New York: Basic Books.

Lindblom, C. E. (1982) 'Another state of mind', *American Political Science Review*, vol. 76, no. 1.

Lindblom, C. E. (1983) 'Comment. on Manley', *American Political Science Review*, vol. 77, no. 2.

Lipset, S. (1960) *Political Man*, London: Heinemann.

Lively, J. (1978) 'Pluralism and consensus', in Birnbaum, P., Lively, J. and Parry, G., *Democracy, Consensus and Social Control*, Beverley Hills: Sage.

Lovell, T. (1980) *Picture of Reality*, London: Methuen.

Lukes, S. (1974) *Power: a radical view*, London: Macmillan.

Lukes, S. (1985) *Marxism and Morality*, Oxford: Oxford University Press.

Lyotard, J. F. (1984) *The Postmodern Condition: a report on knowledge*, Manchester: Manchester University Press.

McFarland, A. S. (1969) *Power and Leadership in Pluralist Systems*, Stanford: Stanford University Press.

MacIver, R. M. (1926) *The Modern State*, London: Oxford University Press.

McLennan, G. (1981) *Marxism and the Methodologies of History*, London: Verso.

McLennan, G. (1986) 'Marxist theory and historical research: between the hard and soft options', *Science and Society*, vol. 50, no. 1.

Madison, J. (1966) *The Federalist Papers* [1788], New York: Doubleday.

Maitland, F. W. (1900) 'Introduction' to von Gierke, O., *Political Theories of the Middle Ages*, Cambridge: Cambridge University Press.

Mandel, E. (1978) *From Stalinism to Eurocommunism*, London: New Left Books.

Mandel, E. (1986) 'In defence of socialist planning', *New Left Review* 159.

Manley, J. F. (1983) 'Neo-pluralism: A class analysis of pluralism I and pluralism II', *American Political Science Review*, vol. 77, no. 2.

Mann, M. (1973) *Consciousness and Action Among the Western Working Class*, London: Macmillan.

Mann, M. (1984) 'The autonomous power of the state: its origins, mechanism and results', *Archives Européennes de Sociologie*, vol. XXV.

Mann, M. (1986) *The Sources of Social Power*, vol. I, Cambridge: Cambridge University Press.

Margolis, M. (1983) 'Democracy: American style', in Duncan (1983).

Martin, R. M. (1983) 'Pluralism and the new corporatism', *Political Studies*, vol. XXXI.

Marx, K. (1909) *Capital*, vol. III, *The Process of Capitalist Production as a Whole*, Chicago: Kerr & Co.

Marx, K. (1968) *Selected Works*, London: Lawrence & Wishart.

Marx, K. (1973) *Grundrisse*, Harmondsworth: Penguin.

Marx, K. (1973a) 'The Eighteenth Brumaire of Louis Bonaparte', in Fernbach, D. (ed.), *Surveys from Exile*, Harmondsworth: Penguin.

Marx, K. (1975) *The Poverty of Philosophy*, Moscow: Progress.

Marx, K. (1976) *Capital*, vol. I, Harmondsworth: Penguin.

Mayo, H. B. (1955) *Democracy and Marxism*, Oxford: Oxford University Press.

Medvedev, R. (1981) *Leninism and Western Socialism*, London: Verso.

Meikle, S. (1985) *Essentialism in the Thought of Karl Marx*, London: Duckworth.

Meiksins, P. (1986) 'Beyond the boundary question', *New Left Review* 157.

Mellotti, U. (1977) *Marxism and the Third World*, London: Macmillan.

Middlemas, K. (1979) *Politics in Industrial Society*, London: Deutsch.

Miliband, R. (1969) *The State in Capitalist Society*, London: Quartet Books.

Miliband, R. (1982) *Capitalist Democracy in Britain*, Oxford: Oxford University Press.

Miliband, R. (1983) 'State power and class interests', *New Left Review* 138.

Miliband, R. (1985) 'The new revisionism in Britain', *New Left Review* 150.

Miller, R. (1984) 'Producing change: work, technology and power in Marx's theory of history', in Ball, T. and Farr, J. (eds) *After Marx*, Cambridge: Cambridge University Press.

Mills, C. W. (1956) *The Power Elite*, New York: Oxford University Press.

Moodie, G. C. and Studdert-Kennedy, G. (1970) *Opinions, Politics and Pressure Groups*, London: Allen & Unwin.

Moore, B. (1969) *The Social Origins of Dictatorship and Democracy*, Harmondsworth: Penguin.

Mouzelis, N. (1986) *Politics in the Semi-Periphery*, London: Macmillan.

Mouzelis, N. (1988) 'Marxism or post-marxism?', *New Left Review* 167.

Munger, F. and Price, D. (eds) (1964) *Readings in Political Parties and Pressure Groups*, New York: Crowell.

Nagel, E. (1961) *The Structure of Science*, London: Routledge & Kegan Paul.

Nedelman, B. and Meier, K. G. (1979) 'Theories of contemporary corporatism. Static or dynamic?', in Schmitter, P. and

Lehmbruch, G. (eds), *Trends Towards Corporatist Intermediation*, London: Sage.

Newman, K. (1983) *Law and Economic Organization: a comparative study of preindustrial societies*, Cambridge: Cambridge University Press.

Newman, O. (1981) *The Challenge of Corporatism*, London: Macmillan.

Nichols, D. (1974) *Three Varieties of Pluralism*, London: Macmillan.

Nichols, D. (1975) *The Pluralistic State*, London: Macmillan.

Nordlinger, E. A. (1981) *On the Autonomy of the Democratic State*, Cambridge, Mass.: Harvard University Press.

Norris, C. (1982) *Deconstruction: theory and practice*, London: Methuen.

Norris, C. (1984) *The Deconstructive Turn: essays in the rhetoric of philosophy*, London: Methuen.

Norris, C. (1985) *Contest of Faculties: philosophy and theory after deconstruction*, London: Methuen.

Nove, A. (1983) *The Economics of Feasible Socialism*, London: Allen & Unwin.

Offe, C. (1984) *Contradictions of the Welfare State*, London: Hutchinson.

Offe, C. (1985) *Disorganized Capitalism*, Cambridge: Polity Press.

Orloff, A. S. and Skocpol, T. (1984) 'Why not equal protection? Explaining the politics of public social spending in Britain 1900–1911, and the United States, 1880s–1920', *American Sociological Review*, vol. 49.

Pahl, R. and Winkler, J. (1975) 'The coming corporatism', *Challenge*, March/April.

Panitch, L. (1979) 'The development of corporatism in liberal democracies', in Schmitter, P. and Lehmbruch, G. (eds), *Trends towards Corporatist Intermediation*, London: Sage.

Panitch, L. (1981) 'Trade unions and the capitalist state', *New Left Review* 125.

Parijs, P. van (1981) *Evolutionary Explanation in the Social Sciences: an emerging paradigm*, London: Tavistock.

Parijs, P. van (1982) 'Functionalist marxism rehabilitated', *Theory and Society*, vol. 11.

Parijs, P. van (1984) 'Marxism's central puzzle', in Ball, T. and Farr, J. (eds), *After Marx*, Cambridge: Cambridge University Press.

Pateman, C. (1980) 'The civic culture: a philosophical critique', in Almond and Verba (eds) (1980).

Pierson, C. (1986) *Marxism and Democratic Theory*, Cambridge: Polity Press.

Plekhanov, G. (1956) *The Development of the Monist View of History*, Moscow: Progress.

Polan, A. J. (1984) *Lenin and the End of Politics*, London: Methuen.

Polsby, N. W. (1963) *Community Power and Political Theory*, New Haven: Yale University Press.

Popper, K. (1962) *The Poverty of Historicism*, London: Routledge & Kegan Paul.

Poster, M. (1984) *Foucault, Marxism and History*, Cambridge: Polity Press.

Poulantzas, N. (1973) *Political Power and Social Classes*, London: New Left Books.

Poulantzas, N. (1975) *Classes in Contemporary Capitalism*, London: Verso.

Poulantzas, N. (1980) *State, Power, Socialism*, London: Verso.

Przeworski, A. (1982) 'The ethical materialism of John Roemer', *Politics and Society*, vol. II, no. 3.

Przeworski, A. (1985) 'Proletariat into a class: the process of class formation', in *Capitalism and Social Democracy*, Cambridge: Cambridge University Press.

Putnam, H. (1981) *Reason, Truth and History*, Cambridge: Cambridge University Press.

Putnam, H. (1983) *Realism and Reason*, Cambridge: Cambridge University Press.

Rader, M. (1979) *Marx's Interpretation of History*, New York: Oxford University Press.

Rigby, S. H. (1987) *Marxism and History: a critical introduction*, Manchester: Manchester University Press.

Roemer, J. (1982) 'Methodological individualism and deductive marxism', *Theory and Society*, vol. 11.

Roemer, J. (1986) 'New directions in the Marxist theory of exploitation and class', in Roemer, J. (ed.), *Analytical Marxism*, Cambridge: Cambridge University Press.

Rokkan, S. (1966) 'Numerical democracy and corporate pluralism', in Dahl, R. (ed.), *Political Opposition in the Western Democracies*, New Haven: Yale University Press.

Rorty, R. (1982) *Consequences of Pragmatism*, Brighton: Harvester Press.

Rorty, R. (1986) 'The contingency of language', *London Review of Books*, vol. 8, no. 7.

Rose, G. (1984) *Dialectic of Nihilism: post-structuralism and law*, Oxford: Blackwell.

Rothman, S. (1960) 'Systematic political theory: observations on the group approach', *American Political Science Review*, vol. 54, no. 1.

Ryan, M. (1982) *Marxism and Deconstruction: a critical articulation*, Baltimore: Johns Hopkins University Press.

Sahlins, M. (1974) *Stone-Age Economics*, London: Tavistock.

Sainte Croix, G. E. M. de (1981) *The Class Struggle in the Ancient Greek World*, London: Duckworth.

Sawer, M. (1977) 'The concept of the Asiatic mode of production and contemporary marxism', in Avineri, s. (ed.), *Varieties of Marxism*, The Hague: Martinus Nijhoff.

Sayer, A. (1984) *Method in Social Science: a realist approach*, London: Hutchinson.

Sayer, D. (1987) *The Violence of Abstraction: the analytic foundations of historical materialism*, Oxford: Blackwell.

Schattschneider, E. E. (1935) *Politics, Pressures, and the Tariff*, New York: Prentice-Hall.

Schmitter, P. (1979) 'Still the century of corporatism?' in Schmitter, P. and Lehmbruch, G. (eds), *Trends Towards Corporatist Intermediation*, London: Sage.

Schmitter, P. (1985) 'Neo-corporatism and the state', in Grant (1985).

Schumpeter, J. (1943) *Capitalism, Socialism and Democracy*, London: Unwin.

Semenov, Y. (1980) 'The theory of socio-economic formations and world history', in Gellner, E. (ed.) *Soviet and Western Anthropology*, London: Duckworth.

Simon, R. (1982) *Gramsci's Political Thought: an introduction*, London: Lawrence & Wishart.

Skilling, G. and Griffiths, F. (eds) (1971) *Interest Groups in Soviet Politics*, Princeton: Princeton University Press.

Skinner, Q. (1973) 'The empirical theorists of democracy and their critics: a plague on both their houses', *Political Theory*, vol. I, no. 3.

Skocpol, T. (1973) 'A critical review of Barrington Moore's *Social origins of Dictatorship and Democracy*', *Politics and Society*, vol. 4, no. 1.

Skocpol, T. (1976) 'France, Russia, China: a structural analysis of social revolutions', *Comparative Studies in History and Society*, vol. 18.

Skocpol, T. (1977) 'Wallerstein's world capitalist system: a theoretical and historical critique', *American Journal of Sociology*, vol. 82, no. 5.

Skocpol, T. (1979) *States and Social Revolutions: a comparative analysis of France, Russia and China*, Cambridge: Cambridge University Press.

Skocpol, T. (1984) 'Emerging agendas and recurrent strategies in historical sociology', in Skocpol, T. (ed.), *Vision and Method in Historical Sociology*, Cambridge: Cambridge University Press.

Skocpol, T. (1984a) 'Sociology's historical imagination', in Skocpol, T. (ed.), *Vision and Method in Historical Sociology*, Cambridge: Cambridge University Press.

Skocpol, T. (1980) 'Political response to capitalist crisis: neo-marxist theories of the state and the case of the New Deal', *Theory and Society*, vol. 10, no. 2.

Skocpol, T. (1985) 'Bringing the state back in: strategies of analysis in current research', in Evans, P. B., Rueschemeyer, D. and Skocpol, T. (eds), *Bringing the State Back In*, Cambridge: Cambridge University Press.

Solomon, S. G. (1983) *Pluralism in the Soviet Union*, London: Macmillan.

Steedman, I. et al. (eds) (1981) *The Value Controversy*, London: Verso.

Stephens, J. (1979) *The Transition from Capitalism to Socialism*, London: Macmillan.

Stone, L. (1981) 'The revival of narrative', in *The Past and the Present*, London: Routledge & Kegan Paul.

Therborn, G. (1977) 'The rule of capital and the rise of democracy', *New Left Review* 103.

Therborn, G. (1978) *What Does the Ruling Class Do When it Rules?*, London: Verso.

Therborn, G. (1983) 'Problems of class analysis', in Matthews, B. (ed.), *Marx: 100 Years On*, London: Lawrence & Wishart.

Thompson, E. P. (1968) *The Making of the English Working Class*, Harmondsworth: Penguin.

Tomlinson, J. (1981) 'The "economics of politics" and public expenditure: a critique', *Economy and Society*, vol. 10.

Touraine, A. (1981) *The Voice and the Eye: an analysis of social movements*, Cambridge: Cambridge University Press.

Trigg, R. (1980) *Reality at Risk*, Brighton: Harvester Press.

Truman, D. (1951) *The Governmental Process*, New York: Alfred A. Knopf.

Unger, R. M. (1987) *Social Theory: its situation and its task*, a critical introduction to *Politics, a Work in Constructive Social Theory*, Cambridge: Cambridge University Press.

Unger, R. M. (1987a) *False Necessity: anti-necessitarian social theory in the service of radical democracy*, Part 1 of *Politics, a Work in Constructive Social Theory*, Cambridge: Cambridge University Press.

Unger, R. M. (1987b) *Plasticity into Power: comparative-historical studies on the institutional conditions of economic and military success*, variations on themes of *Politics, a Work in Constructive Social Theory*, Cambridge: Cambridge University Press.

Urry, J. (1982) 'Duality of structure: some critical issues', *Theory, Culture and Society*, vol. 1, no. 2.

Veen, R. J. van der and van Parijs, P. (1987) 'A capitalist road to communism', *Theory and Society*, vol. 15.

Weir, A. and Wilson, E. (1984) 'The British women's movement', *New Left Review* 148.

Weir, M. and Skocpol, T. (1985) 'State structures and the possibilities for "Keynesian" responses to the Great Depression in Sweden, Britain and the U.S.', in Evans, T., Rueschemeyer, D. and Skocpol, T. (eds), *Bringing the State Back In*, Cambridge, Cambridge University Press.

Westergaard, J. (1984) 'Class of '84', *New Socialist*, Jan/Feb.

Wickham, C. J. (1984) 'The other transition', *Past and Present* 103.

Willis, P. (1977) *Learning to Labour: how working class kids get working class jobs*, Farnborough: Saxon House.

Wolf, E. R. (1982) *Europe and the People Without History*, Berkeley: University of California Press.

Wood, E. (1986) *The Retreat from Class: a new 'true' socialism*, London: Verso.

Wright, A. W. (1979) *G. D. H. Cole and Socialist Democracy*, Oxford: Clarendon Press.

Wright, E. O. (1975) *Class, Crisis and the State*, London: New Left Books.

Wright, E. O. (1983) 'Giddens' critique of Marxism', *New Left Review* 138.

Wright, E. O. (1985) *Classes*, London:Verso.

Wright, E. O. (1987) Review of Bowles and Gintis (1986), *Contemporary Sociology*, vol. 16, no. 5.

INDEX

class polarization theory, 101, 107
Cohen's interpretation of, 62–3
Eighteenth Brumaire of Louis Bonaparte, 101, 102–6
and non-capitalist labour, 107
The Poverty of Philosophy, 106
Sayer on, 70
teleological view of history criticized by, 84
marxism, 259–60, 260–1
analytical, 96–100
anti-reductionist current in, 115–20
corporatism and, 250–3
critique of liberal democracy, 23–4
and deconstruction, 199–200
derivationism and, 202–4
determinism and, 153–5
and disorganized capitalism, 267
and eclectic approach to theory, 201–2
eclectic-pluralist view of, 202–4
essentialism in, 195–6
and feminism, 263, 264
and Foucault, 199
holistic tendency of, 13–14
increased valuation of pluralism by, 4
monism/pluralism in, 58–9
and non-class movements, 263
and political morality, 121–2
and reductionism, 202–4
and scientific realism, 193–7
and state theory, 194–5
structuralist current in, 61–2
theory of history, 59–73
variant interpretations of, 57–8
see also marxism, fundamentalist; marxism,

radical-democratic; marxism, structuralist; Marxism-Leninism; marxism-pluralism debate
marxism, fundamentalist, 129–46, 165
class theory, 136–46
criticisms of new left by, 132–6
and non-class social divisions, 144–6
marxism, radical-democratic, 165–6
and class translation, 146–7
compared with pluralism, 150–1
and democracy, 150–1, 159–60
and determinism, 153–5
and interest groups, 149–50, 152, 156–7
and post-modernist philosophy, 148–9
view of socialism, 157–9
marxism, structuralist, mode of production in, 75–6
Marxism-Leninism, 7, 9
concept of democracy, 9–10, 11–12
marxism-pluralism debate, 166
antagonistic view of, 4–16
'exhaustion' of, 3, 5–6
paradigmatic approach in, 4
philosophical aspect, 5, 6
means of production, control of, and class definition, 139
mechanics, scientific theory of, 154
Meikle, S., 195–6
Meiskins, P., 142–3
Middlemas, K., 249
Miliband, R., 115, 142, 143–4, 215–16
Miller, R. W., 62, 72
Mills, C. W., 37

Index by Justyn Balinski